A HISTORY OF
Bantry
&
Bantry Bay

A HISTORY OF

Bantry
&
Bantry Bay

MICHAEL J. CARROLL

Published 2008 by
Michael J Carroll
Sunville House, The Square,
Bantry, Co Cork, Ireland

ISBN 9780955203930

Printed and bound in Spain by Graphycems

bantrydesigns@iol.ie
www.mjcarroll.eu

ACKNOWLEDGEMENTS

Much of the material in this volume was used in my book *A Bay of Destiny*, published by Bantry Design Studios in 1996. I wish to thank all those who assisted me in my research, in compiling notes, in typing and in the preparation of both that book and the current volume for print, especially Tim Cadogan, Cork County Library; Noel O'Mahony, County Library, Bantry; Paddy O'Leary, Ballydehob; Connie Murphy, Castletownbere; Ted O'Sullivan, Bere Island and Cork; Michael Donoghue, Bantry.

I would also like to thank the archivists of the following institutions: Archives de France, Cedex, Paris; the Heraklion Museum, Crete; the Creek National Museum, Athens; the Barbados Museum; the Jamaica Archives, Spanish town, Jamaica and the British Museum.

Special thanks to the National Gallery, Dublin, the *Irish Examiner* and the *Southern Star* for their kind permission to reproduce photographs and old reports.

Thanks to the University of Oregon for permission to use photographs from the Gifford collection.

*This book is dedicated to
Celia, my mother.*

PREFACE

During the early 1980s I became interested in local history and spent most of my spare time visiting all the known historical sites in the Bantry Bay region. In time I collected a substantial amount of information, especially on the megalithic monuments of the area. I recorded much of this in the *Guide to the Antiquities of the Bantry Region*, which is now out of print.

Trekking over the mountainsides and glens, I found many sites which were not listed or recorded, and I heard tales of a vast number of others which had vanished off the face of the earth while successive governments did nothing to protect this ancient heritage of ours in West Cork. The case of the Kilnaruane Stone is the best example of the government's complete lack of care for our ancient monuments.

Having first concentrated on researching the historical sites in the field, I spent the next few years trying to piece together the pre-history of the region. Consulting the ancient Irish literature, as well as that of Western Europe and the Mediterranean countries, I was able to put together a historical picture of the main events which influenced our local history up to the time of St. Patrick. In fact, the first section of this book in itself would constitute a substantial volume in its own right if expanded with all the information I accumulated.

During the period from the 5th century to the 12th, the history of this part of West Cork, due to its isolated situation, has been very poorly documented. In fact, the events in Bantry Bay were better known in France and Spain than in Cork, Dublin or London, because of our sea commerce with those countries. Even the important Bardic School of the O'Dalaigh near Kilcrohane was better known on the Continent than in the rest of Ireland.

Not until the forced migration southwards, in the 12th century, of the O'Mahonys, O'Sullivans, the O'Donovans and their followers do we get any reasonable documented history of local events. In the following centuries our records are mostly those which were accumulated by the Anglo-Normans who were inclined to record in writing every important event. Even after the Battle of Kinsale in 1601 until the end of the 19th century, most of the recording of history was done by the (English) ruling class and it was not until about the turn of the 20th century that Irish historians began to work in earnest. With the main sources available being the religious writers, along with the plainly biased interpretation of historical fact by the English,our historians were facing an uphill battle.

The 'earliest' recorded history of the country contained in the Irish Annals written from sources of the 14th century is biased and imbued with a primitive Christian doctrine. These were written by the religious for the religious and not for 'common consumption'. The tales and events that they relate are sometimes taken out of the context of tradition and lose their true interpretation amidst the dogmas and accepted beliefs of the religious scribes. Anything that was contrary to the Christian thinking of the time was omitted and only those passages which could be accepted, or changed to suit Christian teaching, were included.

We may ask ourselves what were the main sources of history that the monks used? Many centuries had passed since the demise of the Druid Schools of Learning and the famous bardic tradition. Even though St. Patrick is reputed to have 'burnt over 1,500 pagan books and scrolls' on the Hill of Tara, some parchments or records must have survived throughout the early centuries of Christianity.

Bearing the above in mind, the reader will find in the following pages a somewhat new interpretation of history which I hope is closer to fact than that presented heretofore. Some people will find the contents controversial and not compatible with the accepted norms of documented history. I have not complied with the standard interpretation of historical facts as laid out by many important and eminent historians of the past, but rather attempted to throw a new light on the subject matter.

I do hope that in reading the following pages you will find items of interest which will broaden your understanding of our history and that of Bantry and Bantry Bay.

INTRODUCTION

Situated on the south-west coast of Ireland on the western outskirts of Europe, Bantry Bay has often been referred to as the 'Bay of Destiny'.

The events which have occurred here, from prehistoric times to almost the present day, have changed or influenced the history of Ireland, Europe and, to a lesser extent, the world.

Firstly, there are the accounts in the ancient annals, especially *The Book of Invasions* (Leabhair Gabhala), which describe the first people to come to these shores as having arrived in Bantry Bay. This was Cessair and her followers who disembarked at the well known location outside of Bantry called Donamark or Dunamark (Dun-na-mBarc). This event, even though previously considered as mere legend or myth, is now judged to contain a certain amount of fact, as it had been transcribed by Christian monks despite being a complete contradiction of the Old Testament account of the Deluge.

Sometime later, after the last Ice Age, during the period 6500 BCE to 2500 BCE came the Beaker people and the megalithic builders, who, by erecting various types of stone edifices, converted the bleak and wild countryside into one of the greatest concentrations of prehistoric monuments to be found in Western Europe.

Then, as related in the *Book of Invasions*, the Tuatha de Danaan landed here, to be followed by the Milesians (c.1700–1400 BCE) whose descendants were to rule and dominate the country, as well as the seas around the British Isles, for almost two millennia.

The Norsemen came and made their bases on Dursey Island and at Donamark, from where they plundered and ruled the waves of the south-west coast for a century until they were defeated both at sea and on land by the local tribes.

At the end of the 12th century, the Anglo-Normans arrived and built their castles and tried to dominate the land, while the local tribes fought amongst themselves over territory, cattle and women. However, realising that the Anglo-Normans were the common enemy they joined forces and entrapped the iron-clad horsemen and footsoldiers at the battle of Callan in 1261, thus inflicting on the enemy their first defeat on Irish soil, and also bringing into existence a type of warfare which later became known as guerrilla warfare.

The English adventurers and settlers exploited the natural resources, including the fisheries, woods, forests and the native population. The exported fish fed nations both on this side of the Atlantic and across the ocean in the Caribbean colonies. The timber from the despoiled woodlands built the great warships of English navy which was to dominate the oceans for centuries, and built mansions and country houses, while the native Irish were treated no better than slaves.

A French fleet came in 1689 and, besides landing a substantial force, inflicted on the English navy its first humiliating defeat in what was called the 'Battle of Bantry Bay'. Over a century later, in 1796, came Wolfe Tone and another French invasion force, which, due to severe weather conditions, failed to land an army of over 16,000 to liberate Ireland. If the invasion had succeeded, Ireland would have been liberated, England defeated on both land and sea, and most of Western Europe would have become a collection of revolutionary republics.

From the towns, villages and hinterland emerged a group of dedicated men who infiltrated the British House of Commons by becoming MPs, where they used their influence to change the British attitude towards Ireland and who, by their efforts, became known as the 'Bantry Band'.

Fearing further French invasions the English built their sea fortifications making Bantry Bay one of their major naval ports from the 1800s, culminating in Berehaven harbour becoming their dominant position from which to control the sea lanes of the Western Approaches during the First World War, preserving England and her allies from naval defeat. A point of interest is that the Prince of Wales and the German Kaiser partied, drank and finally shook hands on Bantry pier before war was declared between their two nations. Towards the end of the war Jellicoe sailed with the British fleet from Berehaven to the Battle of Jutland.

To Bantry Bay came the English and European royalty, as well as famous writers, poets and personages of note, to spend their vacations cruising around the Bay in the idyllic surroundings of a semi-tropical climate. Meanwhile, the local Irish were marching on the hidden country roads, learning to drill and bear arms for the eventual struggle which would liberate the country from English rule. The achievements of these local volunteers are well noted in history as having a direct bearing on the final outcome.

Towards the end of the Second World War, when the British presence was no longer visible, the arrival of the Spanish fishing fleet heralded a slight recovery for local trade and commerce. The adoption of Bantry as the second home port for the Spanish and other European fishing fleets brought back the importance of Bantry as a port and renewed its ties with Continental Europe.

The building of a crude oil terminal and the age of the super tankers created a drastic change in the transportation of oil from the Middle East to Europe, which in a way changed the economic growth of Western Europe. Bantry became a 'boom' town but all this changed when the tanker *Betelgeuse* exploded in 1979 and the loss of over 50 lives and the destruction of the Jetty brought a premature end to the economic recovery of the town.

Since that time, Bantry has once again dragged itself out of oblivion to become one of the major shellfish farming sites in Western Europe as well as a mecca for tourism. In addition, the oil terminal has been brought back into operation but with limited tanker numbers visiting the port.

In the following pages the reader will discover events and facts which have only been partially recorded to date, or not at all. In the absence of full written historical documentation, the writer has interpreted the various oral traditions so as to give as accurate an account as possible.

As a final note in this introduction I will just say that it is not my intention to cast aspersions on any belief – local or otherwise – to change recorded facts, or to blame any person or groups for any past event.

I

ANCIENT IRELAND

If all the references to ancient Ireland by early writers and historians are examined, it will be found that there are numerous names given to this country. When we look closely at our own ancient annals of Irish history, we must bear in mind that they were rewritten and framed by Christian monks, bards and scribes. The product of their endeavour is confusing, owing to the revisions and alterations made as concessions to the vanity of their illustrious patrons – the Kings, Chieftains and Lords Abbot.

A good example of this practice is clearly demonstrated in the description and contents of the Book of Invasion, where all events, people and dates were changed to suit Christian dogma at the time of writing. It is also evident that the transcribers were attempting to follow the early French custom of trying to prove a direct lineage back to Noah for their benefactors.

In this context, one could not omit mentioning the instance of the 'poor monk' who rewrote the *Tale of Cessair* – the history of the first inhabitants of Ireland. He placed her landing before the Deluge, the account of which survived afterwards, in complete contradiction to Biblical teaching. It can be asked, how was this event handed down for posterity if everyone perished in the Deluge except those that were in Noah's Ark?

In light of the above, it is an extremely difficult task to extricate facts from our ancient manuscripts. However, with the assistance of early Hebrew, Egyptian, Minoan, Greek and Roman historians some parts of our early history can be clarified. As a result some of the conclusions reached by historians, such as Keating, O'Flaherty and O'Rahilly, are found to be debatable. These eminent historians were over-reliant on existing Irish sources and did not, for one reason or another, consult the many 'foreign' records.

When the references to ancient Ireland, its inhabitants and Bantry Bay made by O'Flaherty and others are examined, it will be found that the name Iernus (Ireland) is used and the inhabitants are called Ierni or Classa Eibheir. Unlike O'Flaherty and Keating who refer to Kenmare Bay as Inmbear Sceine, Ptolemy, the Greek historian, equates Inmbear Sceine with Bantry Bay. Sceine or Sceana is sometimes interpreted as Dannua, the leader of the Tuatha de Danaan. She was a high-priestess and sometimes regarded by earlier inhabitants as a witch in possession of magical powers. Yet, in another historical context both O'Flaherty and Keating equate Inmbear Sceine with Ceann Mhara which in fact is another name for Bantry Bay.

Ptolemy drawing on the sea-faring expeditions of the Phoenicians refers to the island of Ireland as 'Ivernia' and to the inhabitants of Bantry Bay as the 'Vodil' or 'Uodii'. The name Vodil was placed over Whiddy Island in his map of Ireland, while the inhabitants or tribes of the neighbouring coastline were referred to as the Coriondii (Corunnaigh) and the Velaborii (Veliberi).

It has been suggested that Ptolemy's knowledge of the coastlines of Western Europe and the British Isles was limited. This is not true. He had the reports and rudimentary maps of the Phoenicians and other Eastern Mediterranean seafarers who had ventured out into the Atlantic. What has been overlooked is that these seafarers in the search for trade, gold, silver and copper knew every harbour and inlet on the south English coast and Ireland as they left behind them evidence of such activities.

The main sources of early Roman references to Ireland are Caesar's Commentaries (*De Bello Gallico*), Tacitus (*Vita Agriculae*), Dionysius Periegesis, Pomponius Mela, Juvenal and Orosius. In these, Ireland is variously referred to as Hibernia, I-er-ne, Juverna, Ivernia and Iariin. All of these mean the 'Western Isle' or 'Land of the Western Isle'.

The term Gael, or Land of the Gael, has many connotations. The earliest reference to the Gooidhil (Gael) is found in ancient Hebrew as Gadol, according to Hector Boetius, the early historian. In this context, the name refers to the 'followers of Gaodhal' who were in Egypt at the time of Moses. They were later to be found in Crete and then in Scythia. Afterwards, this Hebrew tribe seem to have vanished from the Eastern Mediterranean. It is also interesting to note that Caesar and other Roman historians referred to the first settlers in Ireland as the Gaill or Godill, which means herdsmen or hunters which is not to be confused with the Goths, who are reputed to have fled to Ireland after being defeated by the roman Emperor Vespasian c. 68 CE.

If we examine the ancient Irish Language, we discover that it contains 16 letters, as in early Greek, and had the same basic structure. Taken as a whole, the Irish language was made up of forty per cent early Greek, 30 per cent early Etruscan (Latin), ten per cent Hebrew and ten per cent Berber dialect (North Africa). Taking these facts into consideration, it is strange to find that past historians disregarded the contact between the Eastern Mediterranean civilisations and the south of Ireland in their conclusions on the origins of the various prehistoric 'invaders'. In fact, they arrived at the erroneous conclusion that there was no similarity between Old Irish and Scythian, Coptic, and early Cantabric letters and languages. If a closer look is taken of early Irish, it is found that the numerals are Arabic; alphabetic numerals are early Roman (borrowed from Greek); Irish names of numbers 1 to 100 are Latin; names of trees etc. are early Cycladic Greek (from Phoenicians).

In this context, it is of relevance to note the comments of three early historians. Tacitus, the Roman historian, wrote that 'the harbours of Ireland were better known to the seafarers of the Mediterranean than those of Britain'. Avenius, also Roman, wrote that 'the Carthaginians traded with Ireland which they called Oestrumnides' and Dionysius Periegesis of the third century CE wrote that 'the early Greeks knew Ireland well'.

It is indeed surprising that most of those who wrote about the ancient history of Ireland were unwilling to accept that the early inhabitants of this country could have come from outside the boundaries of Western Europe. In fact, they often seem to have had limited, or 'tunnel' vision as to the origins of the early inhabitants. If they had only studied the rites of the ancient Irish Druids, they could not but recognise their close resemblance to the rites and worship of the Sumerians (early Persians). In the context of our own stone circles and places of ancient worship, we find that the Sumerians had no temples as such, but stone altars or stone arrangements on high hills and dominant positions of the countryside where sacred fires were lit during the rites and ceremonies to the moon, sun and earth.

If we look at Greek references to Ireland, we find that the historians, Herodotus, Hecataeus, Aristotle, Hellanicus and Ephories, mentioned that the 'land of the Gooidhil' lies beyond the 'Pillars of Hercules' (entrance to the Mediterranean). It is very doubtful that the Greeks were referring to the Celts in Catalonia (Spain) or in Northern Gaul (France) at that time, but is more likely that they were referring to a different race of people that inhabited Ireland.

Taken in this context, what follows is a singular viewpoint of the ancient history of Ireland.

II

IRELAND'S EARLY INHABITANTS

It is not known for certain when Ireland was first inhabited – before or after the last Ice Age. It is generally accepted, without evidence to the contrary, that there was a native aboriginal race on the island c. 8500 BCE referred to as 'native Neolithic Man'. The Neolithic Period extended from c. 8500 BCE to the Early Bronze Age, around 3000 BCE.

However, it is also evident that primitive man existed in Europe during the Palaeolithic Age (Old Stone Age, c. 100,000 BCE) or before.

Whether this primitive man existed in Ireland during the same period and had to leave during the last Ice Age is open to question. No evidence of such occupation has yet come to light. As Ireland and Britain were part of the European continent during that time, and as similar animal bones have been found here, it is reasonable to suppose that primitive cavemen lived in this western section of the continent.

With the ever-changing climate, from hot and tropical to Ice Age, primitive man had to be constantly on the move. When he finally did arrive, whether by means of the land connection between Co. Down and the coast of Scotland, or by primitive boat along the east or south coast, he encountered a deeply forested and wooded land, with misty bogs, newly formed lakes, raging rivers and high mountains. The newly found country was inhabited by animals such as elk, wolves, deer, wild boar, foxes and bears while the rivers and lakes abounded in fish.

The land was not very hospitable, and it was extremely dangerous to advance inland. He would have moved slowly along the coastline, either by dug-out canoe or on foot. Living mostly near river mouths, he built a basic shelter with wicker, timber and mud. He surrounded this shelter with a circle of fencing made out of thorn bushes and spikes, in order to protect himself, his family domesticated animals and fowl from the attacks of packs of wolves.

It is interesting to note that, according to historians and archaeologists the great elk existed on the arrival of man in Ireland. But the animal most feared was the wolf, which roamed the country in great numbers and attacked in packs. All early fortifications were built for protection against wolf attack rather than human foes.

As a point of interest the location where the last wolf in the country was killed, in 1827, was in the woods north of Kilgarvan. Wild boar, which can be a very dangerous adversary, were numerous in those early times and remained so, right down to the 17th century, in the wilds of West Cork and Kerry. From the recent discovery of boar tusks, it is estimated that these animals were much larger than the common boar seen nowadays.

From the coastline and river estuaries, aboriginal man slowly explored the interior, following the rivers and streams. In the beginning, his journeys inland were taken with great trepidation. It is unlikely, that he stayed away from his small fortified enclosure overnight, unless he had located a defensible cave or a suitable safe tree. His major aim was to make safe shelters which could be visited in daylight hours and used as outposts so that he could explore further inland.

When a more suitable location for his home was found, he immediately fortified it, and then transferred his family and kin, at least until he found a more suitable location. Sometimes, caves were used as a transition home, as they could easily be defended from the prowling wolves.

In the Bantry area, suitable caves were scarce, due to the types of rock and the last glaciation. Yet, on the northern Caha Ridge there are a number of habitable caves in such places as Borlin, Coomhola, Glengarriff and north-east of Adrigole. Some of these have yet to be examined by archaeologists but some contain Neolithic drawings and scribing. Some examples of this rock scribing are reproduced in the following pages.

The question of when primitive man arrived in the Bantry region is difficult to answer. If we are to accept that the 'shell-midden' sites in Ballyferriter, county Kerry date from c.4300 BCE, and that the two similar middens found at Donemark and Glengarriff date from roughly the same period, further research and archaeological exploration is necessary to find evidence of earlier habitation. Much of the earlier system of dating for prehistory was based on carbon dating alone, but in recent times dendrochronology is being accepted as a much more accurate method of dating. For example, Newgrange has been corrected by over 800 years to c. 3450 BCE, placing its construction prior to that of Stonehenge and the Pyramids of Egypt. This new date for Newgrange, and the possibility that other historical sites have been incorrectly dated, points to a major historical problem, that early primitive civilisation in Ireland possessed the knowledge of building these large stone monuments before the rest of Europe. This question of the accepted diffusion of civilisation will be explained in the following chapter.

Meanwhile, the question remains: where did primitive man come from, and why did he choose this island. Was it from necessity, or was it the need to explore? The accepted explanation is that he was pushed westwards by the influx of other primitive tribes from Eastern Europe.

Maybe there is another answer to this question: that primitive man sought refuge here, not due to the fact that he was forced out of Europe, but because some natural disaster where he previously existed forced him to move on. From what is known about this early period of history, there were only two major events which occurred – and these can be accepted either as fact or myth.

The first is the account of the Deluge, or great flood, which had been recorded by most of the Middle Eastern civilisations. However, most recent research has found that the deluge, as such, only affected that particular part of the world. Whether some of the people fled the deluge and made their way out into the Atlantic is open to question.

The second possible answer lies to the west. Recently, it has been discovered that a meteorite hit the area around the Yucatan peninsula c.9500–12000 BCE. This discovery now supports the idea of the destruction of the legendary continent of Atlantis (as described by the Greek, Plato), which was situated in the North Atlantic between Europe and North America. Briefly, it was described as the most advanced culture of that time, with pyramids, buildings, and palaces which were the forerunners of those that appeared much later in the Middle East and Mexico. Its system of government was based on a monarchy of nepotism, with a powerful priestly class who practised monotheism to the sun-god. It is believed that Atlantis was destroyed by earthquake, fire and a tidal wave, and then sank to the bottom of the ocean.

Returning to Plato, he states that the earliest inhabitants of the Nile Delta, before the emergence of the kingdom of Egypt, related that 'a great seafaring nation came out of the West and settled amongst us'.

Who were these people? According to historians, with the exception of Plato, they did not exist, as the known world was regarded as flat and ended in the Western Mediterranean. Were these people from the West, in fact, fugitives from the legendary kingdom of Atlantis and were they the same early inhabitants of this country as one of the early 'Invasions' of Ireland who are said to have arrived by boat from the west?

There are many conflicting ideas as to the type of boat or sea-going vessel that was used by those who came to our shores in early times.

It has been almost unanimously agreed by Irish historians that the hide-skin curraghs were the main type of sea transport used here up to the arrival of the Vikings around 840 CE. This conclusion is based on the premise that only those types of boats are depicted in copies of early documents, and no evidence has been produced of any other type of boat being used.

To say the least, the historians were rather insular in their belief as modern-day research and discoveries have proved. For example, the recent discovery of dug-out canoes in the Midland bog has been dated to before 500 BCE. Also, a more recent discovery in the Solent of a timber vessel over 36 metres long dated c.4000 BCE gives credence to timber vessels plying off the south coast of England and Ireland. If the inhabitants could build a timber vessel up to 36 metres in length they were able to build vessels of lesser size. Both Tacitus and Caesar describe the sea-going vessels of Western Gaul as being 'beyond imagination' and being larger than the Mediterranean trireme used by the Romans, Greeks and Carthaginians.

However, the question remains as to how this early art of building large timber vessels could have disappeared. The answer is simple, as we know too well today: when the craftsman dies so does his art or was it that Druids or high priests demanded that no large ships should be built so as to protect their position and to keep the country free of outside influences.

Yet, early man in Ireland developed in other directions, and was noted for his ability in the shaping and making of primitive tools as weapons. After a period of time they were able to make and improve spearheads, make flint flakes, borers, scrapers, saws, arrowheads, javelins and axe-heads. With this advance in weaponry early man felt secure in venturing inland from the coastline. He was no longer fearful of the wolf. And so a new age dawned – the Megalithic Age – for primitive man, also known as the Stone Builders.

The Stone Builders

The greater Bantry region which would incorporate the Beara and Sheep's Head peninsulas contains one of the greatest concentrations of megalithic monuments in Western Europe. In numbers, the region contains more monuments than Carnac in France. It is evident that those who brought this art of erecting stone monuments inhabited Brittany, Southern England and Ireland. If we study the early migration of an early civilisation out of the Mediterranean we find that they moved along the Spanish, Portuguese and west coast of France before they arrived here. There are no parchments or early papyri sketching this migration but we do have similar types of places of worship, stone circles, burial grounds, dolmens and standing stones. Many of these were in alignments with the sun, moon, stars and other natural phenomena such as tides and equinoxes.

Unfortunately, our local important monuments, which number in the hundreds, are not preserved or protected like Newgrange,

Knowth, and Dowth. In a sense, they have been forgotten, and suffered the ravages of time, decay and vandalism. In addition, without proper monitoring by the Heritage department, stone circles, standing stones etc. have been removed from the landscape in the name of development. We are surrounded by one of the greatest tourist attractions in the country, and few people realise it. I suppose that it's one of the best kept secrets of West Cork as a whole.

It is difficult to believe that, as the majority of historians suggest, primitive man in Ireland advanced by 'leaps and bounds' during the period 4500-1500 BCE. We are led to belief that Ireland was extremely isolated, and visited only by those who dwelled in the neighbouring island. How primitive man could have advanced so much in knowledge of the sciences, religion, and basic culture without the influence of 'foreign' cultures defies logical thinking.

The supposition that sea-going vessels capable of making the long voyage (say from northern Spain) did not exist during this period rules out the possibility of early sea-going people visiting our shores. However, the absence of artefacts or remains of large vessels on our shoreline does not justify the conclusion that they did not visit. For all we know, ancient wrecks could still be located in our harbours and creeks without us knowing it.

The Phoenicians, those early voyagers and explorers from the Eastern Mediterranean, were already circumnavigating the continent of Africa c. 600 BCE. There is no reason to doubt that they could also have voyaged northwards to Ireland. As a matter of fact, everything points to this fact, regardless of what other historians believed. The Phoenicians were extremely secretive about their sea-faring expeditions and the lands that they found. Having explored the Western Mediterranean, they established a city, called Tartassos, at the mouth of the

Gaualdalquiver (south of modern-day Cadiz) on the coast of Spain. From this base they began to explore the lands to the north and the south, which boarded on the Atlantic. In contrast to the Egyptians, their vessels were built of cedar wood held together by timber dowels. Prior to the introduction of sea-going vessels by the Phoenicians, the Sumerians seem to have been the first to utilize sea transport c.5500 BCE when they transported massive stones by river for the building of Kish, Erech and Ur and explored the Persian Gulf and the coast of India using a 'load-stone' as a compass which always pointed to the north. No doubt, the Phoenicians also used the same method for navigation.

A point worth noting here is that the first known record of Noah and the flood was found on a broken clay tablet in the ruins of the city of Nippur. Some 500 years later the Hebrews wrote their own version, which had wildly exaggerated the original account. Finally, the Uruk people were the first to introduce copper tools; they invented the wheel, and wrote hieroglyphic records on clay tablets.

Returning to the Phoenicians, we find that they had passed Agadir and were already at the Cape of Good Hope by c.600 BCE. During their progress southwards they established various outposts, other vessels followed with families, animals and goods to establish settlements. As they moved northwards along the coast of Spain and Portugal with vessels propelled by both oars and sail, the same system of colonisation followed. Early references show that they were already trading with the 'people of the Northern Isles' for precious metals well before 3500 BCE, and no doubt they had set up their own trading outpost along our southern coastline.

In those early days of trading and bartering, many customs of Middle Eastern culture found their way into usage here.

Communication was probably by sign language at first, until certain important words came into usage. After a time, the interpreters would have come into play and knowledge began to spread. No doubt, when winter storms and gales came early, these eastern traders were obliged to sojourn here for the winter months which resulted in intermarriage and relationships commencing. At this time in local history, our heritage was born.

The investigation of Ireland's pre-history only began in the 1870s and, therefore, we must realise, as many historians and archaeologists have pointed out that we are only dealing with 'the tip of the iceberg'. No statement is more true as far as this part of the country is concerned.

With the absence of artefacts such as implements, utensils, cooking objects, urns, weapon, hieroglyphics, rock painting etc. such as are found in the Middle Eastern countries, we would expect to be totally in the dark as regards this most ancient civilisation and its culture. Fortunately, this is not the case, as we are able to trace the existence of those early people by a variety of means:

1. Religion and religious rites
2. Their systems of burials
3. Their knowledge of astronomy
4. Their rock scribings
5. Their gods
6. The survival of ancient place names

Religion and Religious Rites

In order to consider the earliest of religious beliefs and practices here in the southern part of Ireland, we must first briefly examine the religions of the ancient Sumerian (Urak people), Assyrians, Phoenicians and Carthaginians. We will find certain similarities with these which may be surprising to some people. One of the most important tenets of the early Sumerian religion was dualism: the belief in the existence of two original uncreated principles – good and evil – which were two mighty beings in continuous conflict. One was the creator of life, earth, the heavens and all things spiritual, while the other was the creator of all that was evil. Both of these gods had a number of inferior spirits, and principal amongst them was the good spirit and leader of the angelic host, Serosh, on which example the Christian Archangel Michael was fashioned. With the offering of sacrifice and the burning of the 'sacred fire' these were the origins of a priestly sect from which came our ancient druids. Later, this religion became corrupted into the practise of worshipping the four elements of fire, air (wind), earth and water under the direction of a powerful priest-caste. The fire-altars on the mountain tops and high ground became the centrepiece of their religion, where the high-priest reigned as the chief mediator between the gods and people. Here we see the origins of our Druidic fires and the reverence for water. A point to note is that it was unusual for a woman to be high-priest (see Shubad).

The Assyrians

As for the Assyrians, who were in power in Iraq and Iran c. 5000 to 1500 BCE, we find a few important points which are worth noting. They believed in a supreme god, Ra, and under him existed a triad of minors gods: Anu (chaos), Bel (creative spirit) and Hoa (animate matter), or, in other words, the gods of water, heaven and earth. Of these, Bel is the most important to us as he represents the maker of heaven, earth and the minor sun-god Shaman who is represented as the 'lord of the fire' and 'the light of the gods'. The seventh month, Tisri, was dedicated to him, and he had nine festivals. In the ancient Sumerian 'deluge' tablets, it was he who caused the great flood.

Phoenicians and Carthaginians
Within the limited polytheism of the Phoenicians we find a number of gods which bear a certain similarity to our own ancient gods: El, Baal, Moloch and Shamas. Of those, El had the personality of a supreme or most high god; Baal is the 'lord' or 'master' while Moloch is the 'king'. Baaltis was the feminine form of Baal and so we find that the Phoenicians worshipped goddesses such as Ashtoreth. Baal was really the supreme god or eternal king to whom all Phoenicians were dedicated or consecrated after birth.

Another god worth mentioning here is Dragon, whose worship spread throughout the Mediterranean and further. He is represented as the 'fish-god', deriving from dag, meaning fish and is well represented in Egyptian mythology. Shamas, or Shemesh, 'the sun', was worshipped separately from Baal, and this practice was accompanied by the use of 'sun-images'. The Phoenicians followed the custom of offering human sacrifices to placate the gods in time of great pestilence or calamity. They, however, were not idolaters as such, but worshiped the 'ever burning fire' to Baal. Also, large wooden uprights, or 'Asherahs' were used, and these, together with stone monuments, were worshipped by sung praises, prayer and sacrifice. The 'asherahs' became sacred trees and from this came the worship of certain types of trees in later religious ceremonies. Their festivals were held mainly at the equinoxes, especially at the vernal, when everybody gathered for the festivals.

If we look more closely at the religion of the Phoenicians we will find some very interesting facts in relation to the religion of ancient Ireland. Baal and his fires had a major influence. The Irish word for February, Bealtaine, denotes both the god and fire and when the end of winter was celebrated. In most of the collection of rock scribing found in the greater Bantry region we find many examples of the sun. The worship of stones was also prevalent in the form of standing stones. Moloch became used in place names like the mountain Molochmeise which means the 'altar' to Moloch. Certain trees such as the oak, yew and rowan were regarded as holy, and were worshiped as such. And as mentioned earlier the names of trees derive from the Phoenician. Before I leave this section it is worth mentioning that I located a rock in Leitrim Beg, which had the 'boat of Osiris' scribed on its surface. Also, I located an early Greek script in a cave which has been verified as early Cycladic – 2500 BCE. One wonders what else could be found with exploration and site investigation.

Ancient Burial Sites

When we examine the ancient burial rites practiced by the early inhabitants of this region, the connection with the Middle East becomes more apparent. The profusion of megalithic monuments – stone circles, dolmens, standing stones, cromlechs, and burial chambers – in the area, we must trace back to the commencement of these burial practices in pre-history.

If we follow the trail of identical monuments we trace our way through Brittany, Northern Spain, Portugal, Malta, Libya, Crete, Lebanon, Syria, Iran, Hindustan, the Upper , and the upper reaches of the Ganges River in India. It appears that there was a general migration of early civilisations westwards and some noted historians are of the opinion that this diffusion took place as far back as 8500 BCE. This opinion would give credence to the idea that the Irish round towers were not native but came from some other foreign country. It seems that the only other location of note where these round towers were located was a valley north of Peshawar, in modern Pakistan, where a religious sect worshipped the phallic symbol and built round towers in its image. Also, in this context we must remember that the early Irish celebrated the 'the day of Llama' which originated in Tibet.

Taking but a few examples of the similarity between our ancient burial methods and those of other eastern countries, we only have to look at Catal Huyuk (c.6500 BCE) in Eastern Turkey, Knossos (Crete), Nea Nikomedeia (Macedonia), Dhimini (Greece), Pylos and the Cycladic Islands. If we look at Newgrange we find an almost identical example at Platanos (Crete) and Khiroktia in Cyprus, both of which have been dated as 5800 BCE. The early circular tombs were communal, for families or tribes over numerous generations. Where this system of collective burial came from is open to question, but it seems to have originated in Anatolia (northern Turkey), and to have been introduced to the eastern Mediterranean by a nomadic race, whose custom was to live in round huts surrounded by either timber fences or clay wall for protection. Artefacts prove that the dead of important families had the protection of two mounds, or walls, sometime with a type of dyke between them. It is no wonder, therefore, that the burial places took on the shape of existing living quarters as the abode of the dead in after-life.

Primitive Astronomy

To describe the unbelievable grasp held by early civilisation of the movements of the sun, moon and stars as 'primitive' would seem to be a great misnomer. When we consider astronomy, we have to bear in mind its relationship with mathematics, geometry and the calendar.

Having discussed the systems of burials in the previous pages, and compared them with what we find in Ireland, it is important to mention one major difference, and that is that most of our ancient major burials are surrounded by stone circles. This introduces another dimension, as their alignment coincides with the movement of the sun, moon and stars. Newgrange, for example, was surrounded by a circle of 35 or 36 stones.

Amongst the best examples of the ancient knowledge of astronomy is the Solar Calendar of Heriopolis, while at Carnac there is a wonderful example of the alignment of 'menhirs' (standing stones) while our own stone circles and standing stone alignments have also a direct reference to the movement of the sun, moon and stars, including equinoxes, solstices, tides and an overall grid system within the area concerned.

At this point it is most important to clarify the question of standing stone circles. These are not Celtic druid circles, but are of an age which predates the so-called Celtic invasion of Ireland by several thousands of years. The ancient circles of standing stones consisted of a ring of pillar stones (of any height) which were set on end and enclosed a circular patch of ground. In addition, there was a solitary stone outside the circle, whilst both within, and part of, the circle were the portal stones and a recumbent stone. Through the portal stones was the entrance to the circle while the exact function of the recumbent stone is not known but was probably used for animal or human sacrifice. Some historians, including R.A.S. Macalister, were of the opinion that the various stones of a stone circle represented different deities but this is very questionable as then we would have 8 to 36 gods, which would not conform to the beliefs of the early inhabitants. It is interesting to note here that the largest stone circle in Ireland with stones over five metres high, was situated on the south side of Hungry Hill (Cnoc Da Dia), which suffered from amateurish excavations in the 19th century. Grose depicted the stone circle in one of his books on Ireland.

Ancient Religious Symbols

In this context we see the influence of the different religious beliefs of various civilisations of the Middle East. In order to understand our own ancient religion we must first look at those elements of beliefs that are common to most, if not all early religions, which have been depicted on some of our ancient monuments but mostly explained in the ancient customs which are discussed in a later chapter.

Spirals

This symbol is predominant in all burial rituals and ancient sites. It represents the worship of the 'Earth Mother' or goddess of life and fertility and the return of the body of the deceased to the care of the Earth Mother. It also represents the cycle of life here on earth. Some of the best examples of spirals, sun-shaped drawings etc. are to be found at Kealanine near Coomhola which was known in early times as the 'Valley of the Kings'. In this valley, large souterains, stone circles, and a dolmen are also to be found.

Sun Symbols

There are many variations and examples of this particular symbol, but the basic theme is that of a circle, or solar disc, with interior geometric patterns, or a surround of rays emitting from the centre. This symbol also denotes the place of burial of a ruler or leader, who was blessed by the sun-god through his priests, and which marked his grave or territory.

Boat of the Sun-god

It is generally accepted that all our dolmens were originally covered by mud, earth and stones, to form a mound. Only the basic structure of dolmens now exist, which comprises of three upright stones supporting a reclining cap stone. It is generally accepted that this structure represents a ship with its high prow, supported by the three pillar stones (triad of the gods), which transported the spirits of the dead to the Other World and in the early Egyptian religion represented the 'ship of Osiris' transporting the dead to the Other World.

The most common symbol of the above is that of a boat with some figures on board – the spirits of the dead – being transported to the Other World by the sun-god on his nightly journeys. There is a clear indication here that there was a widespread belief in the transmigration of the spirit in most early civilisation, including Ireland.

There are not many examples of this ship in Ireland but a few have been discovered. One of which, I discovered in Leitrim Beg, between Glengarriff and Adrigole, which was depicted on a large stone which had been moved by a farmer clearing his land.

III

THE LEGEND OF CESSAIR

There are many versions in the old Irish Manuscripts of the arrival on our shores of the first human being – in the person of Cessair. We must not forget that the medieval scribes, who recorded these events, as well as other myths and legends, were imbued with the dominant tenets of early Christianity. They were translating the early Irish language as well as writing down the spoken words of the bards which recorded past history in verse. As the early Irish language did not conform to the grammatical structures of Latin, we must assume that the original stories would have lost something in translation. Therefore, their interpretation of these stories would have been clouded by their own beliefs, and the written records, such as early manuscripts contain only what was acceptable to church teaching at that time.

The exact original contents of the Cessair legend will never be known. However, if we examine closely the various interpretations, we will be able to separate the pagan and the Christian elements of the story. At the time of translating the old stories of the various 'invasions' or incursions in the Leabhair Gabhala (*Book of Invasions*), the notion and practice of filling in the genealogies of all famous people and events from the time of Noah was uppermost in the early Church's mind, so as to give a sense of identity and meaning to all that was written. Accordingly, the story of Cessair has been written in a semi-religious context, with an attempt to discard any pagan symbolism in the process. As the monk scribes were dealing with a very important event, namely the flood, they had to be extremely careful not to contradict the 'Word of God' as revealed in the Old Testament. As things turned out, they failed miserably in their attempts, as by mentioning Cessair at all, they implied that there were other arks besides that of Noah. The story, as related by the early scribes, is briefly as follows:

Having been warned by Noah that a 'great flood' was imminent, Cessair, daughter of Bith, son of Noah, gathered her followers and constructed three 'arks'. When the vessels were ready they sailed out of Mere, upon the Nile, to the open sea. During their voyage, which lasted for seven years and three months, two of the vessels were lost in a storm. Finally, some forty days before the deluge commenced, Cessair and her crew landed at Dun-na-mBarc, near Bantry. On the vessel with Cessair were three men – Bith, Ldara and Fintan – and fifty women. No details were given as to the numbers of people on the vessels that were lost except that they each also had fifty women aboard, but, since we are dealing with a conventional, repeated combination of numbers here, we may assume that there were also three men on each vessel. There is no mention as to how long they remained at Dun-na-mBarc before setting off again. Having arrived at the 'meeting of the three rivers (Suir, Nore and Barrow) the three men divided the women between them – Fintan took Cessair and seventeen women, Bith took seventeen women and Ladra only got sixteen and was unhappy with the division. Fintan, Cessair and their group headed north along the coast leaving Bith and Ladra and their women. In time, word reached Bith and Fintan that Ladra had died of 'an excess of women' so they came together again and divided Ladra's 16 women between them. It is recorded that they all died sometime later of pestilence.

This is recorded as the first 'incursion' to our shores, but when we examine it more carefully we must ask a number of questions. If only Noah and those who he had aboard his ark had survived the flood according to the Bible how was this tale of Cessair passed down to posterity? The early scribes decided that Fintan, having drowned in the flood, afterwards rose from the dead and passed on his story for posterity. So, according to our early Christian monks and scribes, Fintan was the first Lazarus!

However, it is assumed that the story of Cessair was originally placed just before, and after the flood, like all similar tales in the legends of other Middle Eastern civilisations. In actual fact, the first written account of the deluge was discovered on a broken clay tablet in the ruins of the city of Nippur (Iraq): 'for seven days and seven nights' . . . the flood had swept over the land. And the huge boat had been tossed about by wind storms of the great waters, Zuisundra opened a window in the huge boat and . . .'

Zuisundra was the favourite king of the city state of Sumer, and like Noah, was chosen by the gods to ride out the mighty deluge. Some four centuries later, the Hebrews wrote their version, replacing Zuisundra with Noah, and adding his family to the story.

In this context, it is interesting to note that Sir Leonard Woolley, the archaeologist, on his excavations of the cities of Ur and nearby Al-Ubaid, not far from Nippur, had to dig through 3.5 metres of mud deposits before he found traces of the these famous cities. These deposits of mud and clay were dated as commencing between 1200 and 9500 BCE.

The Greeks also adopted the mythology of the great flood in the tales about their gods. When the god Zeus decided to annihilate the human race by burying it beneath the waves of a deluge and flood, Prometheus warned his son Deucalion and his wife Pyrrha to build an ark. For nine days and nights they rode the waves, and on the tenth day they disembarked on Mount Parnassus, which was the only place still above the sea. When they prayed to Zeus to save the human race, they were spared and the seas subsided

Whatever we may say about the other flood stories, the ancient Irish version, before it was tampered with by the scribes, must have been dated after the deluge, as Cessair means 'life to the world' and Fintan means 'the deathless son of Bochna' (or 'the eternal son of the ocean').

Cessair and her followers had set out on the ark, before the flood, on a holy day called 'Lam Di' (Day of Llama) so that they would have the blessings of the gods. We encounter the mystical numbers seven and three: in the setting out seven years and three months before the flood; in the repeated mention of three men and in their second destination, 'the meeting of the three rivers'. We may also note that Fintan was portrayed as a good man, while Ladra was the opposite, being prone to excesses. Thus, together they represent good and evil.

Standing Stone at Scart, Bantry

IV

ANCIENT CIVILISATIONS IN IRELAND

As far as ancient Irish civilisation is concerned, we must examine what these early inhabitants left behind as proof of their existence, and what similarities there were with other early civilisations.

The evidence for early Irish culture consists of megalithic monuments, tumuli, passage graves, stone circles, stone patterns like spirals and other designs etc. In order to find an explanation as to how the mode of burial and monuments happened in Ireland, we must first look at the approximate dates of the prehistoric 'invaders'.

It is fairly certain that Ireland was inhabited towards the end of the Neolithic era, c.6500 BCE and that the builders of the megalithic monuments arrived either around this time or later towards the beginning of the Bronze Age, c.3500 BCE.

The first arrivals were small in stature, cremated their dead and buried the remains in 'boulder burials' (mound of large boulders).

Another race of people arrived during the Middle Bronze age who were tall in stature and who buried their dead without cremation. Later, at the end of the Bronze Age (2000–1600 BCE) yet another race arrived, who again cremated their dead before burying them with urns and implements. Finally, at the beginning of the Iron Age (1000-500 BCE), small numbers of a more war-like race arrived, and overran the country and dominated the previous inhabitants. These also cremated their dead and buried them with urns of food and weapons.

If we identify the above with those mentioned in the early Irish manuscripts as 'invasion forces', we come up with the possibility that the first mention were the Fir Bolg (so called as they wore leather bags on their backs), the tall people with fair hair were the Tuatha de Danaan, and the Iron Age invaders were the Milesians who are reputed to have arrived from north-western Spain.

The question of where these various groups of people came from has been a subject much debated by historians over the past 150 years. Firstly, many question the authenticity of these ancient accounts, believing them to be pure fiction. Others believe that they contain a degree of factual content, while a few are of the opinion that there is a substantial amount of fact shrouded amongst the legends.

If we are to assume that the various invasions mentioned were likely to come from Britain, as the nearest island, why has it been stated that the culture of Ireland was almost a thousand years more advanced than in Britain during that early prehistoric period? Newgrange, for instance, has recently been verified as dating from within an 82 year period of 3880 BCE, which places its construction earlier than Stonehenge and the Pyramids of Egypt. As to the accepted theory of diffusion of civilisation spreading from east to west, there are still many unanswered questions, such as the incursion of the 'Sea People' into the Mediterranean, as related in Egyptian legends, and the arrival of Kukulkan – otherwise known as Cuchulainn – at Yucatan in Mexico as related in Tolmec legends. It is also interesting to note that Kukulkan and his men were dressed like

Phoenician warriors with elaborate head gear, leather breastplates and long beards. The Tolmec and the other inhabitants of Mexico did not grow beards.

The burial places, rites, customs and hieroglyphics of the countries bordering on the Mediterranean, reveal a striking similarity to some found in Ireland. If we look at Newgrange and the minor cist graves found in this area we find that these are associated with similar types of early graves found in the Upper Nile, Anatolia (northern Turkey), Greece, Crete, Cyprus, Libya , Malta and Spain. These tombs or tumuli were communal graves to generations of high ranking families and are dated to the Neolithic period (8500-6500 BCE).

One of the best examples of similarity with Newgrange is found at Platonos, on the Measra Plain in southern Crete. It was constructed above ground, with a sunken floor about a metre deep. No roof remains, but certain evidence shows that it was domed and built in a corbelled or bee-hived fashion like the Tholos tombs. This particular type of burial was widespread throughout the area now known as Greece and the Islands. The thick passage walls lean inwards in an 'A' shape, supporting domes built from stone-bonded clay. The tomb at Platonos and another similar one at Khiroktia in Cyprus are dated prior to 5800 BCE. This system of burial is reputed to have been brought by an Aryan people from the east, who themselves lived in round-shaped huts. These Tholos style tombs are also found at Los Millares, Almeria, Spain.

Returning to Newgrange, we find the influence of an early culture; that of the builders of stone circles, as Newgrange mound was surrounded by about 36 standing stones. The alignment of the Newgrange passage and the stones surrounding it gave an accurate table of the apparent and actual movements of the sun, moon and stars, as well as a type of calendar. It is understood, that Newgrange was built on a Neolithic mound like the Palace of Knossos, in Crete, which has been dated to c.6341 BCE. This leaves us with a serious question – is the date of 3800 BC for Newgrange incorrect?

Standing stones are not unique to Ireland. If we examine closely the archaeological maps of Western Europe and the Mediterranean countries, we can see how a line of standing stones, also known as menhirs or baetyli, stretched from the East to the British Isles. It appears that they had different purposes, such as marking the grave of someone important, a division of land, or a stellar or lunar alignment or were revered as representing a god. There are many fine examples in the Bantry area, especially at Scart, Ahil Mor, Kielnascarta and Millbeg.

Stone Circles and other Monuments

There are quite a number of stone circles in West Cork and the Bantry region, but very few of them stand intact. The best examples are to be found at Kealkil (five stones), Breen More (nine), Colamane (five stones), Baurgorm (five stones) and Millbeg (five stones). There are a number of other stone circles where exact numbers cannot be proven like Kealanine which seems to have had over twenty.

A study of this particular type of megalithic monument is a life time occupation for some enthusiasts, and the various theories and findings as to their exact role in early Irish civilisation would fill volumes. Therefore, we shall have only a brief look at their importance and past usage.

Firstly, when we speak of stone circles, we automatically conclude that they are all perfect, or near perfect circles. This, in fact, is not true. Some indeed are perfect circles but others are well constructed ellipses and are deliberately constructed as modified circles – some with flattened arcs or others pulled out like an egg shape – to conform to their primary use as astronomical clocks, a means to tell the seasons, and then as a solar calendar and a means of telling both solar and lunar eclipses.

Alignment, circle and radial cairn at Kealkil

It must have taken a considerable time of Neolithic man to choose a site which corresponded with know landmarks to give the position on the horizon of the sunrise and sunset at different times of the year.

Taking the position of the North Polar Star and the top of a well-known mountain peak as static points, they were able to chart out the sun's movements through the seasons using the knowledge they had of the use of right triangles.

In addition, with their basic knowledge of geometry, they were able to correlate groups of stones circles with other standing stones and were able to foretell lunar eclipses. In short, in the form of standing stones, we have a 5,000 year old computer whose accuracy was not equalled until the Renaissance.

In establishing a lunar calendar by the study of the phases of the moon, primitive man in Ireland had approached the early Hebrew calendar which is still based on the lunar month and alternate months of 29 and 30 days. This calendar revolves around a period of 19 years, 12 years having 12 months and seven years having 13 months, making a total of 235 months.

This was brought back into line with the solar year by the use of the Metonic Cycle.

On the other hand, the Muslim calendar is purely lunar; making a complete revolution every 33 years and the beginning of the year rotates around the seasons. It is much more likely that the early lunar calendar used here in Ireland was similar to the Hebrew one.

If we are to examine the locations of both the stone circles and the standing stones in the Bantry region, in order to try and correlate their positions with either the sun or the moon, we immediately run into difficulties, mainly due to the absence of stones in vital locations that would assist us in checking alignments. However, by trial and error many possibilities of alignments do appear. Unfortunately, details of these alignments and findings would occupy too much of this book.

In considering the stone circles as astronomical clocks, we should not use the word 'primitive' when we realise the unbelievable grasp that early civilisation had of the movements of the heavenly bodies. Also, we must point out that they are not 'Celtic druid circles', as they predate any so called Celtic influence by thousands of years.

Our boulder burials, or cromlechs, are believed to be the oldest type of ritual burials, and they are mostly found in the south-west of Ireland.

It is argued that they were originally covered in mud and earth in a type of mound, not unlike Newgrange, but have been subjected to the elements and the influence of man over the millennia, leaving them in their present bare state. Then we have the dolmens which consist of a large tilted stone supported by two or three vertical uprights. Some authorities state that the inclination of the covering slab represents a ship with high prow and that the three pillar stones represent the ancient triad of the gods (Father, Son, and Mother Earth) – thus the spirits of the dead were carried in the 'Boat of the Sun' to the other world under the protection of the Trinity. Some of the best examples of the former are to be found at Colomane, Breeny More and Scart. The best example of the latter is found in the Coom (Coomhola) but the covering slab has fallen off its supporting stones.

Pilgrim's circle and cairn, Colomane

Rock art in general has been viewed rather sceptically by both the archaeologists and historians, who believed them to be nothing more than doodling by some farmer or herdsman during bad weather. Now, however, attitudes have changed, following serious examination of various sites in South Kerry. The latest conclusion is that they possibly date from the Middle Bronze Age (2000–1600 BCE). Rock art is particular to south Kerry and the Bantry region, and there are many fine examples, in particular near Massmount (Adrigole), Kealanine and the Coom.

If we are to look at West Cork in general, we find that there are some 6,662 identified megalithic sites at the present time. The general opinion is that this only represents about 40 per cent of what originally existed.

V

EARLY MYTHS AND LEGENDS

Amongst the local myths and legends there are a few interesting stories which are worth noting here – the legend of Cessair, the arrival of the Tuatha de Danaan, and the Milesians. Some of these are discussed at length because of their overall importance. They brought with them their own myths and legends, in the form of a pantheon of gods, customs and beliefs that have influenced our civilisation down through the millennia.

The first group to be mentioned were Parthalon and his followers. As all the other invaders were supposed to have come from the east, he is the only one said to have come from the west. This is the first reference in European mythology of people arriving from the west. This leads to a major question – were they people fleeing from Atlantis? If they were from Atlantis something of their culture should have remained in Ireland.

The next arrivals, called the Formorians, might give us an answer as they were described as a cruel and warlike people who practised the power of 'evil and darkness' and had come from a land of 'ice and gloom' which could at that time mean from northern Europe. Their god was called Balor (of the evil eye) who was represented as a giant, whose death 'by a stone in the eye' is almost a direct parallel to the story of David and

Goliath in the Bible which came much later. They more than likely wiped out the followers of Parthalon. It is interesting to note that "the evil eye of 'Balor'" was referred to by country people up to the 1950s.

Next came the Nemedians who, under their leader Nemed, are reputed to have defeated the Formorians and taken over the island.

Nothing of interest is said in the chronicles about the next two groups, the Nemedians and the Fir Bolg, except that they were inferior and servile and were probably overcome by the Nemedians.

The arrival of the Tuatha de Danaan (People of Danua) – their pantheon of the gods, burial customs, ceremonial rites and the dominant priestly caste – introduced to Ireland a completely new culture and attitude of life. The influence of their science and poetry even permeates life in Ireland today. They had four sacred objects in their mythology: the Stone of Destiny; the Invincible Sword; the Magic Spear and the Cauldron of Dagda. These all have early Greek mythological connotations. Even the name Danae (Danua) has Greek connections, being the daughter of Acrisius, who was to bear a son by Zeus called Perseus who journeyed to the extremities of the world (westward). The story of Danae giving birth to a son through the intervention of the supreme god Zeus is another example of the 'virgin birth' which was a dominant motif in eastern mythology long before Christianity. The last account of Danae in Greek mythology is of her being in the city of Argos, in the western section of modern Greece. Yet, Greek mythology implies that there was another place called Argos in the western world.

The Tuatha de Danaan were reputed to have introduced music and musical instruments as well as the influence of the seasons into early civilisation on this island. Music was supposed to induce sleep and it also invoked various moods, whether of happiness or sadness. In pre-historic times Ireland became known as the land of the harp. Even Hecataeus (550–490 BCE), the Greek historian, observed that 'the inhabitants were almost exclusively harpers and that Apollo must have an influence in this matter'. The harp was described as Orphean, an evident derivation from Orpheus, god of music, who is said to have held back the rivers in their course, made the woods listen and moved stone. The early Irish referred to the harps as 'Clearest' and 'Cruet' – the former identified the musical board and the latter the strings.

It is said the harp was introduced to the Middle East by Indian priests, the followers of Buddha, who had been forced to flee their country by rival sects of Brahma. How it arrived in Ireland is debatable, but it dates from the time that the Tuatha de Danaan were supposed to have arrived in Ireland. Through the centuries the music has not changed and mostly retained its original character, as mentioned in the Book of Genesis, Chapter Four – 'and Jobal was the father of all such as handle the harp and the organ'.

The Milesians

The Milesians are not included in any list of the so-called invasions of Ireland such as the Leabhair Gabhala, Keating's History of Ireland, Ogygia, and the Book of Ballymote. They are reputed to have arrived here from the area around the river Breogan in north-western Spain, under the leadership of Ith. When his father, Milesius, heard that his son was killed by the Tuatha de Danaan, he gathered a large force and sailed to Ireland. They engaged in many battles with the Tuatha-de-Danaan and, according to O'Flaherty, finally defeated them c.1450 BCE. Some historians put the date much later so as to coincide with the Celtic culture moving west across Europe. It is extremely unlikely that the Milesians were Celts who had journeyed across France and England. However, there is the possibility that they were part of another Celtic tribe which had settled in Macedonia and Galatia (Northern Turkey) and who had moved westwards through the Mediterranean and Spain.

The legends say that the land of Ireland was divided amongst the five surviving sons of Ith and Lughaidh Laidhe received West Cork, which became known as Corca Laidhe, as part of his kingdom. All of the West Cork tribes claim their descent from him. In time, the diocese of Ross became co-extensive with the territory of Corca Laidhe which was broadly speaking from the Old Head of Kinsale to the Dursey Sound.

According to the ancient bards and historians, the Milesians attempted a landing at Inmbear Slainge (Wexford) but were repulsed.

They sailed down the coast and successfully came ashore at Inmbear Sceine (Bantry Bay) c. 1600 BCE. According to the Annals, the Milesians, or the various tribes descended from Laidhe, seemed to have for the most part lived in peace, except for inter family rivalry for kingship and raids on each others territory for women and cattle.

The name Tighearnmhas is mentioned as having fought many battles, including one near Kinsale and another on the Beara Peninsula. The latter battle might be identified as the battle of Cnocura (c.1250 BCE), which is mentioned in some sources.

Another episode in the history of the Milesian descendants occurred in Corca Laidhe c. 123 CE, when Con Cead Cathach (Con of the Hundred Battles) came on the scene as high king of Ireland. During his period of kingship, Eoghan Mor (Mogh Nuadhat) was the powerful king of Munster who engaged Con in many battles and disputed his position of High King.

Eventually, during a truce, one of Con's daughters was to marry the eldest son of Eoghan Mor. Con's daughter was the young widow of Lughaidh Niadh of the clan of Corca Laidhe and this marriage was intended to consolidate the friendship of the two kings, as well as being the foundation of the great Corca Laidhe dynasty which ruled West Cork and, at times, Ireland until 1152 CE.

The peace between the two kings did not last long, despite the marriage connection. Eoghan Mor again took up arms against Con, but after suffering two heavy defeats fled to Spain to seek assistance from his father-in-law, having been previously married to Bera, the daughter of the king of Castile. He returned with an army but this was defeated and Eoghan was killed. Oilioll Olum, his son, now became the all-powerful king of Munster. His own stepson, Lughaidh MacCon, requested that he should be entitled to the portion of lands by succession, namely, the lands of Corca Laidhe. This was refused.

Lughaidh sought the assistance of Beine of Britain, who landed in Galway with an army. This was augmented by the fighting men of the High King Art. In the ensuing battle near Athenry, Art was killed even though the forces of Oiloill Olum were defeated. The result of this battle was that Lughaidh MacCon became chief of Corca Laidhe and then king of Munster in 195 CE and ruled for 30 years. Being a wise man he stipulated in his will that the descendants of his two sons, Eoghan and Cormac Cas, should rule alternatively as kings of Munster.

Even though the descendants of Cormac Cas tried to invoke the agreement they were unsuccessful and the family of Eoghan, called Eoghanchta ruled until the time of Brian Boru.

Some historians state that Milesians were also called Goilels or Gaedheal and in fact, were a branch of the Celts who had invaded the Middle East as far as Egypt where they had befriended the Israelites.

They were supposed to have travelled along the north coast of Africa and crossed over to Iberia and then journeyed to the north-west corner of that country before they moved to Ireland.

As far as can be ascertained, the Milesians (Goidels) had their own language. This supposition is very interesting in that the ancient language of this country which is now called Gaeilge or Gaedhilge contained a high percentage of Hebrew words. In fact, according to linguistic experts, the language is made up of ten per cent Hebrew.

Of the early tribes which inhabited the region of Corca Laidhe who were descendants of the Eoghanachta, we find the following mentioned: O'Driscolls, O'Falveys, O'Sheas, O'Connells, O'Coffeysss, O'Cowhigs, O'Flynns, O'Ceadagain, McAuliff, O'Dowlings, O'Hogan, O'Doogans, MacKeadys, O'Keevans, O'Mangans, O'Macken, O'Barr, O'Kennedy, O'Ruirce, O'Hennessy, O'Downe, O'Dineen, O'Downing, O'Cullen, O'Horan, O'Hyne, O'Hussey, O'Fehilly, O' Field, O'Corman, O'Nolan, O'Cronin, O'Hea, O'Haye, O'Donnell, O'Lynch, O'Kelly, O'Murray, O'Gavan, O'Downey, and O'Leahy.

Generally speaking, the public have been brain-washed into believing that all our prehistory dates from the so-called 'Celtic Age' As for the 'Celtic Invasion' of Ireland, many are now of the opinion that the idea is but a myth. What migrated was a culture which we might label 'Celtic' rather than a people. It can be accepted however that different groups of colonists who shared this Celtic culture did reach our shores, integrating with the Irish natives and becoming part of the framework of that society. These were not great inventors, as history suggests, but rather they were gifted to improve anything they found to be of interest like gold and silver work.

Much has been written about the Celtic druids and their influence in ancient Ireland, especially in the context of their ceremonial rites in and around the megalithic monuments such as stone circles. This is presented as if the Celtic druids were the instigators of the construction and usage of these monuments. Nothing could be further from the truth, and this belief should be obliterated from Irish history.

In fact, the precursors of Celtic society did not make an appearance in Western Europe until c.700 BCE when they introduced their type of 'culture' at La Tiene, in the Swiss/ Austrian border region. The Celts were not a race as such but a mixture of various tribes which came south from eastern Poland and the Ukraine and fanned out to Greece and Turkey in the south, Austria, Switzerland, France and Spain to the west and eventually to Ireland. In what order these countries were partially occupied is open to question.

On the other hand the various earlier invaders or incursions, whatever name you give to them, came to this country from the south and by sea. Some historians say that the Tuatha de Danaan were Minoans fleeing Crete at the time of the early Greek conquests, but palaeontologists have refuted this argument by showing that the Minoans were of small stature, with black hair and dark eyes. Also, there are no murals, for which the Minoans were renowned. Yet, evidence of bull-worship, the same pattern designs and identical burial customs are to be found here. A much more plausible explanation would be that the Tuatha de Danaan were Dorians, who had overrun the Eastern Mediterranean c.2000 BCE. Having been defeated by the Egyptians under Rameses II, the Dorians scattered all over the Mediterranean, even as far as south-west Spain. They were noted for their fair hair and blue eyes, which were more akin to Nordic features than those found in the Near East. During their short occupation of Crete, they had adopted some of the Minoan religious ceremonies and customs, such as reverence for the bull and the use of the double-headed bronze axe. After their decimation by the Egyptian forces, the surviving Dorians fled in sea-going vessels taking with them their advanced culture with a pantheon of the gods, who buried their dead in dolmens, tumuli and passage graves, their emblems of a double-headed axe and the bull's head, and their language which was a mixture of early Greek, Etruscan and Hebrew. After the eruption of Santorini in 1626 BCE the Dorians seem to have vanished from the Eastern Mediterranean.

Before leaving the Dorians we should look at bull worship which seems to have infiltrated the Eastern Mediterranean civilisations from the Hittites of Anatolia. We read that the Hebrews, during their wandering through the deserts, made a cast of a bull and began to worship it before Moses intervened. The Egyptians worshiped the Apris Bull and the god Amun who had the horns of a bull. Centuries later we find the inhabitants of Spain worshipping the bull and in Ireland the famous saga called the Táin Bó Cúalnge was written. Spain and Ireland seem to have been the only countries in Western Europe who worshiped the bull in some form or other.

In early times, Ireland had native animals such as the giant elk, wild boar, deer, wolf etc. Nothing so far has been excavated showing the presence of other animals. These had been left behind when the land bridge between the North and Scotland disappeared. Contrary to legend, Ireland did not have any snakes and, when reference is made to St. Patrick banishing snakes from Ireland it is not the cold-blooded reptile that is alluded to but the god Dagda of the old pagan religion of the Formorians who was represented as a snake. The snake is also a common image for mother goddesses and the Patrick story represents the defeat of a matriarchal, earth religion by a patriarchal, air god. There is a connection also with the biblical story of Adam and Eve and the evil snake.

One interesting animal which deserves mention here is the humble donkey. This animal is not native to these Isles or to Europe, but to the Middle East and Africa. How it made its appearance here is debatable – maybe he was brought by sea by one of the early invaders who came from North Africa or the Middle East! In those early days it was not unusual for seafarers to carry on board their ships fowl and animals in case they were marooned on some foreign shore.

The ancient names of some of the local important historical sites may cast some light on the early connection between the Middle East and Ireland. For instance, the Bull, Cow and Calf rocks, off Dursey Island, on the end of the northern peninsula of Bantry Bay have been known since c. 1600 C.E. by these names which derive from folklore concerning the 'Cailleach Beara' and her two sisters. However, according to early references to the south-west of Ireland the names of these rocks were completely different. The Bull rock was known as 'Mosdah' (Big Sea), 'Mikologh' (Great Beyond) or 'Teach Don' (House of Dagda). The Calf rock was known as 'Crelagh' (Ashes); referring to the cremated dead, while the Cow rock was called 'An Torann' or 'Tonnai, denoting rough and stormy seas.

On the north side of the Bull Rock was a large cave, before the action of the sea tunnelled right through the rock. This cave or aperture, was referred to as the Entrance to the Other World – a direct reference to the entrance of Hades as related in Greek mythology, where Aeneas is helped by Sybil to cross the black river Cocytus when she offers a golden branch to the old ferryman, Charon, whose first refusal was because he only ferried those who had received proper burial rites.

It is interesting to note here that Sybil, in Greek mythology, is said to have possessed prophetical powers and the power of magic. Maybe there is a link here between Sybil and Sceine (An Cailleach Beara).

As for the local equivalent of Charon, the ferryman, the only reference encountered is to Manannan the god of the sea like Poseidon, who manned the ferryboat which departed from the mainland (Coite).

Situated to the east of Bantry town is the mountain known as Mullaghmesha. This mountain in ancient folklore was regarded as a sacred place. The name itself lends itself to a variety of interpretations – the high round summit, or the altar to the god Mulloch (Phoenician Melek or high god). Whether the top of the mountain was a ceremonial site in ancient times is open to debate and requires further site investigation. Also, there is the tradition that a type of passage grave was to be found on the north side of the mountain as well as an extremely large cave which could hold a few thousand people and could have been dedicated to Mulloch (Melek).

Here we have a connection with the Greek god Zeus and his cave in the island of Crete.

Another interesting site is that of Milbeg, which has been mentioned elsewhere, which has a tradition that this apparently insignificant location was or was near the burial ground of kings. Who these kings were, or what period of prehistory is in question, nobody knows. Examination of the site itself which consists of the remains of a stone circle with a sacrificial stone in the centre indicates that it was a place of ceremonial ritual and possibly burial. There is only one reference to an ancient battle being fought in the vicinity and that was between the inhabitants and a new group of invaders – possibly the Tuatha de Danaan or the Milesians. As mentioned before, there are a number of souterains, a damaged dolmen, a stone circle and some ancient script rock writing within a few miles of the location. The last time I visited the souterains which have man-made stone entrances, was with a number of terriers and when they entered, their barks were heard from a hollow distance when they encountered a fox. As far as I know nobody has entered the souterains or carried out an investigation to date.

Millbeg ritual complex

As mentioned elsewhere, the practise of building Christian settlements or churches on old pagan sites was very common. Some of the most important sites, like Colomane, Kilmacomoge and Kilcaskan (Adrigole) were three such sites. The latter site, is most intriguing, as it contains a bullaun-type hollow on a large rock from where a snake-like arrangement of boulders snake their way to the nearby river indicating that it was some sort of ceremonial site to Manannan, the pagan god of water. Nearby are the ruins of an early Christian church and graveyard with an Ogham stone.

Colomane is also an interesting site. It contains a stone circle with five stones, a cairn, a well and a large barites stone which was used in some form of ancient ceremony. It is reputed that St.Colman had a hermitage here with a number of monks. This seems to be verified by the presence of the remains of a rectangular stone building, a graveyard, and the conversion of the well into a holy well.

Returning to the Beara peninsula, we have the old name for Hungry Hill which was 'Cnoc Da Dia' (the Hill of Two Gods). Why it was called this name is a bit of a mystery. However, the former existence of one of the largest stone circles in Ireland (no trace now remains) might give an indication that it was the conflict between the earlier pagan religion and Christianity that gave it its name.

One of the most important myths of the region is that of the Cailleach Beara. The Irish word 'cailleach' means priestess, witch or a person who has magic powers which can be good or evil. She has also been referred to as 'An Sceine', 'Boi' or 'Bui' – in this context remember that 'Inbhear Sceine' is the old name for Bantry Bay. According to legend, the 'Cailleach' was also the goddess of the harvest and the wife of Lugh, the sun god, who gave his name to Lughnasa, which was the ancient harvest festival which fell on the last day of July or the Day of Llama. Associated with 'An Cailleach Beara' are the other two cailleaghs of Dingle and Bolus Head.

She is also known as the wife of Manannan, the god of the sea, who has been mentioned above as the ferryman to the cave (Underworld) at the Bull Rock. If Manannan is compared to Poseidon, the Greek god of the sea, we find that the scope of Manannan's powers and identity are much greater and much older in history. Besides being the god of the sea, he was also the god of water, the god of rivers and streams as well as the snake god. However, 'An Cailleach' does not bear any resemblance to Amphitrite, the wife of Poseidon.

As to the connection of 'An Cailleach' with the stone overlooking Baycrovan Harbour, which bears the same name, we have to look into a folktale which has survived down through history. It states that when St. Catherine fell asleep outside her monastery at Coulagh, the Cailleach snatched her prayer book and ran away to Gortgarriff, where St. Catherine caught up with her. As a punishment for stealing the prayer book St. Catherine turned the Cailleach into stone. This has a strong connection to the Greek myth in which anyone who looks at Medusa is turned into stone. With the connection between 'an Cailleah' and the snake god Manannan, plus the snakes around the head of Medusa these should be related somehow in mythology.

Another local legend concerns the exploits of Fionn MacCubhal, the famous Irish mythological character, where he fought a battle with the carrion of death which appeared as a giant black eagle at Inchnagaum, near Coomhola.

Moving on to more recent centuries, the popular myth of the Priest's Leap deserves some mention. The most common story relating to this is the account of a priest being pursued on horseback by a detachment of English soldiers. Coming up the north side of the mountain with the English closing in, and having arrived at the summit, his further escape was doomed because of the terrain. Facing death and with a bounty of £5. on his head, he had no option but to urge his horse to jump off the steep cliff face. Instead of falling to their deaths, both horse and rider took off and flew through the air until they finally came down to earth at Newtown, just outside of

Bantry. A commemorative plaque marks the spot. As far as can ascertained, the story seems to have originated c. 1603 CE, after the fall of Dunboy Castle and refers to a Fr. Archer, a Jesuit, who was in the Beara at that time. This particular priest was not known for his pious works but rather for his other exploits, especially with the fair sex. The old traditions around the Coomhola area state that, if Fr. Archer was the priest in question, it was not by the power of God but of 'the man below' that his horse flew through the air.

VI

PLACES OF HISTORICAL INTEREST

With over 500 historical monuments in the Bantry region, it would be an almost impossible task to enumerate or give detailed accounts of all of them here. Many of them have been noted and marked on the Ordnance Survey maps by the relevant authorities – the Board of Works, the Archaeology Department of UCC and others. Full details of these can be found in the Archaeological Survey of West Cork. Therefore, this chapter will deal with the history, location and ancient use of a limited number of monuments and sites.

Monuments

The exact dating of the earliest monuments in Ireland is very difficult, as it depends on two factors – the presence of wood (charcoal) and implements (ware, weapons or bones). The dating processes for these are dendrochronology and carbon (carbon 14). If either of these two dating processes cannot be accomplished then the approximate date of similar monuments is taken into account.

Here in the Bantry region there are many ancient sites and monuments which for one reason or another cannot be accurately dated. The most important and probably the oldest of these are – the stone circle, cromlech alignment, standing

Standing stones at Scart

stone alignment and sacrificial stone at Mill Beg, Coomhola; the Kealkil ritual complex which consists of a stone alignment, a five-stone circle and a radial stone cairn. The stone circle and cromlechs at Breeny Mor and the stone circle, quartz cromlech and cairn at Colomane. These four sites are believed to be amongst the oldest in Ireland and it is thought that they were used, possibly over millennia, as places of worship, ceremony and sacrifice. The exact time of their construction has not been ascertained either by dendrochronology or carbon dating even though attempts have been made since 1963. However, it is possible that these date prior to c.4500 BCE.

The next oldest type of megalithic monument of importance, is the 'boulder burial', which consists of large boulders resting on smaller ones and which are located adjacent to a stone circle or else in groups on their own. These probably date from the Early Bronze Age c.3500 BCE and are also known as 'cromlechs' or 'gallauns' in Ireland, which means god and stone. In other words they are to be adored like a god. The worship of some particular stones was widespread during prehistoric times. The custom seems to have originated in the Far East where the early inhabitants of the upper reaches of the Indus River adored stones and called them Lithoi. From north of the Black Sea in the lands of the Cimmerians, this religious practise came westward, through the Middle East, the Mediterranean, North Africa, Portugal and Spain where the stones were referred to as baetyli and were of Canaanite or Phoenician origin (see Appollonius, the Roman historian). In Ireland, they were also called 'gallauns and in certain townlands where there was a proliferation of such stones the name gallauns was applied to the region. The practise of adoring stones became so prevalent up to the Middle Ages that the Lateran Council of 1672 prohibited it. Later, the Council of Paris decided that all such stones connected with this ancient religious superstition should be destroyed. Here in Ireland these stones were usually situated on high ground or in a prominent position overlooking the countryside. As the main pagan ritual sites had earlier been converted to Christian usage by the building of Christian settlements or churches on their locations most of the remaining stones avoided destruction.

The standing stones and cist graves in the region are too numerous to be listed in full. The standing stones can be found in rows, in pairs, or singularly. The ones in rows usually stand

Cappanaboul stone circle and cromlech

Scribed rock markings at Coom

on a NW-SW axis. Those in alignment are graded in height – with the tallest at the SW extremity. These also are probably dated from the Early Bronze Age and were used to tell the changes of seasons, or marked a grave or an ancient battle site or a boundary. In the countries bordering on the Mediterranean and the Near East, they are referred to as menhirs or baetyli and were venerated as representing some god or other.

Some mention must be made of 'rock scribing' or rock art as there are a number of good examples in the area. These consist of various motifs cut out of a rock face and are mostly circles with interior designs. Some, however, are of unique design and appear to represent certain constellation of stars in the night sky. Most of these rock scribings are found at Kealanine, Coomhola and near the Mass Rock at Adrigole and the valley of the writings north of Hungry Hill. Some years ago, the author took samples of rock scribing found in a cave in the Coom at Coomhola which appeared to be a type of hieroglyphics or writing. These were studied by the British Museum, Yale and Harvard, and were found to be a type of early Cycladic script – a type of early Greek writing. How people with this type of writing found their way from the Aegean Sea to Bantry Bay is another question. This script may be a key to one of the early prehistoric invaders during the early Bronze Age.

Dating from around the same period, Fulachta Fiadh are found. These were sunken rectangular pits lined with wooden planks, filled with water which was then heated by the addition of large stones from a nearby fire. The uses of Fulachta Fiadh is not known but may have involved, cooking, bathing, sweat lodge rituals or all of these. They are usually found near other megalithic monuments and the source of water. Most of the known examples in this region are to be found in Coomhola, Borlin and Kealkil. They were however extremely common in some areas. During recent archaeological work before the construction of a new stretch of road north east of Cork City, ten Fulachta Fiadh were recorded in a ten kilometre length.

In the general archaeological field, it is worth noting the importance of 'shell middens'. These are mounds of discarded edible sea shells encountered near the existing seashore. Here in the Bantry region two such shell middens have been found – one at Glengarriff and the other at Donamark. They have been dated from around the end of the Bronze Age. Due to the fact that a shell midden found a Ferriter's Cove, near Dingle has been dated to the Mesolithic/Neolithic Period, c. 12,500 to 10,000 BCE, the dating of those found near Bantry Bay could possibly be of the same period.

Forts and Ring Forts
Most of the forts that exist or existed in the countryside were built during the period – 800 BCE to 500 CE but some were

built even later and were occupied up the 16th century. Before describing the different types of forts, it would be useful to look at the structure of society in Ireland at the time.

The most important unit in land ownership was the tuath, which was an area of up to 1,600 square kilometres. The size of the tuath varied according to the success or failure of its ruler or Righ. Usually those who inhabited a tuath were of the same family and surname, and the head of the family was chosen by the members of Tuatha. In practice, it was one particular family and its descendants who were most likely to rule. A number of families of the same name (descendants of the same ancestor) were called a sept, while a clan was a number of septs from the same common ancestor. Finally, a tribe was made up of several clans, where all the families were related to one another.

The forts, whether as abodes of families, clan leaders or tribal leaders, were of different construction. Firstly, there were the ordinary small forts with the defensive ring built of earth, mud and stone, which was usually the abode of a single family unit and their livestock. Then there was the double circular fort, which was where the head of the family, or sept, resided, and then the double ringed fort with a dyke, which was usually occupied by the clan leader, and, finally, there was the three ringed fort (with or without dykes) where the tribal chief resided. In addition to the above, there were promontory forts which were built on headlands or on high ground overlooking the coastline. The main function of these was to keep watch on the activities of ships, in case of attack by sea. There were also some stone built forts, which were established on main access routes to particular territories as a focal point for defence.

Generally speaking, the ring forts (rath or lios) were enclosed farmsteads with interior buildings and stables built of timber laths with walls of wattle and mud, and thatched roofs where families and animals dwelled. They were not very defensive, but were generally adequate as protection against predators such as wolf packs and a deterrent against cattle raids which were prevalent during that period. Most of the forts were built on locations where in time of attack, smoke signals could be seen by those in other forts in the general area to summon help.

The majority of the larger forts had souterains, which usually consisted of a number of cells or chambers linked together by small narrow passages which opened into the interior of a main dwelling. Opinion differs as to their exact usage – either as a place of refuge at times of attack, or else as a place of storage. Both are possibly true.

In fact, there are two different types of souterains – those that are interconnected within the fort complex and those that have an exit either near the boundary or further away. These latter were sometimes even cut through rock, as archaeological excavations have proved.

The forts in the Bantry region are too numerous to mention individually. One of the best examples is Ardrah (Ard Rath) which originally had three rings and a moat (dyke) and a souterain running from the interior under the main wall to the northwest.

Castles and Fortified Houses

The remains or ruins of stone castles are scarce in the Bantry region due to their destruction from Elizabethan times onwards. Beginning in the extreme west, there was Dursey Castle and further along the north side of the Bay were Dunboy and Castletown Castles, all of which were almost completely destroyed c.1601 CE. Glengarriff Castle cannot be called a castle as such as it was a gothic replica built by the local landlords, the Whites (see Glengarriff). Nearer Bantry at Ballylickey the

Castledonovan

ruins of Reendesert Court are to be found and further up the Ouvane River are the remains of Carriganass Castle. Nothing remains of Donemark Castle except a few stones and the same is true of Scart and Baurgorm castles of the McCarthys. Further east are the remains of Castledonovan Castle which suffered during Cromwell's invasion. Finally, on Whiddy Island there are the ruins of Reenavanig Castle of the O'Sullivans, which now only consists of one wall. Most of these castles, if not all, are discussed in other chapters of this book.

There are many other important historical buildings and sites in the area which have yet to be examined and defined, such as a possible Crannog, caves, early mines, medieval settlements, possible beehive settlements and other sites. Only with archaeological surveys can the true identity of these sites be clarified.

Before leaving this section, it is worth noting that there were a number of large residences in the area which were mainly built by English settlers. These include, besides Bantry House, Bantry Lodge at Glengarriff (Whites); Inchiclough (Whites); Balliliskey (Hutchinson); Gurteenroe (Lawlor); Dromroe (Whites); Newtown (Murphy); Ardnagashel (Hutchins); and Beach House (Bird).

Abbeys and Churches

As Bantry Franciscan Abbey was totally destroyed over the centuries, little or nothing remains today except for some of the original stones – sculptured or plain – which now make up an altar on the grounds of the present graveyard. The exact location of the abbey is, however, known – it occupied the ground to the north of the present stone steps ascending at the top centre. The entrance to the Abbey grounds was about 50 metres above the present upper entrance and was called the 'clapper gate' Near the gate were a number of bothans with some more near the Abbey itself.

Over the course of the years, the local monument erectors and grave diggers have encountered sections of the cobbled floor area and the floor of the kitchen. As there are no paintings, sketches or plans, it is difficult to know what the exact shape or form of the monastery was. The one thing that we do known is that there was a large bell tower at the north-west corner, where the choir was probably located. The records of the Franciscans in Ireland do not give details except for a brief paragraph. There is an ancient map of Bantry c.1598 CE, which gives some idea of what the Abbey looked like.

There is controversy regarding the exact date of its foundation, whether in 1340 or 1460 CE. The monastery did not figure in Irish history until it was mentioned in military circles in the 1580s. Yet, since the 15th century it had become well known in maritime affairs on the Continent as an entrepot or a base for wine and brandy smuggling from Spain and France. In fact, it had the reputation of being the centre for smuggling on the south-west coast of Ireland. Whether the monks themselves were involved is not known but it seems more than likely.

Most monasteries in Ireland were built by powerful local leaders and the Bantry Abbey was one of these, being financed by the O'Sullivan Clan. Many of the O'Sullivans, O'Mahonys and other high ranking members of the local septs were buried there.

During the general suppression of the monasteries c.1542 CE, the abbey seems to have escaped due to its isolated position in West Cork. However, in 1580 an English army came and, having ousted the monks, occupied the building for a short period. Events connected with the Abbey during 1601/02 are dealt with in the section on Whiddy Island.

Following the 'scorched earth' policy of Mountjoy and Carew, after the fall of Dunboy Castle in 1602, little is recorded as to the fate of the then ruined Abbey except that two monks remained in the vicinity and lived in a hut behind the present Marino House. It is recorded that some of the building stones were removed, first by the Revd. Davys, local rector, to build a 'fish palace' on the area now taken up by the north side of Bantry Square. More stones were taken by Lord Bantry for the construction of the 'stables' and an additional wing of Bantry House. It is not known what happened to the Abbey bell, but there is a tradition that Donal Cam dropped the bell into the sea off the Abbey Point when last he departed the site with some wine and brandy casks.

On the shoreline near the Abbey there were at least two bothans which were later (in the 1800s) occupied by a John O'Sullivan and a Downey family. West of the Abbey near the

Black Strand were a number of fishermen's huts, while at the end of Beach road a coastguard station was built. Only parts of two walls are still visible.

Two friars were captured by English forces in 1667 CE and there were reports that other friars were in the area as late as 1703, one hundred years after the final destruction of the Abbey.

VII

ANCIENT FESTIVALS AND SUPERSTITIONS

Considering the concentration of megalithic monuments, including stone circles and other places of ancient worship, in the Bantry region, it is interesting to try and envisage the activities of those early inhabitants and our ancestors during the sacred festivals of the year, the first of February, the first of May, Midsummer, and the first of November. Of these, the most important was the first of May, which was called La Baal-Tinne (Bealtaine) or the Day of the Fires of Baal.

Bealtaine

At this time fires were lit to Baal, the sun god. Baal was also the sun god of the Canaanites, the Phoenicians and the Hebrews c. 3,500 BCE. It is more than a coincidence that these civilisations worshipped the same sun god as the early inhabitants of this country on the same day and with almost the same ceremonies.

All domestic fires were put out on the eve of La Baal-Tinne, and, when the head priest had lit the sacred fire within the most dominant stone circle, burning embers were carried to the nearest hearths, and from these to others, until all the home fires were relit. Sometimes two fires were lit close together within the circle, between which a bull and cattle were driven in order that they be 'marked by fire' which was almost the same practise followed by the Minoans of Crete.

It is said that the Baal fires were used for human sacrifice in those early times in Ireland, but there is only one vague reference to this practice concerning a tribal ceremony in the midlands. It is more likely that the sacrifices to Baal were those of animals. In addition, people also had to pass through the flames to be purified from evil spirits and then water which had been boiled over the fires was sprinkled on the recipients by the priest as a sign of cleansing. It is worth mentioning that the fires were started by rubbing two pieces of ash timber which was considered sacred. As with the Sumerians and the Phoenicians, the early Irish religion had Baal as the Supreme Being and worshipped him in fire, trees and water. Fire was the most important aspect of the ancient religion as it protected people from evil spirits.

As the dawn of La Baal-Tinne approached, with fires burning within the circle, the festivities commenced with the people dancing around a large May bush, decorated with multi-coloured garlands of cloth, which had been placed near the circle. The women wore ribbons in their hair while the men carried a branch of leaves in their hands. Then, holding hands, they danced around in two circles to the sound of music and drums, which began with a steady rhythm and then built up to a pulsating and hypnotic beat which put the dancers into a state of trance. This type of dancing, according to some sources, was known as the baila, the dance of Baal. The sacred fire of Baal was a source of revenue to the druid priests who demanded some payment of food or goods in return for receiving the burning embers to light the hearth fires.

Every three years, the sacred fire at Tara (Tamhair-na-Righ) was ceremoniously lit, and from this all the sacred fires in

Ireland were kindled at the feast of Baal. This fire was started with a primitive lens or mirror, which diverted the sun's rays onto dry straw or by the friction of two pieces of ash if the sky was cloudy.

As the first of May was the beginning of the Old Calendar Year for the early Irish, there were many rituals to be performed. Amongst these was the gathering of herbs for curing diseases during the following year. These were usually collected on May Eve and blessed by a high priest, and were then distributed amongst those chosen to be one who practised the 'curings' on the local population.

This was also the time of prophecy. The high priest or members of the priestly caste, gave their prediction for the coming year by observing the 'signs' of nature visible on that morning, such as the direction of the wind, the fall of the ashes or the sighting or sound of particular birds.

Midsummer – The Feast of the Baal Fires

The celebrations and activities of the priest and people were something similar to those on La Baal-Tinne. On the eve of Midsummer Day the people began to gather fire wood and to make preparations for the important feast. Everyone gathered at the stone circles in the locality which were held most sacred for all the major celebrations. When the high priest lit the main fire, it was a sign for all others to light their fires. When the prayers and incantations of the priests were completed, the young men were purified by leaping back and forth over the flames three times. After the fires had subsided somewhat it was the turn of the young women, and then finally it was the turn of the older women, who walked through the embers in their bare feet. These particular customs originated in the Middle East, especially in the festivities of the Minoans of

Crete c. 2800 BCE. These rituals were then followed by singing, dancing and relating old tales of the might and valour of the gods. With dawn approaching, the festivities came to an end, and everybody took a burning sacred branch home with them for good luck.

Whitsuntide

Another of the three elements held sacred by early inhabitants was water, represented by the god Manannan, the Irish version of the god Neptune. This was celebrated at Whitsuntide when all of the people gathered at the 'holy wells'. All over Ireland the sacred wells, surrounded by trees and usually in a sheltered location, were regarded as one of the most important places of worship. A stone circle, pillar stone, cromlech or some other ancient monument was nearly always to be found in the same locality. The worship of spring wells is one of the earliest rituals of humanity and was brought to our shores by those who came from the East, where it was first known to be practiced by the Aryan races of northern India and Pakistan, around 5000 BCE. This ritual of well-worshipping was practiced throughout the eastern Mediterranean civilisations, but had special significance in the Hindu religion further east, in relation to the 'sacred cow'. During ceremonies cattle were herded together, garlands were thrown on their horns and they were sprinkled with water from a holy well. Like the Hindus, the ancient Irish threw tufts of grass into the well to protect them from evil. Here in Ireland, the bubbling springs were held in high esteem by the high priests and became focal points of the ancient religion. One of the special ceremonies connected with the sacred wells was the ancient ceremonial snake dance to the water god Manannan.

This ceremony reached a new height in Ireland where young people, their heads garlanded with flowers and greenery, danced in a snake-like formation from west to east, and then, in rotation of three, six, and twelve circled the well throwing small stones into the water for good luck. Others, mainly the older people, circled the well on hands and knees while invoking Manannan for protection. More often than not, the well was located near a whitethorn or an ash tree, each revered as symbols of health, happiness and protection from evil spirits. One of these sacred wells is situated at Colomane, outside of Bantry.

La Samnah

The second half of the ancient calendar year began with La Samnah, the first of November, otherwise known as the Season of the Moon.

It was the beginning of that period of long dark nights, and short days when the spirits of evil were out and about. Belief in the power of evil was very strong amongst the primitive people, who lived in fear during the following months. It was a time when the dead were believed to wander about, and during darkness it was unsafe to leave one's dwelling or abode. If someone did venture forth in the darkness, there was always the fear that the risen dead would assault them and drink their blood so that they could come back to life. According to Mary Shelley, the idea of Dracula did not come from Transylvania but from these ancient beliefs.

All that the people had for protection were the sacred fires and the ash tree. As during the other festivals, the fires were lit and the nearest ash tree was decorated in long coloured ribbons before sacred music and song began. Then after incantations by the priests to the gods for protection, people bound their heads with the pieces of cloth and also hung cloths on the horns of animals, to protect them from evil spirits. When the festivities were over everyone carried home a piece of burning ash from the sacred fire to protect them against evil spirits during the darkening nights.

Many interpretations of these rituals were incorporated into early Christian ceremonies. Where once there were 'pagan' rites, now there were Christian rituals, such as the Mass, reciting of the Rosary while circling the well, doing the 'rounds' – where people walked through two parallel mounds of stones, picked up a pebble, and before depositing it on another mound said prayers and made the sign of the cross. This custom was subsequently modified and, until recent times, people still picked up the stones and blessed themselves three times before proceeding to the next mound. The best example of this custom is at St. Colman's site at Colomane, near Bantry, where the well and the heaps of stones are still visible. In time, each pagan well was called after a particular local saint, and each person, having partaken of the 'holy water', hung a coloured ribbon or handkerchief on a nearly ash or whitethorn tree just like in ancient times. Instead of throwing a pebble into the water, a coin subsequently became the norm. It was never accepted by Christian teaching that the waters of the wells had any particular power for healing infirmities, but they claimed that any apparent cures were as a result of intercession by a particular saint, and, likewise, any miraculous healing was said to be the result of prayer rather than of an inherent power in the waters of the wells.

While dealing with the ancient festivities we should examine how they evolved in time. About 1000 BCE they were called 'gatherings' and were principally held on the main festive days like the first of May and the first of November. The festivities became a three day event and were also called 'the fair days' and the 'scattering day'. Like the ancient festivities of Greece and Minoan Crete they became known for their horse riding, bull baiting and games. The gatherings were held under the auspices of the tribal chief and his head priest.

On the first day, the division or allotment of land was decided and the Brehon Laws were invoked for disputes. Marriages were arranged, dues were paid to the chief and future cattle raids were planned. On some occasions important marriages took place.

These marriage events commenced with the arrival of the bride and groom, their first meeting taking place by a decorated hawthorn tree situated near a nearby stream. They were then joined by children with flowers and greenery on their heads, who led the way to the sacred site; they were accompanied by musicians playing flutes, pipes and goatskins in a steady rhythm, while others rattled bones and stones in their hands like Spanish castanets. Arriving at the sacred location, the pair had to jump through the fires, which symbolised future protection from evil spirits. They were then sprinkled with 'holy water' and pronounced married by the high priest under the sign of Baal. After the bride and groom had kissed the celebration commenced.

With the advent of Christianity, the old sacred ceremonial sites were mostly taken over by the early missionaries, and some were converted to Christian usage. Many of the stone circles and other sites were uprooted and replaced by rudely made churches of mud and thatch. This is especially true of Kilmacamogue church and graveyard near Bantry where one of the finest examples of a stone circle was said to have existed.

Having briefly examined the various ancient festivals in the first part of this chapter, we will now consider the customs and superstitions which were closely related to our ancient culture. In fact, most of these, both good and bad, are slowly disappearing from daily life in the countryside, where they have existed up to the present generation.

This means, of course, that Irish rural life has moved into a new phase of behaviour and beliefs. Yet, for some living in the countryside, there is still a strong regard for the ancient piseoge or beliefs. These ancient superstitions were passed down from the earliest times by tradition, or by word-of-mouth, through the continuity of the Irish bards and local storytellers.

We have already considered some of the religious beliefs and practices of our predecessors and the fact that local Christian religious traditions are very similar. Combined with these worship practices was a deep superstitious fear of good and evil, and from this grew a multitude of customs designed to ward of the spirits of evil whether they be the ancient gods and goddesses of evil or the Christian devil and his cohorts of fallen angels. In addition, sacred trees were not cut down or tampered with, the stone monuments were revered and the holy wells were not interfered with, while the priestly caste dominated the lives of the ordinary people.

Anything connected to the elements of fire, wind, earth and water were held as sacred, and to violate the rituals associated with them brought the evil spirits amongst the guilty. Baal's fire was the protector from evil, especially at Samhain, when the dead came out of their graves and walked the paths and byways trying to find their homes. Before the people departed from their homes for the celebrations of Samhain, food was always left out at the doorstep for the wandering spirits. Whitsuntide was the most unlucky time, as the god Manannan searched the oceans, rivers and streams for victims to take into the Otherworld. Death was close at hand at Whitsuntide, and the evil spirits were always waiting to claim a victim. In the huts fires were always kept burning and the sick were never left alone.

The Banshee

The Banshee could not be omitted from any account of Irish superstition. In fact, when I commenced research into the Banshee in Irish folklore I was under the misguided impression that this superstition started around the Middle Ages, but this I soon found to be completely incorrect. Superstition, or the belief in the unknown and unseen, the mysteries and the spiritual, had been with man from earliest time, when he first came to believe that the material and the spiritual worlds existed side by side. In fact, after the need for food, the fear of the unknown dominated the life of early man, and elements of the old pagan customs and traditions have filtered down through the ages to the present day.

This is especially true as regards the Banshee, or Beanshee, in Ireland. The name itself means 'the woman of the fairy race' and can be identified with the Greek goddess Hecate who was regarded as the queen of ghosts at night but during the day was a helpful maiden.

If the name Banshee is spelt as ban-sidhe, we find that it means 'the spirit of the dead', while its counterpart was called leeanan-sidhe, or the spirit of life. In Irish mythology, both of these are one, i.e. a spirit who appears as a beautiful young woman during daylight or as a witch at night and it is the latter interpretation that took hold in ancient Irish tradition. She has been described as a shrouded, veiled old hag who emitted an unearthly wailing at night-time which indicated that someone was about to die. This belief comes directly from the Greek Hecate who was said to frequent graveyards.

Although she was seldom seen, and then as a passing shadow, many people have testified on oath that they heard the wailing cry of the Banshee before somebody close to the family had died either nearby or far away on distant shores. In olden days, when she was heard, people would rush to get some ash tree branches, twigs or leaves and scatter them around the cattle in the pen, and around everyone in the family in their hut for protection.

When one considers the role of the Banshee, one automatically thinks of fairies, as both are intertwined in Irish folklore and tradition. The forts, caves and music and dancing of the fairy folk comes immediately to mind.

Many historians relate the fairies to the Tuatha-de-Danaan who had mystical powers and who were permitted to live in the caves and forts by the conquering Milesians. This idea cannot be based on any historical fact or tradition, as the Tuatha-de-Danaan were supposed to have come to Ireland c.1700 BCE and it was another 500 years before the Milesians arrived. Also, the lis, or forts which were supposed to be inhabited by the fairies were not, however, built until the 8th or 9th century BCE at the earliest.

Yet, regard for the fairy folk, whatever its origins, grew almost into a cult in earlier days, especially at the time of the festivals. While the young women were enjoying themselves at the Midsummer festival, the fairies were also enjoying themselves with song and dance in their forts. Nobody would approach an old fort on the eve of a festival for fear that they would be taken and changed into a fairy. Families feared for their young girls, as the fairy king, Finvarra ascended from his underground kingdom, and his followers were always on the prowl to carry away the prettiest girls to the fairy kingdom. Those they succeeded in entrapping were held for seven years, until they had lost their beauty, but in return were given the gift of magic herbs. Sometimes, in order to capture the young girls, the fairies were supposed to approach the fires of Baal as a whirlwind, in order to extinguish the fires and leaving the festivities in darkness. Up to recently, the phrase 'the fairies will take you' was used to frighten disobedient children.

Ancient Cures

The most important herbs were ground ivy, vervain, eyebright, groundsel, foxglove, bark of the elder tree and young hawthorn saplings. It is said that the powers of herbs was bestowed on those who had been in the Fairy Land and those that had been chosen by the druidic priests.

The cures were many and include the following:

Wild sage when boiled was used as a cure for a bad cough.

Nettle soup was supposed to purify the blood.

Dock leaves were used to cure nettle stings.

Fever was cured by drinking a mixture of whey and boiled wheat.

Boils were cured by applying a poultice with the poisonous river parsnip and button grass boiled in sea water. Also, to be rubbed into a limb affected by rheumatism.

Wood anemone used in plaster for wounds.

Yarrow had many cures and could be mixed in potions.

Freckles cured by distilled water of walnuts.

Burns cured by a mixture of boiled lamb suet and rind of elder tree.

Stomach pain – placing band of mint around wrist.

Nettles boiled were good for dropsy.

Ring of iron around fourth finger was supposed to cure rheumatism.

Spoonful of aquavitae and sugar plus bread crumbs was a protection against colds.

Boiled carrots were suitable for purifying blood.

Rubbing morning dew on the face gave good skin.

VIII

THE BREHON LAWS

The Brehon Laws were the code by which the country was governed from about 1200 BCE. They were said to have been introduced into Ireland by Amergin, son of Milesius, who was known as 'An Ollamh Fodhla' (the wise man) and reigned as high king around 1185 BCE. These laws are similar to those that came into existence around the time of the destruction of the Assyrian empire and during the birth of the three kingdoms of Nineveh, Babylon and Media.

The Brehon Laws can be compared to the Roman (Etruscan) Code – the Twelve Tables – being founded on the natural law and conforming in part to the written law of that period before the foundation of Rome itself. Both sets of these laws have the same Aryan roots and are not dissimilar to the ancient Hindu law. The Brehon Laws, unlike the Roman which were transformed and modified to suit the advances of Roman culture, survived in a purer form, due to Ireland's isolation from Roman and other early conquests.

The ancient legal code was expanded by the introduction of the 'Commentaries' of Ugoni the Great, who lived c.350 BCE. However, during the following centuries, the laws became unmanageable due to the influence of some Irish druids whose incorrect interpretation – to their own advantage – caused much distress throughout the land.

King Connor Mac Nessa of the kingdom of Ulster produced a revised code of laws which were easily understood by all the people. These were later known as the 'Breatha-Nimhe' (the Judgement of the Heavens). Amongst these were the writings (interpretations) of Moran, son of Cabrie, King of Ireland, who was the chief Brehon c.85 BCE.

In addition, King Cormac Mac Airt, when he was in power, assembled all the 'ollamhain' (judges) of Ireland to collect together the chronicles of the country. These latter became known as the 'Saltair of Teamhair'. He is also believed to have commissioned the 'Teagasc-no-Ri' (Teaching of the King). The Saltair itself contains the list of dues or levies which were payable to the high king by everybody – from the poorest peasant to the provincial kings – as well as the exact boundaries of each kingdom and even each small holding.

As to how this code of law came to Ireland in the first place, we have only to trace its path westwards from the Far East (Hindustan). The Sumerians practised a code of law which found its way to Egypt – as identified on the Rosetta Stone – and then to Crete, where the Law Code of Gortys was discovered in 1884. This Law Code, written in early Greek, parallels our Brehon Laws almost word for word in many passages.

The connection of the Brehon Laws of Ireland with the Middle East is further substantiated by ancient references to Tara as the 'Palace of Ben Hedar (Arabic for Heber). As the Phoenicians traded extensively with Crete their laws were probably adopted in many parts by these sea traders and explorers.

The original Brehon Laws were preserved in rude verse or in rhythmical prose, Sumerian style, as were the early myths and legends. If we are to compare the exploits of the Sumerian king Gilgamesh with those of our early explorer, Mael Duin, we immediately see the relationship between the two odysseys which were preserved in the same style. This method of recording the past and identifying the laws changed with the arrival of Roman Christianity and the introduction of the Roman alphabet which followed the original Irish language by almost a millennium. We read that St. Patrick made many important changes and modifications to the Brehon Laws to conform to Christian teaching. While he was doing this the Roman alphabet was also introduced.

The Brehon Laws existed in this new form and the only change enacted was in 697 CE by Adamnan, when he introduced a new law exempting women from taking an active part in wars. It should be remembered that the English Parliament was founded, and modelled on the legislative body at Tara, by Alfred the Great, who had been educated in Ireland. The Brehon Laws remained in force until the Statutes of Kilkenny were passed in 1376 CE when they were denounced as 'wicked and damnable' by the English. They seemed to have forgotten that their own laws derived from the Brehon Laws as practiced in Ireland. This opinion was upheld by English writers and historians through the centuries mainly due to ignorance, prejudice and religious hatred, as well as hatred of all things Irish.

IX

THE ANCIENT LANGUAGE
AND OGHAM SCRIPT

The old Irish language was based on an alphabet which was known as the 'Beith-Luis-Nion' where each letter represents a type of tree and where the name itself derives from the letters b, l, and n, which are the first, second and fifth letters of that alphabet. In addition, there was a type of script known as 'Ogham' or 'Orhum-Coll' which represented the branches of a hazel tree. This type of script, which no doubt, is connected to the original alphabet in some way, is peculiar to the South West of Ireland and the western fringes of Great Britain.

Some historians say that Ogham script was introduced to Ireland by the Celts, c.500 BCE, at about the time of their arrival in the country. However, no discoveries have so far been found in Europe to justify any connection with westward movement of Celtic culture across Europe.

The script seems to have been based on early Etruscan which is itself based on the alphabet of the Phoenicians. On examination of the early types of hieroglyphics, scripts and writings of the prehistoric period in the Middle East there appears to be only one type of script which comes near 'Ogham' and that is Middle Cycladic (Northern Aegean Sea) script of 1900-1500 BCE in which a base line for consonants and vowels was used. A number of examples are set out in one of the following pages which give a glance at the similarity between the two types of script.

It is very strange that this Cycladic script was peculiar to a few islands in the Aegean Sea and was not found in any other part of the Eastern Mediterranean civilisations. Therefore, we have two almost similar types of early script which are located over a thousand miles apart. The best example of the early Cycladic script found in the South West is in a cave near Coomhola, Bantry, which may prove that 'Ogham' is derived from the early Cycladic script.

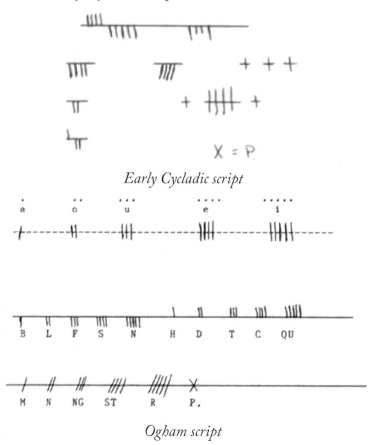

Early Cycladic script

Ogham script

Early antiquarians and historians were at odds trying to explain the origins of both the 'Beith-Luis-Nion' and the 'Ogham Script' without reference to early Mediterranean civilisations. This put them in a quandary, as they refused to accept that no mention of the languages was contained in the early Annals so they must have been invented by the early Irish civilisations. If we are to accept this fact, then we must conclude that our early ancestors were as highly gifted in intelligence as the Phoenicians! The only logical conclusion is that both alphabets were brought to Ireland by the Phoenician sea-farers to assist them in trade and to communicate with the native Irish. To verify this connection we must not forget the supreme god of the Thuatha-da-Danaan was called Dagda or Og, and the divine writing of the priestly cast was called Ogham. If St. Patrick had not burned hundreds of druidic documents at Tara, we would probably have much more information on our pre-historic ancestors.

If we refer to the writings of Caesar, we find that 'the Irish Druids never committed their mysteries to writing, except in their public acts in which they made use of a type of Greek characters'. This information was passed on to him when he was thinking of invading the country. This type of behaviour was only practised by the priestly caste of the Middle Eastern countries like Egypt and Greece.

The material used for the writings of the 'Beith-Luis-Nion' was the inside of the preserved bark of the ash tree which was laid out flat after a certain period of time. As for the 'Ogham Script' it was preserved on thin square lengths of preserved oak. The former was used to record history and genealogy, while the latter was reserved for ceremonial rites such as ceremonies honouring the gods, funerals and marriages. The use of letters was very important to the early Irish, as it helped in the retention of the genealogical family lines of the clans for the purpose of heredity and the right to fill important positions in their society.

The Ollam Fodla or the Highest Judge, who lived and reigned c. 500 BCE, founded the triennial assembly at Tara. He established the seat of antiquity in each of the provinces where all records were to be preserved. Each and every document had to be examined at the gatherings at Tara, and under his supervision copies were made of everything recorded. This volume of copies was called the Psalter of Tara and was written in verse in the manner of the ancient Egyptians, using the Beith-Luis-Nion alphabet.

As for the alphabet itself, it had only seventeen letters. Ancient Greek also had seventeen letters, but lost one, namely F, during the early period. Their alphabet was originally called 'Phoinika, having derived from the Phoenicians, and also because the letters were written on leaves or tablets of the palm-tree (Phoinix), and consisted of twelve consonants and five vowels, with each consonant and vowel having a short and long sound which was the same as the Irish tongue. It is clear, therefore, that our language had no equal in the world as a complete language, either then or now.

X

THE CELTS

In the context of Irish or local history mention must be made of the Celts, who are said to have originated in eastern Poland and the Ukraine. They were not in fact a race of people, but a band of several warlike tribes who spoke the same language and had the same customs. Due to the advance of more powerful tribes from the east they found it necessary to move further west. Having arrived at the Danube River they split up into two groups – one following the river southwards and another into Austria. The latter group divided into further groups – one heading south into Italy and the other into France and eventually into Spain conquering every tribe on the way including the Etruscans in Italy. Some of them settled on the borders of northern Switzerland where they built up what is known as 'La Tiene' culture which became the major influence in western European civilisation.

But, for our interest, the most interesting movement of the Celts is the southerly one into northern Greece – as related by Hecataeus, Aristotle, Hellanicus and Ephories (c.500 – 350 BCE) – who wrote that the Celts 'practices justice and righteousness and at the same time could be frenzied warriors when imbued with potent drink when going into battle'.

Having conquered the northern tribes and the Illyrians with their superior iron weapons, they marched south and then sacked the city of Delphi in 273 BCE. They then made a truce and an alliance with the Greeks in which they agreed to protect the northern borders in return for lands and to assist their struggle against the Persians and Carthaginians. In fact, the Celts played no small part in the preservation of Greek civilisation and culture.

When Philip of Macedonia was attacked by the Thracians and the Illyrians, the Celts came to his rescue and defeated the enemy. Afterwards, a strong bond grew between both races and when Alexander the Great, Philip's son, began his invasion of Asia Minor (Turkey) in 330 BCE, to conquer the Persians; his best soldiers were the Celts. Their appearance alone was enough to put fear into any enemy, covered as they were from head to toes in white powder or chalk, shouting wildly, hammering their swords on shields and with an apparent disregard for their own lives. They often threw away their shields and this act alone was sufficient to put the enemy to flight. Their battle chant, preserved in ancient Greek, to the rhythm of beating on their shields, was:

We fear no man; there is one thing we fear, namely
That the sky should fall on us and crush us.
May the earth gape and swallow us up
May the sea burst out and overwhelm us.

If the 'Tain Bo Cuailnge' is consulted, as related in the Book of Ulster, the scenes described of the early Celts going into war are almost identical – as they gathered speed on their horses and chariots they shouted:

Heaven is above us, the earth beneath us and the sea
Around us, we shall never retreat and death shall only
* defeat us.*

Even the custom of covering their bodies in white powder is identical. However, these particular customs do not seem to appear in any other early European civilisations at that time. When the exploits of the northern band of Celts which invaded France and then southern England are considered, no documented record exists that they actually crossed the Irish Sea and invaded Ireland. It is more likely that they came in small groups c. 350 BCE and slowly subdued the existing Irish inhabitants by the force of their stronger weapons made of iron as opposed to bronze. Another theory is that a southern tribe of Celts who were in the Eastern Mediterranean found their way by land and sea to the south of Ireland. However, the similarity between the Irish Celts and their counterparts in Greece requires further study.

In all their invasions and conquests throughout Europe, the Celts were noted as fearless warriors, but they did not exterminate their defeated foes. Instead, they spared the former enemy and became the dominant class and imposed their customs, art forms, traditions and way of life while adopting or integrating that part of the religious customs of the defeated which they found similar to their own.

The presence in Ireland of Celtic influence before any incursion from La Tiene or from Hallstatt via France or Britain (c.300 BCE) presented some major problems for early historians. The place names preserved by Ptheas, who sailed the north Atlantic in 400 BCE give us an indication that these names are in fact a type of Illyrian or eastern Celtic, i.e. Hierni (Ireland), Orcades (Orkneys) and Albu (Britain).

It is therefore, obvious that one of the most important facts in ancient Ireland is the existence of a unique and well-structured language. A language, in fact, that had no similarity with the Western European tongues of that time and which cannot be defined as Teutonic or Middle European, but which was similar in its alphabet and construction to Phoenician and early Greek. Due to its similarity with the southern dialect of the Celts it was adopted by them.

Finally, it should be pointed out that the term 'Celtic' or 'Celt' is a misnomer. There was no such thing as a Celtic race, but rather a number of tribes which shared the same original homeland, customs, beliefs, art, military skills, dialect and the desire to fight and conquer.

The word 'Celtic' is, in fact, a mixture of Etruscan (early Latin) and Greek and is a quasi-ethnic term. It identifies a certain group of people who are devoid of any fixed geographical location or homeland.

Even though Ireland, south-western Britain and France were areas still occupied by the Celts during the Roman conquests, these regions were never identified by Caesar or Roman historians as being Celtic. Instead, Ireland was described as the 'Goidelic' speaking nation which had been influenced by the 'iron culture' of Celts. It was also noted that women of the Celts took up arms like the men and were feared more than the men in battle. Maybe this was one of the reasons why Caesar never invaded Ireland!

XI

CHRISTIANITY IN THE REGION

The exact date of the arrival of Christianity in the south-west of Ireland is a very much debated subject. Those records that do exist concerning the period of 400 – 600 CE differ in many respects. It is hotly contested amongst historians even whether there was more than one St. Patrick, leaving aside the separate and earlier introduction of Christianity into the South West. Before we refer to such records as do exist, let us briefly examine Ireland as a whole, in relation to the introduction of Christianity.

It is generally accepted that there were Christian congregations in Ireland prior to the mission of Palladius in CE 431. His chronicles state that 'he was sent to the Scots living in Ireland who believed in Christ'.

As most writers do not refer to the earlier life of Palladius, it is worth noting that he was a follower of the holy hermits who lived in the upper regions of Palestine, probably amongst those who did penance, prayed and fasted on Mount Carmel. It is said that Palladius, who had been under the guidance and direction of a holy monk from his early years, embraced the life of a hermit at the age of twenty. Having spent some time in Jerusalem, he journeyed to Rome where he became a deacon, and was made a bishop by Pope Celestine to go to

Ireland ('to a land lying under the winter cold') and to preach the Gospel, a request which seemed rather unusual at that time considering the distance. If we refer to Tacitus, the Roman historian and writer of that time, we find that he states that 'the ports of Ireland are better known to the Romans than those of Britain'. The persecution of Christians by the Roman emperors Diocletian and Maximian in all parts of the Roman Empire caused many believers to flee from Europe and England and to seek safety in Ireland. Sedulius Scottus refers to Scotus Hyberniensis and the southern part of Ireland in this regard (c. 430 CE).

Prosper states that Palladius travelled to Ireland as Bishop, landing somewhere near Wexford, and in time established a number of churches where he kept the relics of St. Peter and St. Paul as well as his 'tablets' which probably mean his own copies of various books from the Old and New Testaments. One of the churches built by Palladius was referred to as 'Teach na Romanaig' or Church of the Romans. This may have a connection with Kilnaraune, near Bantry, but more than likely refers to the new form of Christianity introduced by Rome.

As to Prosper's assertion that paganism had disappeared from Ireland around the sixth century, this conflicts with other writers writing about early Christianity in Ireland. It appears that Prosper's judgement was influenced by the erroneous reports arriving in Rome from Ireland to the effect that Palladius had converted all Ireland to Christianity. This, however, was not true, as the powerful druid priests had influenced the tribal leaders to expel Palladius from the country.

Before he departed, he organised a number of his followers, unknown to the pagan priests, to remain in Ireland and preach to the people. A year after his departure, c. 432 CE Palladius died. Some years later when Patrick arrived, he found an infant church, based on the Eastern monastic form, which he considered wise to follow, rather than introduce any major changes dictated by Rome.

If we consult Usher's 'Third Order of Saints', we find that he states that 'there were those holy priests and a few bishops who dwell in remote places and who live on herbs water and alms. They had divers rules and Masses. As for tonsure, some had the corona and others with their hair. They differed also in Pascual Celebration in that they honoured the Resurrection from the fourteenth day of the moon while others from the sixteenth'.

Amongst those mentioned by Usher, are a Colman, a Carthagh and two St. Mochoemogs, one of which was the son of Cuaith, a disciple of St. Carthagh and a bishop whilst the other was the illegitimate son of Vairt, also a disciple of St. Carthagh (CE 540-580). He also mentions details of three brothers, Gobban, Garphan and Laseran, the sons of Nescainn. Gobban is mentioned later as a bishop and a saint by the historian Colgan.

Of the above one of the St. Machoemogs and St Gobban were connected with the Bantry Region, as were a St. Colman, St. Fineen, St. Gobnait and St. Canera. St. Machoemog is mentioned in connection with the ancient church and graveyard near Kealkil, St. Fineen with a monastic settlement to the south of Bantry town and St. Canera with her hermitage at Ballylickey. It is said that St. Colman, having converted the people around Roaring Water Bay, moved to Colomane, Bantry. The place he picked for a religious settlement is rather a puzzle as the original site contained an early megalithic site with standing stones, a stone circle, a cairn, a bright barytes stone and a ceremonial druidic well. Under the directions of St. Colman the druidic well became a holy well with lines of penitential stones on sides, a graveyard and a stone burial site where the saint is reputed to have been buried. Remains have also been detected of a rectangular stone settlement which the followers of the saint may have occupied. We are led to believe that this was an important religious site during early Christian times and up to the 1940s it was a place of religious visitation for the local rural population.

Another important Christian site was at Kilmacomoge near Kealkil. According to local tradition this was a druidic site before the arrival of Christianity in the area with a stone circle and a druidic well which in later years was reputed to give relieve to the infirm. There is now a Mary shrine here which is signposted from the main road and accessed by following the path over the field beyond the modern grave yard.

There were other early Christian settlements in the region including Kil-na-Romanig (Kil-na-Ruane), Kil-atha-Fineen, Kil-More, Reen-a-Disert, Reen-a-Ban-Oige, Kil-na-mBan-Oige and Maul-na-Monaig.

One of the earliest Christian monuments is that found at Kilnaruane situated on a high field overlooking Bantry harbour. There were no indications of any ruins until an aerial photo was taken of the area some time ago by Dr. P. Mould. This showed an outline of a square building surrounded by a circular outer ramp indicating that this was a substantial settlement. Due to the lack of early records it is impossible to connect any local saint to the settlement except St. Gobnait.

As for the Kilnaruane Stone, we don't know if it has a connection with the site or not. It is possible that what remains of the cross or ankh could have been brought from another location. The only reference to an important cross in the locality is to that which was placed on Horse Island by the monks of Cuinge to advise ships that they were entering a port controlled by the religious monks. The idea of a connection between the Horse Island Cross and Kilnaruane is strengthened by the depiction of a boat crewed by monks on one side of the upright.

The following is a detailed description of the Kilnaruane Stone.

The cross in the top panel represents both the symbol of the supreme sun-god of the ancient civilisation, and the sign of Christianity. The strands of interlacing would suggest the influence of the ancient sea-god Manannan, as he was usually portrayed by the sign of the sea serpent or snake. Thus we have the conflict of the old religion with Christianity – and good or evil.

The lower panel depicts an orans, or praying figure, wearing a simple ankle-length garment. The two feet, clearly defined, represented a holy man of God in early Christianity. Before that, the symbol represented the feet of the Egyptian sun-god Osiris. The figure is therefore praying or instructing his audience on the liberation from past beliefs.

The next panel is a Greek-style cross of the early Christians and represents the introduction of the converted to Christianity.

The lower panel displays two figures with one knee on the ground, hands extended to a wafer-shaped bread on a pedestal or altar and it appears as if the bread has been dropped by a bird, possibly a dove. This represents a passage about St. Paul, written by St. Jerome, as the taking of the Bread of Life after conversion.

The twin interlacing spirals, on the top of the other side, are believed to represent the spirals of life.

The central panel shows four animals, symbolising the four Evangelists of the early Church, or, more accurately, as in Revelations 4 (4:8), signifying the throne of Heaven.

The Kilnaruane Stone

The Kilnaruane Stone

On the bottom panel is the symbol of a boat which derives from ancient Mid-Eastern religions, especially Egyptian, representing the ship of Isis transporting the 'beatified dead' to the Other World. Here it could possibly represent the ship of Christianity or else the early voyages of the early Christian monks like St. Brendan.

Mention must be made of some of the other early Christian settlements or 'churches' that were to found in the greater Bantry region. These would include –

Kil-atha-Fineen
The name means the 'church of Fineen's Ford' The original site was reputed to have been on the high field to the south of Bantry town.

In ancient times there was a stream running down what is now Scairt road with a timber bridge further up. At present there is little to see of the church or settlement except the general outline of mud walls indicating some sort of rectangular enclosure.

Kil-Mor
Kil-More means 'large church'. It is situated on Whiddy Island. Today, all that can be seen are the ruins of a stone church and graveyard. This is not the ruins of the early settlement or church but dates back to c. CE 1500. From an aerial photograph the outline of three circular enclosures can be seen – two near the church ruins and one between the two lakes to the south.

Reen-a-Disert
At Ballylickey, to the north of Bantry, there is a small isthmus at the entrance to the almost enclosed river's mouth, where it is reputed that St. Canera established a priory. Little or nothing remains due to sea erosion but there are some building stones

in an old wall. As there were two old stone dwellings built nearby, it is assumed that the original stones were used in their construction.

Reen-na-mBan Oige

The name means the 'knoll of the young women'. It is reputed to have been located to the north-east of the ruins of the O'Sullivan castle on Whiddy Island. The priory is said to have been connected to St. Canera.

Kil-na-mBan Oige

This priory was located on the north side of the disused Church of Ireland building on the north side of the road to Gearies. There are some references saying that it was connected to a St. Mineog. The ancient Irish poem called 'Caoine na mBan Oige' relates the plunder, rape and removal of the young women by a Viking raid. On a hillock to the south are the remains of a souterrain and a burial ground.

Ard-na-Monaig

This name means 'The Height of the Monks' and is situated west of Ardnagashel on the headland. Little exists today of this settlement which was supposed to have been located between two hillocks.

Nearby is Ardnatourish where a holy well was a place of pilgrimage in the past and a bothan where Mass was celebrated.

There are many other locations in the region where there were possibly early Christian settlements, such as Farranamanaigh (monk's land), Kilnaknappoge (church of the hillocks), Maulavanaigh (knoll of the monks), Gortnakilla (field of the church), Gortnascreena (field of the shrine), Kilnascarta (church of the shrubbery) and Kileen (little church).

Before ending this chapter we should mention the various 'children's burial grounds' or Cilineacha where un-baptised children were interred such as – Derrymacilla, Kilnacknappoge, Dromlicacaroo, Lisheens, Cloonygorman, Dromclogh West, Baurgorm, Derryginagh East, Gortacloona, Ardrah, and at Dromliegh South, near the hospital in Bantry (old Workhouse site). Also, we should not forget that there was leprosy at one stage in the region like in other parts of Ireland and that there were a number of colonies where those stricken by the decease had to go. With few if any references to the locations there is a tradition that two of these were located at Brenny Beg and Glanbanoo.

Mention must also be made of the 'holy wells'. Some of these have already been discussed such as Tobereen Mhuire at Kilmocomogue.

Some of the others were at Cahirmukee, Gortroe, Breenybeg, Ardnatourish, Ballylickey Bridge, Beach and Whiddy Island.

Penal Mass Sites

During the Penal Times there were many locations and hidden sites where Mass was celebrated by priests who were on the run.

In the Mealagh valley there is a place called Cnocan-na-h-Althbrach where Mass was celebrated. Those that were old and unfit, like many others, who could not make the journey recited the Rosary at home. Another location was at Cappaboy south which was known as Clais an Aifrinn. Nearby was a place where the priest used to hide called Pluais-an-Tsagairt. At Coomleigh north is a place called Coom-an-Tsagairt. It is reputed that people in the area used to light a bonfire when a priest was needed for someone that was dying. At Breenymore, there is an altar stone called Cloch-na-hAlorach near Breenymore hill. Based on tradition there was another altar stone at Maghanasilee where Mass was celebrated and one at Derrynacille.

Another debatable site was at Kealkil where there was supposed to be an altar stone which has been referred to as 'shelter church' – probably the antecedent of Kealkil church. According to tradition Mass was celebrated in a cave at Scartbawn and also there was a thatched building at Dromacappal at a location called 'Ard an Tseipeil' where Mass was celebrated during the period 1730 to 1764.

CHURCHES

Kealkil Churches

Between the years 1648 and 1665 a small thatched church existed in the village of Kealkil. From 1700 to 1750 a building known as Farrell's rock was used as a church and this was replaced by another thatched church, referred to as O'Reilly's haggard, which was located in the present graveyard. This was used from c. 1750 to 1840. This was followed by the building known as the church of the Immaculate Conception c. 1840 which was built by a Fr. Barry. This was just before the Famine hit the area in 1842.

Ardnaturish Church

This was not a church as such but a family cabin or hut where Mass was celebrated. It was known as the 'barracks' and belonged to a Mr. Lyons.

Cooricamade (Coomhola) Church

The first reference available indicates that Mass was celebrated in a temporary structure at a place called the 'Gairdin' which was located at the junction of the old road to Glengarriff and the Priest's Leap road.

It seems that Mass was also celebrated around this time (1806) at a building known as the 'barracks'.

The present church was built in 1806 by a Fr. Daniel O'Crowley, on a small plot of land. It is now referred to as St. Joseph's Church or Coomhola Church.

Kilmocomogue Church

This was probably one of the oldest churches in the Bantry region as there is mention of its existence in 1199 when there was also a chancel and a rectory where some priests lived together. In 1437 the church, chancel and rectory were separately taxed and the rectory etc was connected to St.Catherine's of Waterford. It seems that the buildings and rectory constituted a monastic or religious community which was taken over by the Protestant church during the Suppression of the monasteries by Henry VIII or Queen Elizabeth but fell into disrepair in 1615. By 1699 the church which measured about 20 metres by 12 metres was in ruins. It could be argued that this was an ecclesiastical establishment which was pre-Norman.

The Protestant church was then transferred to Bantry in 1703 at a location known as Garryvurcha – See Protestant Churches.

Bantry Catholic Church

As far as we know the first church in Bantry was built in the location where the priests' houses now exist. It was a thatched building of about 20 by 10.5 metres. It came into existence about 1795 when the then Bishop of Cork, Dr Moylan, leased the plot of ground from Hamilton White for 300 years. It is also said that the first church near Bantry was at Dromacappal near Donamark and existed before the thatched church at the location of the presbytery. This church had a bell to summon the local congregation. It was demolished when the new church was built at the site of the presbytery at Bantry.

This Bantry church was used up to 1825 when a new church was built by a Fr. Barry to a design prepared by M. Augustine Riordan, a Presentation Brother. The transepts were added in 1846. The site includes a cemetery which was purchased under the Land Purchase Acts in 1889. Serious faults were found in the roof and ceiling in 1944 and the church was almost rebuilt and reopened in 1946. The site of the old church was cleared and three houses were built there prior to 1852 and this became known as the presbytery. In front of the church near the road a boys' primary school was built. Tim Healy's father taught there as well as a Robert Kelly. It should be noted that Greek and Latin were two of the subjects.

Garryvurcha Church – Protestant/Church of Ireland
Garryvurcha means 'Murphy's Garden' and was the location of a small cabin which was used as a church after the Protestant congregation left Kilmacamogue church due to its condition. It was not legally a parish church until 1703 when an Act of Parliament was passed. A new church which is now in ruins was built there c. 1720. A number of the Earls of Bantry are buried there as well as members of prominent Protestant families.

Bantry Protestant Church (St Brendan's)
This replaced Garryvurcha church and was built c. 1818 and was extended in 1858. It is located on the north side of the Bantry Square and is noted for its fine wood carving and stained glass windows. About the turn of the 19th century additional work was carried out which included laying a marble floor,

installation of an organ and a church bell which weighted 16 cwt. At that time the church catered for a population of about 300 souls.

Snave Protestant Church

This small church was built about the same time as Rooska Church c. 1886. It was used by the small local Protestant population who lived in that area. With the introduction of vehicles and easy access to Bantry, the church was closed in the late 1970s and later sold as a private dwelling.

Kilavanoige or Rooska Protestant Church

This church was built in the middle of the 19th century c. 1866 to cater for the Protestant population in that area which numbered about fifty. It occupies a section of the land where the ancient priory was located and which was sacked by the Vikings. With the dwindling Protestant population. The church was closed in the 1960s and later sold. It was a part of the parish of Durrus.

Mention must be made of the Methodists in the Bantry area. In 1783 it is recorded that a James Vickery was using his house at Rooska as a meeting place of prayer. Despite his religious beliefs he was also reputed to have been involved in smuggling. In 1803, a small Methodist chapel was built at Pig Lane. This was replaced by a more suitable chapel at the same location. A new chapel was built at the junction of Marino Street and Bantry Square. This was completed on the 13th of September 1866 with a school in the basement. Due to the fall in numbers of the congregation, the chapel was closed in the 1980s and is now occupied as a doctor's surgery.

XII

THE ARRIVAL OF THE VIKINGS.

The Viking invaders and their exploits in Ireland are related in the book known as 'The war between the Gael and the Gaill'. These Vikings or Norsemen were either from Norway or Denmark. Those that came from Norway had fair hair (Fionn Gaill) while those who came from Denmark had dark hair (Dubh Gaill). The historical records of Ireland including the above make no reference to the conquest of Bantry Bay by the Vikings.

The Vikings first made their appearance in Ireland when they raided the monastic settlement on Lambay Island off the coast of Dublin in 795 CE, and after this first lucrative raid they commenced a general conquest of the coast of Ireland during the following centuries. For the most part they were pagan warlike tribes, goaded on by their chiefs whom they regarded as demi-gods. Their raids at first were aimed at the monastic churches and settlements which were adorned with articles of gold, silver and precious stones. They then directed their raids against the native settlements for women and slaves.

The first wave of Viking raiders arrived on the north coast of Scotland and then proceeded to plunder along the whole east of Ireland. Their first appearance on the south coast was in Cork in CE 822 and then in CE 827 they entered Kinsale harbour and proceeded up the Bandon River as far as Innishannon. Moving further south they attacked Timoleague Abbey and all those settlements within thirty kilometres of the coast. In 827 they moved further south and raided all the monasteries and settlements as far as Cape Clear and Sherkin Island.

It was not until 882 CE that references were made again concerning the Vikings, when Donnchadh, King of the Eoghanacht (West Cork tribes), engaged the Vikings in battle near Glandore harbour, which encounter ended in his death and total defeat of his army. During the next hundred years the newcomers sought to entrench themselves in West Cork against the will of the local tribes. In 916 CE the Vikings were defeated and then in 960 another battle was fought and being victorious the Vikings laid waste the countryside. Finally, they were defeated at a place called Oneachach.

Meanwhile, during those centuries of war on the east and south coasts of Ireland between the Vikings and the Irish tribes, another force of Norsemen had moved down the west coast and in 807 CE they ravaged Inishmurry off Sligo and plundered the other off-shore islands.

Four years later, in 811, they moved further south and attacked Valentia Island, the Skelligs and the Kerry coastline. During that same year the local Kerry tribes defeated the Danes in a sea battle off the coast. Despite this defeat, the Danes returned to the Kerry coast in greater numbers and while the local tribes fought amongst themselves, the Danes established a base on Dursey Island. It would appear that the name Dursey derived from the Norse Thor Iy, or the Island of Thor, the god of war. Having established themselves on this island they ventured up Bantry Bay. A monastic settlement near Blackball Head was first sacked before they entered Castletownbere harbour, where they plundered two monastic settlements on the mainland

– one west of the ruins of Dunboy castle and another near the native settlement. Moving across to Bere Island, they sacked and plundered a number of religious settlements and then built another stronghold at Lonehart, there they built a breakwater to protect their vessels in the small harbour from southerly and easterly winds. From here it is assumed that they destroyed the small hermitage at Adrigole, the monastic settlement in Glengarriff harbour and the small hermitages on the various islands. Also destroyed about this time were the monasteries or settlements at Ardnamonagh, Reenidesert, Kilmacomogue, Whiddy Island and Killnavanoige.

One of the strongest local traditions which supports the above account is the story related in the ancient poem called 'Caoine na mBan Oige' which relates the story of the sack of the priory at Gearies by the Norsemen who, having raped the older nuns removed the younger nuns to their stronghold on Dursey.

It is understood from local tradition that the Norsemen took over an old fort at Donemark and eventually made a settlement there. The dykes were deepened and two large sluice gates were built on the river's edge to retain the water within and thus prevent attack. It is reputed that they stayed in this base for about 50 years until the local tribes came together with the intention of driving the enemy out of their fortification. Having attacked the fort, the Irish withdrew as if in flight and allowed the Norsemen to follow them inland.

The Irish made their final stand at Curran, on the Priest's Leap road, and defeated the enemy. It is said that the last of the Norsemen to die were buried near the ancient stone cairn. This event seems to have been the last of the occupation of the Norsemen in Bantry Bay and Ireland in their conquering mode as from then on they integrated with the local population in other parts of Ireland.

When we discuss the Vikings and their explorations and conquests their migration southwards and especially westward must be taken into account.

When they sailed westward on their voyages during the summer months they discovered the Faroe Islands and Iceland and found that they had been preceded by Irish Anchorites who lived in bee-hive structures. These were referred to as Papor and their settlement as Papey, both of which refer to followers of the Pope. Between 930 CE and 984 the Norsemen landed in Greenland and built a number of settlements. With no timber available in Greenland the Norsemen under the leadership of Eric the Red are reputed to have voyaged further west to the coast of Labrador in 985 where they cut and gathered timber and transported it back to Greenland. Nothing much more was known about the Norsemen's exploits in Canada until a complete village was found on the southern shore of Lake Michigan, which is about 2,500 kilometres from the mouth of the St. Lawrence river. Only further investigation and exploration will give us a better idea of the exploits of the Norsemen in the American continent but it seems obvious from the amount of megalithic monuments found in Maine that the early Irish and then the Irish monks had already made these sea voyages earlier.

In the context of voyages and discoveries the legendary journeys of St. Brendan, who is reputed to have reached the eastern seaboard of the American continent, should be mentioned. There are many versions of St. Brendan's voyages and one has to separate fact from fiction. Most of these texts were written in the ancient form imbued with myths and legends. A text, dated c. 945 CE, and called the 'Navigatio Santi Brendani', reveals an account which is devoid of the bardic style and seems more factual.

To discover more about the voyage of St. Brendan, one has to look at other details which related to seafaring at that time – for instance, the existence of an ancient seafaring people who lived on the Kerry coast and who were referred to as the 'Ciarraige'. They are said to have made regular voyages north to the Hebrides, Shetlands and further. They also voyaged to the south coast of England and France and plundered villages taking away women and slaves.

Amongst the 'Ciarraige' was the renowned Mael Duin, whose exploits are famed in legend and history. The voyages of Mael Duin and St. Brendan were referred to as Immrama, which denotes a physical sea voyage and not a spiritual voyage of the mind. If the date 525 CE is accepted as the commencement of Mael Duin's voyage north, then St. Brendan followed him some twenty years later in 545 using the same knowledge of the course to be followed. It is worth noting here that the Greek historian Pytheus refers to Iceland in 370 CE and there are further Greek references in 795 and 800 CE.

In the account of Mael Duin and St. Brendan a detailed topography of the west coast of Ireland is mentioned giving an indication of the veracity of these voyages. Furthermore, they were not recorded to prove that these known islands existed to the north, nor were they a means to claim ownership. They were but a documented history or account of inter-island voyaging by the seafarers and then the monks.

The historic voyage of Mael Duin is related in the ancient Book of the Dun Cow. Leaving the obvious mythical content aside, the sea journey was up the west coast of Ireland, across to the west coast of Scotland, onto the Hebrides and then the Faroe Islands. From here the voyage was westwards to Iceland, Greenland and then to the coast of North America. Various aspects of the voyage are fascinating, such as the volcanic eruptions and the spouting waters or geysers on Iceland, the silver pillars (icebergs) in the sea, the silver (snow) islands of Iceland and Greenland, the large birds (albatrosses), the giant trees of Labrador, beast-like oxen (bears or caribou), and the hairy people (wearing animal heads and skin) who blackened their skin in time of mourning. For anybody interested in further research the last reference is the most remarkable, as it may show that Mael Duin did reach North America and encountered some of the native people who were Inuit or Eskimos.

At that time, there were many small tribes of Inuit in northeast Canada, including the Labrador Inuit, the Ungave and the Western Territory (Lakes) Inuit. They spoke a common language called Inuktitut, which was made up of six different dialects. The Inuit had a very strong family culture due to the harsh terrain where they lived.

This culture could be described as pure Shamanism. The most interesting point of their Shamanism was their elaborate 'feast of the dead' (Potlach) which has not been properly investigated. This festivity of mourning commenced with gifts been presented to the bereaved around the funeral pyre. Then the men painted their faces and bodies and, having smeared their bodies with fish or seal oil, coated their bodies with ashes from the burning pyre. This is exactly what Mael Duin described of the Inuit people he encountered during the latter part of his voyage.

XIII

THE ARRIVAL OF THE ANGLO NORMANS

From 950 to 1175 CE there was relative peace in West Cork until the arrival of the conquering Anglo Normans c. 1150. With their chain-mail, iron-clad horses and decorated shields they must have presented a fearful sight to the native population, especially to the clan leaders and their fighting men who were clothed in leather and carried small shields and short swords or rudimentary spears. Like the Vikings, who had preceded them by a hundred years or so, the Normans advanced along the coast with their ships accompanying them off-shore. Having picked a suitable location they started to build their fortifications, which evolved into stone castles where they could be safe from the local natives.

The Irish chieftains had no military answer to the Normans on the open field of battle or in their castles. They resorted to short skirmishes and fast running battles, wherever they saw an advantage. Laying siege to the newly built castles did not prove any success as the Normans could be supplied with food and water by sea and the Irish soldier was nothing more that a peasant called to arms, lacked battle experience and had to return home to tend to his animals and crops.

As a result of the Anglo-Norman conquest of north Munster and the occupation of all their lands, the O'Sullivans, like many other clans, were forced to move from their hereditary lands around Knockgraffan in Co. Limerick, and ended up in West Cork and South Kerry. There were two main branches of this powerful Sept: O'Sullivan Mor who settled in South Kerry and the O'Sullivan Beare who settled around Bantry, Castletown and west of Kenmare.

In 1531 Dermod the Elder who built Carriganass, Reenavanig, Castletownbere and Dunboy castles, married into the Mac Carthy clan when he took Sheena, the daughter of Donal Mac Carthy Reagh of Kilbrittain Castle, as his wife. When he blew himself up experimenting with gun powder, their son Donal should have succeeded him as head of the O'Sullivan Beare. Donal was underage, however, and the chieftainship passed to his uncle Owen. Meanwhile, Donal Mac Carthy of Kilbrittain submitted to the Anglo-Norman Crown in 1565 CE and was made the Earl of Glencar. Owen O'Sullivan, like many of the other West Cork chieftains, also submitted and he became Sir Owen O'Sullivan, Lord of Beare. This entitled him to hand down his title and property to his firstborn son which would mean disinheriting Donal, in contradiction to the Old Brehon Laws. Sir Owen was now the dominant power in the region and a period of inter-tribal feuding began between the young Donal, his brother Philip and Sir Owen as to who was rightful heir to the leadership of the O'Sullivan Beare. In the meantime, most of the local chieftains had submitted to the English Crown in order to keep their titles and their lands which were constantly under threat of being taken over by avaricious Norman knights.

The conflict regarding the chieftainship of the O'Sullivan Beara clan was placed before the English Commissioners in 1587 for a decision and after six long years the verdict arrived whereby Donal received the lands west of Adrigole, Sir Owen received the lands around Bantry and Philip received a few acres at Ardnagashel, near Bantry. By this division, in the space of some six years the O'Sullivans lost a large proportion of their lands to English settlers.

When Sir Owen O'Sullivan of Carriganass castle died in 1594 his family were led by his son, also called Owen. He fought with the English at Kinsale and afterwards took their side in the conflict with Donal Cam even aiding the English forces in the destruction of Dunboy Castle which was the hereditary seat of the O'Sullivan Bere.

Donal, after his epic march to Leitrim with over a thousand of his followers after the fall of Dunboy Castle, fled to Spain with some of his family and followers. Following his departure Sir Owen became the lord of all the O'Sullivan property, but in name only as Sir William Petty became the owner of much of the abandoned O'Sullivan property. In fact, Sir Owen never retrieved a single acre of the O'Sullivan lands which were previously under the ownership of his cousin, Donal Cam O'Sullivan. Sir William Petty arranged a marriage between his daughter and Fitzmaurice of Kenmare (Marquis of Lansdowne) so that more property would become his, while Owen O'Sullivan lost what little he possessed following the Irish Uprising of 1641. This ended the reign of the O'Sullivan Bere.

Sir William Petty did not have everything his own way, as Arthur, Earl of Anglesey secured for himself some ninety-four thousand acres (38,000 hectares) of forfeited lands between Bantry and Beara in 1679. By Royal Charter 'these lands were erected into the Manors of Bantry and Altham (Beara) each with 2,000 acres in demesnes with the power to hold courts, 'leet and Baron'. Permission was also granted to hold two markets each week and three fairs annually at Ballygobban in the 'Manor of Bantry'.

The O'Donovans

One of the most important clans in the area from around 1100 CE were the O'Donovans, who had a stronghold called Castledonovan east of Bantry. They are supposed to have been descended from Fiach Fidhgeinte and also from the family of Cairbre Aehbda and Ui Connaill Gabhra at Cochma in County Limerick. There were two branches and the head of the clan could come from either one until the tenth century when Brian O'Donovan came on the scene.

It is generally accepted that, fed up with the raids of the Dalcassian tribes from across the Shannon, Brian led his clan in arms and, with the assistance of Maolmuadh of the Uibh Eachac tribe, defeated the Dalcassians at Bearna Dearg (Red Gap) in 976 CE, resulting in the death of Mahon, son of Cinnedi, brother of Brian Boru.

Incensed by his brother's death, Brian Boru raised an army and invaded the territory of the Ui Fidhgeinte in 977, defeating the O'Donovans and their allies. Brian O'Donovan, the leader, was killed as was his Danish ally Amhlaff of Limerick. Not satisfied with this victory, Brian Boru engaged the forces of the Eoghanacht and defeated them in 978. They were then forced to give up their hereditary lands and move further south into West Cork in the beginning of the eleventh century and immersed themselves in almost continuous warfare with the existing tribes.

From the thirteenth century onwards the O'Donovans were lords of a large expanse of territory in West Cork which had previously belonged to the O'Driscolls and the O'Mahonys. This area stretched from Castledonovan in the north to the coastal castles at Rahine and Glandore.

Following their participation on the English side against their old enemy, the O'Sullivans, their territory was confirmed by the English Inquisition held in Cork on October 1607.

This happy outcome was soon to change when Cromwell arrived in Ireland and came west as far as Bandon. Leaving a substantial force in Bandon he instructed his officers to attack and destroy all the strongholds held by the Irish clans in West Cork. The O'Donovans suffered like everybody else with the confiscation and forfeiture of their territories. Later, when Charles II came to the English Throne the O'Donovans sought the restoration of their properties but only got the lands and demesne around Rahine castle.

The McCarthy Scarteens

To the east of Bantry is a townland called Scairt which had a castle and a ring fort called Ardragh. Before the 1600s this branch of the McCarthys occupied land stretching from Scairt to west of Durrus. The castle was completely destroyed in the time of Cromwell and all the lands were confiscated.

The O'Driscolls

These were one of the oldest clans in Ireland and their domain stretched from Cork to Dursey at one time. From c. 500 BCE they were engaged in commerce with France and Spain, mainly in fishing, and the export of hides and cured meats. Their name derives from the Irish word of interpreter. Their mini-kingdom was laid under siege by the Irish tribes who were dispossessed of their traditional lands in north Munster and who had moved south, especially the MacCarthys, the O'Donovans and the O'Sullivans. The hold on their territory became impossible especially when the Anglo-Normans arrived in West Cork. Being unable to sustain themselves in their customary style they mortgaged their lands to a number of powerful Norman families and when they were unable to repay, their lands were lost and they became small landowners like their tenants. They lost their lands around Bantry Bay to the MacCarthys who became the new landlords.

The MacCarthys brought south with them the MacSweeneys who were mostly galloglasses(mercenaries) and these settled on Whiddy Island, where they built a large fort, and also on the fertile valleys of the region.

XIV

THE ENGLISH PLANTATION

B efore discussing the major confiscation and occupation of the land by the English in the 1600s, we should examine how the land was held and divided before that time. Within the tribes or clans, the land was let by the chief to his subjects on the basis of a 'gneeve', which equalled a twelfth of a townland. The term of the lease was usually for 21years and a life, or for life, or for 31 years, or for a period of three lives.

The lowly peasant only obtained about half an acre on which to survive by growing food and grazing an animal. There was little left over from what they grew after they paid their rent to the landlord or chieftain. They also had to dedicate themselves to work for free for the benefit of the landlord or chief. It is interesting to note that the same system operated with both black and white slaves in the colonies of the West Indies and the Americas.

As far as the author is aware, there are no records of the early English settlers in the Bantry area from 1150-1600 except for the mention of a John Galwey of Kinsale having a fish palace at the estuary of the Dunamark river c.1410. It is also recorded that Sir Owen O'Sullivan gave leases to two English settlers named Derbyshire and Broigley on Whiddy Island around 1604. These leases were transferred to a Major George Walters and Rev. Davies by the Earl of Anglesea when he was awarded his large tracts of land around Bantry Bay. A John Davies got the patent to hold fairs in Bantry c.1702. During this period the pilchard fisheries became very important to the area and in 1622 there were a number of fish palaces on Whiddy Island. About 1702 CE the lands that were leased by Major Walters were transferred to a Richard White of Whiddy Island and in 1714 those lands near the harbour leased by Mr. Hugh Hutchinson and John Despard from Lord Anglesea also came into the hands of Richard White.

About this time the pilchard fishery was at its height and large quantities were landed. A Mr. Meade built a fish palace on the north side of Bantry inner harbour and exported over 6,000 barrels of cured pilchards during a calendar year in the early 1700s. His partners in this venture were Galwey and Rev. Davies and a Mr. Young. As far as can be ascertained there were a number of fish palaces on the mainland near the sea and these were at Bantry, Donemark, Ballylickey and Snave. In addition, some 40 tons or 36,000 kilos of butter were also exported about this time.

With the proceeds of the pilchard fisheries, Richard White continued to lease or purchase lands including Blackrock House and demesne which he bought in 1765, when he changed the name to Seafield House.

This building was not Bantry House as we know it today but a two storey building nearer the sea and overlooking the 'Black Rock'.

Looking back a number of years to the 1641 Uprising, most of the English settlers on Whiddy Island had their houses destroyed and their cattle driven into the sea, while those living ashore lost all their cattle, houses and goods. Most of them fled to the English stronghold of Bandon. Carriganass Castle of

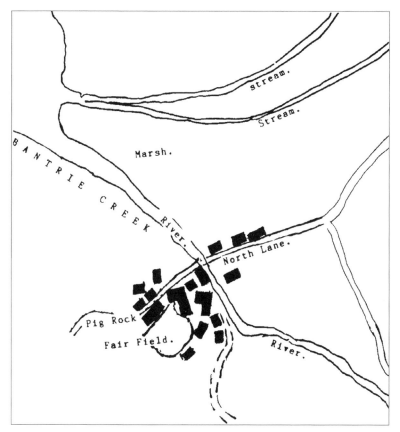

The clochan of Beantrie in Medieval times

Sir Owen O'Sullivan was taken and remained in Irish hands for almost a year. After Cromwell's expedition to Ireland, his son, Ireton, became the Lord Deputy for the short period 1650 to 1651 when he died. During his term of office, the star shaped fort at Newtown came into existence. It was too far from the sea to be of much use and could not protect the inner harbour so it was no surprise when it was abandoned after a few years.

Ireton was succeeded as Lord Deputy by Ludlow. After ten long years of wrangling an Act of Settlement was passed in

1651. This was to repay the Adventurers who had subscribed a total of £336,000 which financed Cromwell's War in Ireland. It was also designed to repay the soldiers and consisted of the allocation of parcels of land. A body called the Irish Commissions was set up to oversee the 'plantation' of forfeited lands. The division of the country into counties in 1562 was used as the basis of allotments, and the county of Cork was reserved for the Parliamentarians themselves. The seven baronies of County Cork, including the tithes to church property, were allocated to both special Adventurers and Cromwellian officers. As often happens in these circumstances, the Adventurers who were favourites and friends of the Parliament received the best lands while the officers and soldiers got gorse and mountains. The allotment of lands was made regardless of who already occupied them – whether Royalists, Royalist sympathisers, early English settlers or the native Irish.

As mentioned earlier, a Major George Walters received the lands of Whiddy Island. He seems to have been connected to the Bristol slave traders and the planters in Barbados as the family name appears on the list of landowners in Barbados. It is recorded that Walters leased part of his land to a Mr. Skinner, who in turn sold the 'use of the lands' to a Mr. John Davies of Middle Temple, London, who happened to be a friend of Sir William Petty, the cartographer of Cromwell. But, then again, the leases for the 'use' of these lands and others were yielded to Annesley, Viscount Valentia and the Earl of Anglesea. To complicate matters further, some of the lands were released by a Mr. Hutchinson, a Mr. Depard and a Richard White.

As far as can be ascertained, the Hutchinson family held large tracts of land in and around Bantry. These included the lands south of the town of Bantry (Blackrock House etc), Reenrour to the north and parts of Ardnagashel. Depard lands were to the east of the town. From his home on Whiddy Island, Richard White accumulated sufficient funds from fishing and smuggling to buy out Depard's leases and lands and by 1712 he had purchased the leases held by the Hutchinson family which included the house and demesne to the south of Bantry. As the Whites moved into Blackrock House, the Hutchinsons moved to Reenrour House and then later to Ardnagashel. The Whites by this time had extended their operation to the export of timber and bark as well as setting up a number of iron ore smelters. By 1751 Richard White Jr. had amassed a fortune big enough for him to acquire most of the lands around Bantry Bay which were originally ceded to Lord Anglesea and White became the major landlord of Bantry.

XV

BANTRY – A PIRATE PORT

The period of time – 1550 to 1745 – when pirates used the port of Bantry as a safe haven could be described as one of the lost chapters of Irish and local history. In contrast to the Dutch and the English pirate activity the Irish mostly concentrated on the south-west coast of Ireland. Some of them roamed as far as the Caribbean and the East Coast of the United States and became as well known as Blackbeard, John Racham, Captain Kidd and others. Those who didn't have vessels of their own joined the most notorious pirates as crewmen awaiting their opportunity of commanding a captured vessel of their own. The life of a pirate was extremely dangerous. The majority ended up dead but a few survived to live out their lives ashore in relative luxury either on the south-west coast of Ireland or the eastern seaboard of the States. It is said that the colonial towns of the eastern coast of the United States including Boston and Charlestown were built on the proceeds of piracy.

The discovery of the New World gave an impetus to piracy especially when many of the English crews and ships used to defeat the Spanish Armada found themselves redundant. Having obtained a lettre de marque from the Crown, many captains ventured as far as the Caribbean to attack the Spanish bullion ships which were transporting gold and silver back to

Spain and those ships which were supplying the new colonial settlement with food and goods. When the prey was scarce, the pirates and privateers moved up along the east coast of America seeking plunder. However, most of the Irish pirates remained in home waters where they plundered foreign vessels passing the south-west coast to and from the European ports including those in England. In fact, any foreign vessel was fair game.

Life on board a pirate ship was much better than on a British warship at that time. Food was a hundred times better with an almost limitless quantity of captured wine to wash it down. There was also a plentiful supply of rum and beer. Each crewman got his share of any captured booty. This division of spoils was made by the quarter-master and not the skipper.

Each pirate ship operated as a democracy and those who suffered injury were recompensed on a sliding scale. Thus, each crewman that was injured or lost a limb knew that he would have sufficient funds to look after himself and his family when he was obliged to live ashore.

Those pirates who operated in European Waters around Ireland, England, the English Channel and the Bay of Biscay organised themselves into a loose band of some forty pirate ships, which had an admiral, vice-admiral and rear admiral. When a ship was taken, these individuals would have the say as to who would take over the captured ship or ships if they were in good condition and could join the fleet.

During the reign of King James I there were ten times more pirates active around the British Isles than during the reign of Queen Elizabeth. These were recognised as the greatest threat to the economy of England and other European countries and the peak of their activity was during the period 1603 to 1625 when the Crown had only three ships seeking out pirates in their safe havens on the coasts of Ireland and Britain.

Coastal communities entertained crews, bought their loot, supplied their needs and at times financed them when business was quiet. They regarded the pirates as benefactors as they supplied cut-price goods, such as sugar, tobacco, silk and spices which the people could not otherwise afford. Those who traded in these goods were called 'Land Pirates' and they carried out this business with impunity due to the absence of proper laws. The English Statue of 1536 against piracy made no mention of 'Land Pirates'. Those who benefited most were those in high office like the English High Admiral and the numerous Vice Admirals, stationed in Ireland, who were supposed to suppress piracy.

It came to such a stage that no merchant ship was safe on the high seas. As a result, merchants ashore, faced with losing their income, equipped and manned their own privateer vessels and sent them to sea with hand-picked captains and crews. However, things changed when peace was declared between England and Holland and Spain in 1609 and there was a general clamp-down on pirates on the Devon, Cornish and south coasts of England. Knowing the south-west coast of Ireland, where the Irish pirates had their bases, provided many safe havens, the majority of the English pirates move over to the coast of Cork where English authority did not exist.

Amongst the ports and inlets where the pirates found safe havens were Glandore, Castlehaven, Baltimore, Leamcon/ Crookhaven, Castletownbere, Bantry and Ballinskelligs. Every ship that passed within range of these ports was in danger of being attacked by pirates.

When the pickings became scarce off the south-west coast, the pirates headed for the Caribbean and the east coast of the States especially during the winter months. Sailing in fleets of up to seventeen vessels they stopped and boarded every vessel that they could out-sail and overtake. They even attacked the fledgling settlements, regardless of what nationality the occupants were.

With the approach of summer and fine weather in the Home Waters the pirates returned across the Atlantic and sought refuge in the main refuge ports such as Crookhaven, Baltimore and Bantry where they disposed of their pirated loot, careened their vessels, took on supplies and generally enjoyed themselves ashore in the ale houses. Finding no safe port in the Caribbean or the East Coast of the States to sell their pirated goods, some of the pirates escorted their prize back across the Atlantic to Ireland where they disposed of the cargoes for a good price.

Bantry, in those days, was only a small fishing port with about 2,500 inhabitants but grew rapidly from the pilchard fishing industry. The town also became noted for smuggling due to the arrival of many ships from France and Spain. A number of English 'adventurers' took up residence in the town and on Whiddy Island to trade with the pirates. They even transferred cargoes, like sugar, from one ship to another and sent her to Cork or across the Channel to dispose of the goods.

One of the most noted pirates who used Bantry as a safe haven was Captain Easton who was Admiral of the Pirate Fleet. On occasions, he arrived in Bantry with most of his fleet of seventeen vessels after returning from the Caribbean. Here, they disposed of their loot and took on water, supplies and additional local crewmen. Another frequent visitor to Bantry was the pirate, John Stevenson, who had a woman in town while other pirates had moved their families to the area. Some of their descendants are still living in the region. The pirate ships ceased to visit Bantry after about 1745.

XVI

THE FISHING INDUSTRY

In accounts in the ancient Irish manuscripts of the first people who arrived in Ireland mention is made of three Iberian fishermen who were ship-wrecked on the south-west coast. This event is deemed to have happened many millennia before our era. Following on this report, it is noted in the early histories of West Cork that Iberian fishing boats were accustomed to fish off the south-west coast and that the O'Driscolls carried out a lucrative trade with these foreign fishermen from 500 BCE onwards. The surname O'Driscoll means 'interpreters' in Irish so perhaps they were able to communicate with Iberian fishermen in their own language. It is assumed that these fishermen continued fishing off the south-west coast as mention is made that they settled in various ports where they built 'smoke houses' for the curing of fish such as hake, cod, ling, haddock and pollock which they caught by the use of long lines.

With the arrival of displaced clans of the MacCarthys, O'Sullivans, O'Mahonys, O'Donovans etc. to the region there was conflict as to who was to benefit from the fishing. It seems that the O'Driscolls were recompensed by barter of those goods brought from Spain but now a tariff or duty was levied on all vessels entering the ports held by the various tribal chiefs. This also applied to the native fishermen whereby one tenth of the value of fish landed was paid to the local chief. In addition, certain days' fishing was dedicated to the chieftain. When the Anglo-Saxons became entrenched along the coastline, the proceeds from the fisheries became their main income.

Early in the 1600s, when Sir Owen O'Sullivan of Carriganass Castle granted some land on Whiddy Island to two Englishmen, Broigley and Derbyshire, they immediately saw the advantage of getting involved in the pilchard fisheries. Another English settler, who joined them in their efforts to get involved in the fisheries, was an Edward Davenport, a brother of John Davenport, Bishop of Salisbury. It is interesting to note that Davenport, during his early period in Ireland, had borrowed too much money from his friends in England and had made some dodgy investments, but further assistance from his friends enabled him to establish himself in the fisheries by building a fish palace on Whiddy Island.

Pilchard fishing usually commenced in July and lasted until December. During the first three months the pilchards were full of oil and difficult to handle, being soft and brittle to handle. Despite this, their yield of oil was high, which increased their value. Pilchards were caught by day and by night. During the day watchers took their places on high ground around the Bay and, as soon as a shoal of pilchards was seen schooling on the surface word was quickly sent to the fishermen who were waiting in their boats just offshore. The nets used were called 'purse seines', which were from 100 to 150 fathoms (300 metres) long and from six to nine fathoms (12 to 18 metres) deep.

The net was dropped into the sea making a circle around the bank of fish, then the larger seine boat and its 'follower' brought the two ends together and hauled on the footrope to close the net at the bottom.

Baskets were then used to scoop the fish out of the net and into the boats. If there were too many fish remaining in the net, one of the boats went to shore to discharge its catch before returning to the net. Some of the large open seine boats could carry up to ten tons (9,000 kilos) of fish aboard.

In order to cope with the enormous quantities of pilchards landed many people were employed. Around the inner harbour some seven fish palaces were built where the fish were processed and barrelled. One was situated at the north side of the Square in the space occupied by the Church of Ireland and the large houses, three were on Whiddy Island, another at Newtown then there was one at Ballylickey and one at Snave. The largest was the one located in the town which was built using some of the material of the ruined Abbey. This fish palace was a stone walled enclosure with a number of small buildings in the interior used for the preparation of fish and storage of barrels etc. On the outside was a gently inclining cobbled pavement where the workers first covered the fish with salt and then laid them out with their heads facing downwards on the slope so that the brine would run off. After a few days more salt and fish were added until the heap reached over a metre in height. After about twenty days, the fish were removed, the salt brushed off and the fish were dipped into fresh water a number of times until they were completely clean. The fish were then carried in basket loads to the yard and emptied into casks (large barrels), where they were closely packed. The casks were pierced with holes to let out any water, blood and oil that remained in the fish.

As soon as a sufficient number of the casks were full they were lined up against the press-wall on timber stands. Using a long plank with a round piece of timber attached, which was hinged to the wall, the workers squeezed the fish down in the casks by applying pressure on the artificial top covers. As the fish were compressed, the casks were topped up until they were completely full and ready for the market.

It was mainly women and older girls who worked in these fish palaces, the ratio being ten women to one man. The women carried out most of the work which involved the laying out of the fish, salting, carrying baskets of fish and collecting the oil. The men handled the presses and the casks and barrels. With over 600 barrels of fish being landed in one day, a large labour force was required. It is said that over a thousand worked in the Bantry fish palace on some occasions.

Bantry grew rapidly during those years of the pilchard fisheries. In fact, the saying that 'Bantry was built on the pilchard fishery' is fairly accurate. There are no records as to how many people were involved in the industry but a rough guess would be about 3,500 given the number of fish palaces in the vicinity. With exports of some 15–20,000 barrels per annum many ships entered the port. Some records say that there was an average of two ships sailing and two ships entering port each day during those years. However, only a few of the ship's names are mentioned. Most of the cured fish was exported to Spain, Portugal and Italy and to the new colonies in the west. In addition to fish being exported direct to these countries, some fish was sent by sea to Cork for export from that port.

At the beginning of the 1700s the shoals of fish decreased drastically. This coincided with the arrival of large French seine boats with very large nets fishing at the entrance of the bay where they continued fishing for over three years. This, combined with over-fishing in the bay itself, was probably the main cause exacerbated by a change in sea temperature as the pilchards seem to have declined around the south-west coast generally. Yet, the pilchards did not disappear completely as a Mr. Young cured over 500,000 fish in 1748 and a Mr. Meade who operated the Bantry fish palace cured over 380,000 fish in 1749, all of which would be equal to 1,500 medium-sized barrels. Some 20 years later there was a serious complaint sent to the British naval authorities in Cork that over 50 large French boats were fishing off Bantry Bay.

During the next 100 years various efforts were made to revive the fisheries by changing to sprat and herrings. Long lining for cod, ling, and hake continued, but insufficient fish were caught to sustain the large numbers previously involved in the industry despite the fact that some of the local yawls and small sailing fishing boats began to fish outside the confines of the bay.

From the 1780s there was a gradual changeover to herring fishing, using the same type of seine netting. It is recorded that in one haul, in 1785, over 200,000 herring were landed; the equivalent to about 1,500 boxes. It is not known exactly how many seine boats and crews were engaged in this type of fishing during the following 100 years, but a rough estimate would be 12 to 15 seine boats plus their followers, employing over 150 men. In addition to these, in the 1830s, there were eight half-deckers, five decked, 59 sail and 641 small rowing boats, giving employment, some seasonal, to about 3,000 men.

The history of the fishing industry during the famine years is vague, to say the least. It appears that the industry was again in decline due to the absence of the herring shoals but long lining continued as did the mackerel fishery. Many people gathered periwinkles, clams, small crabs and seaweed along the shoreline to cook and eat. Many of the fishermen, due to the scarcity of fish, sold their nets and boats to make enough money to feed their families. This forced sale denied them the opportunity of ever fishing again if fish became plentiful in the bay. The gathering of shellfish from the beaches unfortunately stopped when it was reported that there was a 'disease' in the water. This was the first report of the 'red tide' in Bantry Bay.

In the years prior to the Famine, the herring and sprat fisheries were in serious decline and the fish palaces had been forced to close down, after which they deteriorated into ruins. Then, after the Famine, the stone work was removed and used for building houses, so that almost nothing remains today of the many fish palaces although their locations are known. Yet, some of the buildings on the north side of the Square built in 1830 do retain some of the old walls.

With the advent of steam, a number of steam-driven trawlers from England and France began fishing along the coastline and even up the bay, to the detriment of the local fishermen. Where trammel nets and long lines were anchored on the good fishing grounds, these trawlers would often trawl right through them, thus destroying the nets and long lines. On one occasion, c.1861, when a number of fishermen – C. McCarthy, two O'Mahony brothers and a Denis Bohane from Muintir mBaire, set out to recover their trammel nets, they were all lost.

During the same year, the building of a new pier was proposed to promote sea traffic and fisheries in the port. This proposal was delayed for some six years by the objections of the Castletownbere ratepayers, who would have to foot some of the costs. They saw no advantage to them in subscribing to a project which would be in competition with their own port. Eventually, the government of the time granted a sum of £3,000 and an interest-free loan of another £1,600 over six years. Work was started by W.M Murphy, a local contractor, using stone from Scart and from the quarry near the hospital cross. The pier was completed within two years.

The first steam trawlers were introduced to the local fishing fleet by Messrs Pike, Murphy and Tisdall. At this time only four or five eight-man seine boats remained fishing for herrings. These belonged to the Downeys and O'Driscolls of Whiddy Island, the O'Donovans of Bantry and two owners from Gearhies. These continued fishing for herrings up to the late 1940s.

During the 1930s a number of half-deckers were converted to diesel engines and, with the setting up with the Fastnet Fisheries Company by Messrs Biggs, a number of larger, fifty footer, diesel trawlers were introduced. These included the *Mary Audrey*, the *Angela*, the *EDJ*, the *Connie* as well as the *St. Ita*. The motor vessels called the *Donemark* and the *Togo* were also from this period. Later, in the 1940s, a number of larger diesel trawlers were introduced. These included the *Deirdre*, the *Johanna Mary* the *Star of Maeve* and the *Hidden Treasure* which continued fishing up to the late 1950s.

In 1966, the herring shoals returned to Bantry Bay and there was a short lived fishing boom in the Gearhies fishing grounds. Small thirty-footers came from all over the south-west coast to join the small number of local boats. Tempers flared as the locals with their open boats were 'pushed off' their own fishing grounds. Nets and marker buoys were cut but eventually there was peace when many of the 'outside' boats departed. Then large fishing trawlers came to reap the harvest and the smaller fishing boats could not compete; loosing their nets on a regular basis.

Some Sea Tragedies
In addition to the four fishermen from Whiddy Island who were lost in the middle of the 19th century there were two more local tragedies.

On the 11th of October 1895 an open boat with five men departed Adrigole to fish on the south shore of the bay with trammel nets. When the weather began to deteriorate they decided to return to Adrigole but somehow they went up on the Colla Rock and the boat capsized throwing the crew into the water. No alarm was raised and all of the crew were drowned. Two of the bodies, namely John and Michael O'Sullivan, were found floating off Blue Hill near Bantry. The bodies of Tim O'Shea, Maurice Abbot and another John O'Sullivan were never found.

Another seine boat disaster occurred on 25th of September, 1918. While lifting the net aboard a false wave came over the stern and swamped the boat. The 'follower' was full of herrings and despite suffering the same fate, the crew somehow kept their boat afloat and managed to get to Whiddy Island and raise the alarm. Immediately, a boat was sent to the mainland to

Steam Yacht in Bantry Bay

*Old engraving showing the inner harbour and town
from the area of the pier.*

alert the fishermen there. Boats departed from both Bantry and
Whiddy Island despite the very bad weather and sea conditions.
Two of the crew were located hanging on to oars but they were
dead. There was no sign of the rest of the crew or of the seine
boat. Those that were lost were Henry Driscoll, Johnny Leary,
William Donovan, Jeremiah O'Neill, Christy O'Neill, Denis
McCarthy, Jeremiah McCarthy and Ned Griffin.

XVII

BANTRY THROUGH THE AGES

As mentioned earlier the question of land division was a most important issue amongst the local tribes, especially the rights to pathways, country routes and river crossings, where more often than not a toll was levied. River crossings became very important as trade increased. Many castles were built at major crossings and small clusters of mud huts were built at the minor vantage points. In time, small markets and fairs were held near these crossings.

In Bantry the main crossing of the mill river and the tidal creek was half-ways up the present Bridge Street. On the right is an alley way where a cluster of mud huts existed between the rock and the river bank together with a small clearing which was used as a market for cattle, pigs and farm produce and called the 'Fair Field'. This is now a private car park. In time, this little village grew and extended along the river-bank of what is now Bridge Street. In addition, the village began to extend on the north bank with further huts and with a timber bridge crossing the river.

It is not known when exactly the little hamlet of Bantry came into existence but various sources indicate that it probably was about the middle of the 12th century when the parish of 'Cuinge' was established. However, we find that there are references to a

Spanish settlement in the area which engaged in fishing and the smoking of fish – 'Fumadores' – in earlier centuries.

From approximately the middle of the 16th century, when the pilchard fishery commenced and pirates began to visit, we note the 'creek of Bantry' being mentioned as well as the village of Ballygobbin.

Early mariners do not mention Ballygobbin in their logs but refer solely to 'Bantry creek', and it would therefore appear that the commercial centre was Bantry on the south side of the river and that Ballygobbin was situated on the north side of the river. Ships, on high tide, came up the river and berthed on the south side of the creek. Even in those early days, there were about 60 ships visiting the small port each year. At that time, there was a small island at the entrance to the inner harbour where a fisherman and his family lived.

One of the first references to Ballygobbin or Bantry in English correspondence was the charter of 6th of February 1679, to the Earl of Anglesea by the Crown whereby fairs and markets could be hold in Ballygobbin and Newtown. In 1702 this was followed by the granting to a John Davys of the right to hold fairs at Bantry. This would indicate that Ballygobbin and Bantry were separate villages at that time.

Ballygobbin being described as a small hamlet, where 74 people lived, consisting of four houses and a collection of mud huts. The inhabitants were made up of 58 natives and 16English settlers.

When an English fort which was built by the sea, north of Ballygobbin, for the defence of the harbour against any possible French Invasion, fell into disrepair after a few short years the 119 settlers who had decided to live nearby returned to Ballygobbin. From about this time both villages amalgamated into one using the name Bantry which began to grow in size.

The pilchard fishery was the main reason of this development with many people coming in from the surrounding region to work and to try to earn a living.

With the expansion of the town many small industries sprang up including a number of small tanneries, timber yards and coopers. With the number of ships visiting the creek there was a flourishing import and export business, with cured and smoked fish, hides, wool, and cured meats being exported. Amongst the goods which were imported were wine, spirits, cloths, crockery and hardwoods. As previously mentioned all the ships moored along the creek from what is now known as New Street and down as far as the A.I.B. Bank on the Square.

With the arrival of a French invasion flotilla in the Bay in 1689 there was a general exodus of English settlers from the town, Whiddy Island and the surrounding area. Most fled with what they could carry on carts and carriages to the walled town of Bandon which was under English control. This event is covered in more detail in one of the following chapters.

When the French had departed, the village returned to normal and most of the English settlers returned. At that time it was noted that there were only about six decent houses in the village and the rest were bothans of various sizes.

From 1690 onwards the pilchard fishery expanded with nearly every inhabitant, in some way or other, engaged in the industry.

The English who were involved in the fishery and with the export of barrelled fish, made substantial amounts of money. These included Richard White who purchased leased lands in 1739 and then bought Blackrock House near Bantry along with its demesne. He changed its name to Seafield House in 1765.

With the improvement of pilchard fishing, a Robert Young leased lands on a beach in the harbour area for the building of a fish palace.

Photograph of a local girl taken in 1917 or 1918

He was already in the fish export business with Mr. Meade who had the fish palace on the north side of Square and is recorded to have exported about 1,000 barrels of pilchards and 231 barrels of sprat in 1748. The following year Meade exported about 800 barrels of fish.

During the following 40 years, as people grew more prosperous the town grew in size and stone houses with thatched roofs replaced the mud huts. Richard White demolished Seafield House and construction began on a new and larger house which later became known as Bantry House. This consisted of the centre section of the present house. In addition, the Whites got involved in the felling of oak trees in the locality. These were exported to England for the building of ships. Also, a number of ore smelters were set up in Bantry and the outlying area.

As for the position of the Protestant and Methodist populations in the Bantry region, the Protestants had their first church and glebe house at Kilmacamogue, which is about five miles from Bantry town. This was previously a monastic settlement. When this building fell into disrepair, a new church was built in 1720 at Garryvurcha, Church Road, with an adjoining graveyard. A British Act of Parliament was necessary for the building of this establishment.

After a short period of time the building deteriorated seriously and work commenced in 1816 on the building of a new place of worship situated on the north side of the Square. This was completed in 1818 and further work including the tower was completed c.1898. In addition to this new church there were a number of small churches and glebes especially at Cappanaloha (Rev. Charles Smith), Durrus, and Snave.

In 1796 there was general pandemonium when a French fleet was sighted in the Bay. A general alert was sounded as people feared an invasion and a landing force. Only a small English

Engraving dated 1779 'Cataract of the Bantry River'

garrison of some 26 men were present to oppose the French. Notice of the invasion was dispatched to Cork by Richard White. All that happened after this is contained in the second next chapter.

Life returned to normal after the French fleet had finally departed in early January. Fishing recommenced and ships began to use the creek once again. Ashore, woods and forests were cut down and the smelters resumed working. Many more houses were built and the covering in of the Mill River as far as the end of the present New Street was being considered. Most of the ships were now using the timber pier at the Black Rock where they could stay afloat at all tides.

During the early 19th century civil unrest began to take hold of the countryside. Renegades called the 'White Boys' began marauding throughout the countryside. Their main objective was to loot and burn everything English and redress the hardships of the poor and those evicted. Two of the agents of Bantry House called Payne and Bird were noted for evicting those who could not come up with their rents on the appointed day. As a result of one particular eviction, Mr. Bird was shot dead in his office on Barrack Street and the culprit, found guilty on false evidence, was hung at Cork Jail.

Originally, the 'White Boys' were made up of the dispossessed Irish peasants but were later joined by some men whose sole objective was to prey on the English settlers and even their own countrymen and their families. In January 1822 a band of about 200 horsemen entered Bantry. They had attacked and looted the houses of the outlying English settlers. One of those houses belonged to a man called Mellefont. Having paraded around the town the 'White Boys' departed and were soon followed by the Earl of Bantry and a force of horsemen. At the Pass of Keimaneagh, a skirmish took place and a number were killed on both sides. This incident is recalled in the popular song 'Cath Ceim-an-Fhia'.

Towards the end of the summer of that year, the potato crop failed, which in a way heralded the calamity of the Great Famine which was to occur some 23 years later. This crop failure was accompanied by an outbreak of cholera which commenced in Belfast and spread rapidly south as far as West Cork. Some 38 adults were admitted to the small hospital but many fled the town spreading the disease inland. On the 14th of August the town was free of that dreaded disease.

According to the Desmond Commission, in 1826 5,060 tons of corn was exported by Bantry Mill which had been taken over by the Galwey family. The sea traffic through the port in 1832 was 31 inbound with cargo and 28 outbound also with cargo. At about the same time, Michael Murphy

Bantry before the famine

had taken over the mill and brewery at Donemark as well as a mill on Main Street. Another mill belonging to the McCarty Scarteens was situated on the quays. Amongst the tanneries were the ones at the present Warner Centre and the location of the present Post Office. It is also recorded that the porter brewery at Bantry, run by Michael Murphy, Mr. Plummer and S. Young, was dispatching barrels of porter to Cork. Records show that there was a cider brewery near the Hospital cross and another on Whiddy Island.

Imports consisted of iron ore for the smelters as well as coal and sugar. Also imported were 17,000 gallons of spirits, 2,500lbs of coffee, 3,600lbs of tea and 38,000lbs of tobacco, not to mention what was landed by smugglers. As for fishing, there were twenty four hookers and 360 men engaged in long lining as well as 12 seine boats catching herrings and sprat. During the year 1835, thirty one vessels sailed with cargoes of corn while some 28 entered harbour with various cargoes. Two of these vessels were the '*Kingston*' and the '*Deeley Bridge*' which plied between Bantry, Quebec and Nova Scotia with cargoes of timber for Bantry and emigrants to St.John's, New Brunswick.

With the ever increasing population of the town living from day to day and in squalor, the ravages of hunger and fever began to appear. To combat this, a relief fund was organised and subscriptions were made by the well-off which financed the setting up of soup kitchens around the town for the first time. More funds were allocated by the government in Dublin and London. These were to be used to purchase seed, to construct piers and to build the English Market at the end of Main Street. Up to this time Main Street had been an open market with stalls selling everything from meat, fish and farm produce. Fishing and fish curing continued but on a lesser scale. So as not to be reliant on one industry, Lord Bantry introduced

Donemark Mill

the growing of flax and the making of cotton (vitries – coarse linen for making sacks). When this proved successful, the linen trade became restricted to a few of the well-established merchants, including Vickery, Kingston, Clarke, O'Connell, Young, Murphy and Bird (agent for the Earl of Bantry). One of those who received a grant for the spinning wheels was a Mr. Dursey while a John Kingston took out a lease on the Mill.

In 1821, Mr. Galwey leased the Bantry Mills from Lord Bantry and started production of grain once again. Five years later, the existing small cottage hospital was demolished for the building of the Workhouse. Meanwhile, work continued on filling in the Square and the river was only now open from the entrance of New Street to the Slob area. Two timber bridges were used to cross the river – one opposite the Bantry Bay Hotel and the other opposite the Gift Shop. Lord Bantry started to rear deer about this time. The Deer Parks were at Whiddy Island, Seafield, Parkana, and Seskin.

About 1830 plans were proposed by Lord Bantry for the building of a Bridewell (jail). Up to this time, anyone guilty of a serious crime was transported to Cork on a prison wagon and those who were found guilty of murder or the likes were hanged locally either on the hanging tree on the Rope Walk outside the southern gate of Bantry House, or on Whiddy Island, Reendisert and east of Dromroe. The original courthouse was burnt down during the Troubles in 1921.

During the early 1840s there was a general decline in local trade. The once thriving export of grain and bagged flour had fallen drastically. The mills were working only at about 15% capacity. The fishing industry was experiencing poor catches. The linen industry was almost wiped out due to export tariffs to England. If this was not enough, the sudden appearance of potato blight on the crops caused much hardship. Then, just as the population was recovering the blight returned in 1845 plunging the country into the abyss of hunger and despair.

Bantry was lucky in that a workhouse had been built by the Poor Law Union and had been completed in 1842 on land purchased from Lord Bantry. With a capacity for abut nine hundred inmates; it was designated to serve the baronies of Bantry and Beara. For further details on the Famine in Bantry read the chapter concerned with this event.

By the early 1850s things had gradually returned to near normal except for the serious decline in the population. Employment increased and fishing improved. In 1858, due to weeks of heavy rain, there was major flooding in the town as the main culvert could not cope with the river in flood. All those that had premises in the low lying centre of town suffered flood waters up to four feet high. This however, did no lasting harm

Local man with basket of turf 1918

to the growing economy of the town. The Munster & Leinster, at Bridge Street, became the first bank to open in Bantry. Shipping increased with the import of Indian corn, timber, coal and general goods. Finally, by 1868 the pier was completed. Work commenced on the supply of fresh water for the growing town. A substantial underground reservoir was built across from the Catholic presbytery. Supply was from the stream and by pipes from two spring wells on the hill-side. Piping was laid to the English Market and to the Square. During that same year, there were only 100 souls in the Workhouse.

As most of the fisherman had sold their nets and boats during the Famine they were without a means of subsistence. The number of seine boats had dropped from nine to four. Those that had smaller boats reverted to dredging coral sand and gathering seaweed off the shoreline. In 1861 money was donated to the fishermen to purchase trammel nets. Instead of exporting corn it was now imported from Odessa and the American Colonies. Two ships involved in this trade were the 'Margaret Ann' and the 'Ellen' while the 'Heinkringla' transported timber from Quebec.

On the first of November 1861, four fishermen lost their lives in Bantry Bay while trammelling for hake and cod. These were Charles McCarthy, Daniel and Denis O'Mahony and Denis Bohane of Gearies. I can find no record that their bodies were ever recovered.

Meanwhile, ashore, various slate quarries were opened. There was a good production of high quality slate which was shipped to Cork and exported to England. Unfortunately for the many workers these quarries closed after a few years due to lack of investment. Many other types of mining commenced but these also suffered the same fate. Mining is covered in one of the following chapters.

During 1871, James Capithorne reopened the Bantry Mill for wool dying while the Murphys continued with their grain mill off of Main Street. The wool and grain was mostly imported from Australia. Other activities included the importation of grain for G.W.Biggs' mills and timber imports for the saw mills of W. Murphy on the quayside. Before the building of these steam driven saw mills it is estimated that there were over 50 small carpentry enterprises in that lower docks area.

A Mr. Harris commenced the manufacture of paint at Donemark Mill and also the export of barytes. During the period 1878 to 1880 the fishing improved. The conflict between the trammel fishermen and the trawlers continued. A temporary agreement was sorted out whereby the trammel fishing took place at night and trawling during the day. This meant that the trammels had to be lifted at dawn.

Although the 1880s brought a new depression to the economy in Ireland, Warners from Whiddy Island opened their butter factory on William Street in 1880. Despite the depression, the section of the railway from Dunmanway to Bantry was completed in 1881. The station was situated in front of the present hospital. Carriages and carts owned by Vickery's, Waters and the Railway hotels brought the passengers and goods to the town. A few years later, in 1883, the Bantry Bay Steamship Company was formed and the first ship to commence plying on Bantry Bay was named the 'Countess of Bantry'.

Bantry Woollen Mills.

Irish Tweeds,

Serges, Friezes,

Homespuns,

UNEXCELLED FOR PURITY, DURABILITY, CHEAPNESS, AND FASTNESS OF COLOUR.

Supplied direct from the Mills.
Any Length Cut.
Carriage Paid on Suit or Costume Length.

PATTERNS FREE, on receipt of Post Card, from

Thomas Copithorne,
Woollen Mills,
BANTRY, CO. CORK.

Visitors to Bantry are invited to visit the Mills, where they can inspect the Goods in every stage of progress (in actual Manufacture), from the Fleece to the Finished Cloth.

Bantry Woollen Mills and the Catholic Church

Meanwhile, the buttery of Warner's and Mander's, situated on what is now the car park on William Street, was exporting some £2,000 worth of butter per week.

Oil lamp lighting was installed on most of the streets of Bantry during the early 1890s. Previous to this, only the area around the Mill had a supply of light generated by the water-wheel when this was working.

When the work of filling in the Square was completed it was named Egerton Square in memory of the White family, the Earls of Bantry. But a few weeks later in 1897, it was unanimously agreed in town that the Square be called Wolfe Tone Square in memory of the failed invasion of 1796.

Around the turn of that century the population of the town was estimated at about 3,000 people which was only about a third of what it was before the Famine. Still, the majority of the people lived in base accommodation with no sanitation facilities. Marino Street, Blackrock Road and Barrack Street were considered to be in bad condition but the worse was Tower

The Prince of Wales and Kaiser Wilhelm arriving at Bantry Pier

Bantry Square flooded in December 1948

Street. Yet, the town seemed to have prospered and instead of thatch, the roofs of the small houses began to be covered with slate or corrugated iron.

With the English Fleet based in the Bay, and many of the English government and aristocracy visiting, Bantry House was the scene of many lavish parties including the last great party at Bantry House in honour of the cessation of hostilities. In the town itself there were 52 pubs, six hotels and many eating houses where the officers and crews of the ships had the opportunity of eating something different to that available aboard ship. Also, when the crews were ashore the Square was used for drilling and marching.

One of the major events of 1912 was the arrival of the Prince of Wales and the German Keiser in their yachts, escorted by some naval vessels. Both the Prince and the Kaiser landed at the Railway pier and proceed up to the town where they dined at a hotel. This was the last time they met before the declaration of war between their two countries.

XVIII

WHIDDY ISLAND

In the map of Ireland attributed to the Greek historian and cartographer Ptolemy, the name 'Vodii' appears over Whiddy Island, Bantry Bay (Inver Sceine). This name 'Vodii' seems to denote the tribe that inhabited the island and the adjoining coastal area and is understood not to be a place name.

Whiddy Island almost embraces Bantry Harbour on its north side. It measures a little less than 5 kilometres from east to west and is 1.6 km at its widest points with three undulating hills or hillocks. The highest part of the island is the centre hillock which is about 37 metres high. The island is devoid of megalithic monuments. Whether these were removed when the land was prepared for cultivation is not known, but it seems unusual in comparison with all the megalithic monuments on the adjoining mainland.

In early Christian times the island became known as 'Insula Sancta' or Holy Island. We know from tradition and ancient remains that there was a religious settlement in the vicinity of the ruined church of Kilmore at the western end of the island. This settlement consisted of three round enclosures – two adjacent to the present church ruins and the other located between the two small lakes to the south. If my memory serves me correctly, I remember seeing a reference somewhere stating that these settlements were of mixed sexes. The existing ruins of the church seem to indicate that the church replaced an earlier one on the site. As far as this writer is aware no archaeological digs have been carried out on these sites to-date.

Near the eastern end of the island a nunnery was located. This was sited about 100 metres from 'Reenavanig' (Hill of the Young Women) castle ruins. Nothing remains of this nunnery today except the holy well and some stones which were incorporated in the building of a nearby ditch. Up to the 1950s people were accustomed to visit this holy well on the 15th of August, the Feast of the Assumption. This nunnery and holy well were attributed to St. Canera. These various religious establishments more than likely gave the name 'Insula Sancta' to the island.

Having set up a base at Dursey Island, the Vikings commenced raiding up the Bay c.850 C.E. It is probable that they sacked the settlements on Whiddy as they referred to the island as 'Vod Iy' or Holy Island. Later the name 'Vod Iy' was changed by the local inhabitants to 'Faoidi Island' which was probably the nearest that they could get to the Norse pronunciation. This name still remained in use by the island people until the 1950s when the name Whiddy came into common usage.

According to Friar O'Sullivan of Mucross Island, in his 'Ancient History of the Kingdom of Kerry' there were many Spanish settlements along the South West Coast in the sixteenth century. These were principally at Dingle, Valentia, Ballinskelligs, Castletownbere, Kilmacomogue, Bantry and Baltimore where they had 'fish factories'. We understand that these were factories involved in the curing and smoking of fish such as herrings, mackerel and sprat and were called 'fumadores' by the Irish at that time. Ships came from northern Spain loaded with wines, sherry and brandy and then loaded cured meat and smoked fish as well as cow hides and sheep hides for the return voyage. It is recorded that one could purchase a salmon for a gallon (four and half litres) of wine and a good hide for ten gallons. At that time Whiddy was noted for its fisheries of herrings, pilchards, sprat and scallop, and for its oyster beds. It is recorded that, after the declaration of war between Queen Elizabeth and Spain in 1585, with the Anglo-Norman advances into the South West of Ireland the Spaniards had no option but to leave their homes and businesses and return to Spain.

In the early medieval maps of the island a number of settlements or clusters of houses appear. These 'Clochans' were situated at Reenaknock, Tranahilla, Tranahaha, Kilmore, Gurrarthy, Croangle and Reenavanig. The number of huts (bothans) would indicate a population of about 250 people who probably existed on fishing, farming and the raising of a few animals.

When the powerful clan of MacCarthy moved south into West Cork as a result of the Anglo Norman invasion in the twelfth century they occupied by force the territory which encompassed South Kerry and West Cork and they became the overlords to all the local tribes. They were followed south by the O'Sullivans of east Limerick who became their vassals.

The O'Sullivans broke up into two groups, the O'Sullivan Mor who occupied South Kerry and the O'Sullivan Bere who occupied the Beara Peninsula and the lands adjoining Bantry Bay. The Bere branch built four castles – Dunboy, Castletown and Carriganass on the mainland and Reenavanig on Whiddy Island. In addition to receiving tributes from the inhabitants they also claimed a tariff on ships entering Bantry Harbour and on the fishing grounds. Reenavanig castle became the centre for observing shipping and the collection of dues.

Old postcard of the harbour with Whiddy in the background

Growing in strength, the O'Sullivan Bere clan, following the example of the McCarthys, began to raid other parts of the country for cattle, women and booty. On one such foray the MacCarthys had raided north as far as the lands and the monastery of Cong in Co. Mayo. When the High King of Ireland was notified of this event he sent a messenger to the MacCarthy Clan leader demanding recompense for the raid or else he would send an army south and lay waste their territories. In 1134 Cormac MacCarthy the Clan leader gave up to the monks of Cong, Whiddy Island and the other islands in the harbour as well as the lands bordering the harbour from League Point on the south to Ardnagashel Point on the north side of the bay along with the rights to all dues and tariffs from shipping and fishing. This parcel of lands became known as the parish of 'Cuinge' and was later amalgamated with the local parishes of Kilmacamogue and Durrus which stretched from the Kemineagh Pass to Mount Gabriel.

According to tradition Chapel Island (Inis Cuinge or the Isle of Cong) in the harbour got it's name from a small church of the monks which was situated at the east end of the western hillock. This small church and its adjacent graveyard are recorded as existing up to 1199. It is quite probable that this was where the monks settled and had also their accommodation. Near the site of the church is a pure spring water well which must be fed from an underground reservoir. The ridges of cultivation can still be made out on the slopes of the western hillock. On Horse Island to the east, which was much larger in those days, the monks had a small tower to regulate the shipping and the fishing boats entering and leaving harbour. It is also said that the monks had stone walls protecting a high cross on Horse Island which gave notice that ships which entered the harbour that it was controlled by the monks. The townland of Croangle (Cro-Ceangaill) which is situated in the middle section of Whiddy where the pier is now located is difficult to translate but probably means the enclosure or garden of those wearing a belt or binding which would mean the monks. It is reputed that the monks only remained about 50 to 75 years in the locality and when the last ones went back to Cong the Mac Carthys regained their territory and subsequently passed it over to the O'Sullivans, while the ancient parish was absorbed in the local parishes of Kilmacamogue/Durrus.

The only extant vestiges of the church are the walls of the building which were incorporated into a house where a family lived for a number of years. When these departed the building was covered by a corrugated iron roof and used as a shelter for cattle. At this stage the island was owned by Murty O'Sullivan. Nearby was the ancient graveyard where some of the monks were buried.

West of Chapel Island, which later became the property of the Earl of Devonshire is the Rabbit Island or Cooney Island and to the north is Hog Island. Both of these islands were much larger in Medieval Times. A family of five lived on Rabbit Island up to the 1900s according to Lewis in his Topographical Dictionary. The island also later became the property of the Duke of Devonshire and part of the Bandon-Boyle Estates. Also, both the nearby Hog and Horse islands became the property of the Boyle Estate.

With the departure of the monks from Whiddy Island the O'Sullivans consolidated their grip on the income of their subjects. In spite of the vast revenue (c. £ 2,000 pa) from shipping, fishing, the land and the unknown income from smuggling they still had to pay a substantial tribute to their overlords, the MacCarthy Clan. Reenavanig castle was the administrative centre and even had a dungeon at ground level where those who failed to pay their dues or tithes were incarcerated.

The castle was a tower house originally built by Dermod O'Sullivan and became the property of Sir Owen O'Sullivan of Carriganass after the division of the O'Sullivan territory by the Crown. A few years afterwards Owen mortgaged the lands around the castle to the Englishmen Hugh Broigley and James Derbyshire.

However, things turned to the worst when the Irish forces were defeated at Kinsale in 1601. As the O'Sullivan clan leader, Donal Cam, became the nominal leader of the defeated Irish, the English marched south with a substantial force of over two thousand men to eradicate the O'Sullivans and their allies. Fearing that the English would use the Franciscan Abbey at Bantry as their stronghold, Donal Cam had his forces demolish the abbey and retreated by sea to his stronghold at Dunboy Castle at Castletown Bere. When the English force arrived at Bantry, the Earl of Thomond camped near the Abbey while a garrison was placed at the ruins. The rest of the army camped at Donamark and Whiddy Island near the abandoned Reenavanig Castle. Seizing the opportunity, Donal Cam sailed from Dunboy with a force of about five hundred men and arrived at Traclonna, on the north side of Whiddy Island, in darkness. Waiting for his diversionary attack by Captain Tyrell on the main force at Donamark, he waited until just before dawn and then attacked the sleeping English force. It was a complete disaster with the English abandoning their guns and equipment and trying to get off the Island on a small number of boats. There is no record of how many were killed on both sides but the rout of the English army was overwhelming. Losses would have been far greater only for the timely arrival of a number of boats from Bantry. Donal, having collected all the arms, powder, and equipment that his forces and the boats could carry sailed back to Dunboy where he began to fortify the defences of his main castle.

While Donal was preparing for the onslaught of the English forces on his castle at Dunboy, his uncle Sir Owen O'Sullivan of Carriganass castle, who sided with the English, joined the army at Donamark with his small force. He and Donal were bitter enemies since Donal had been granted half the lands of the O'Sullivan Bere Clan but mostly because Donal had snatched Sir Owen's young wife and taken her to Dunboy Castle. When Donal was defeated by the English and Dunboy Castle destroyed he marched with over 1000 of his followers to his allies and friends in Leitrim while Mountjoy returned by sea to Whiddy Island where he remained overnight in Reenavanig Castle. In the morning he ordered his men to blow up the castle with gun powder. The castle was not totally destroyed and parts of walls remained as there was insufficient powder. After The Earl's departure from Bantry, all the O'Sullivan territory reverted to Sir Owen.

Sir Owen, to strengthen his position and gain influence with the English Crown, invited English and Welsh settlers to Bantry with promises of good land and fishing. Those who had supported Donal Cam were either hung or evicted from the island and their holdings were transferred to the English. The hanging tree is still to be found on the island and the location is marked on the map. Around 1660, a Cromwellian Major, called George Waters, leased some lands on Whiddy from the Anglesey's Estate. He lived in the house which was later occupied by the Whites, Vickerys, Warners and the O'Driscolls. Four of the other settlers, Davenport, Davies, Addis and Snelling gained larger tracts of land on a 31 year lease from Sir Owen O'Sullivan. These gentlemen got involved in the fisheries and smuggling with vessels frequently arriving from Northern Spain, Portugal and France with wine, port, sherry and brandy.

In addition, Pirate ships began to arrive in numbers making Bantry Harbour one of their main bases. The pirates landed captured loot which was sold to a few individuals such as Mr. Devanant, Nicholas Snelling, Richard Addis, Richard White of Whiddy Island, James Galwey, Hugh Hutchinson and Thomas Roper. John Hutchins of the mainland distributed the loot throughout the country. Seized vessels with their cargoes were even brought to Bantry Harbour from as far away as the Caribbean and the East Coast of America. Many shiploads of sugar were discharged both at Whiddy Island and the 'Black Rock' timber pier on the south side of the mainland foreshore which was located on the shore in front of the present Bantry House.

In the meantime, the pilchard fisheries grew in importance. Numerous 'fish palaces' were built by English settlers both on Whiddy Island and the mainland. The largest of these was located on the north side of what is now Bantry Square and was built by a Mr. Meade and the local rector, a man called Davys. The fish palaces on Whiddy Island were located at Tranahaha, Croangle and Reenavanig. It is estimated that the men of Whiddy had at least eighteen large seine boats with their 'followers' (smaller boats) employing fifteen men in each group. Most of the curing and barrelling was overseen by men and carried out by women and boys, many of whom came from the mainland when the fishing was good. It is estimated that for every fisherman there were ten women working ashore. Many took the short sea trip from Beach where there were three little hamlets or clochans (clusters of bothans) at the south side of the present airstrip and under the Abbey graveyard where some families of the Downeys, O'Driscolls and O'Learys lived. Barrelled and cured pilchards and herrings as well as smoked sprat were exported to Spain, Portugal, Italy, Morocco and the West Indies. Many people got rich but these were mostly the English settlers who included Davenport, Snelling, Meade, Hutchins and especially the Whites.

It is not known how many people lived on Whiddy Island during the 17th century but with all the activity of fishing, barrelling, and pirate trade it must have approached a thousand people. We find that in the census of 1831, the last one before the Famine, 942 people were registered as living on the Island despite the fact that by this time the pilchard fisheries had seriously declined. To try and compensate for the loss of earning from the pilchard fisheries, Richard White began to rear deer on the island which were much valued in England as a specialised dish. During the 18th century, the fishermen gradually changed their boats to herring fishing as well as long-lining for cod, hake, pollock and ling and in spite of these activities being seasonal they seem to have sustained the income of the inhabitants when not farming. In addition, there was the coral sand trade where boats dredged the bottom deposits and loaded up with sufficient cargo to land on the island or ashore. This, when dry, would be used as a fertilizer on the island or sold to the farmers on the mainland to be added to their pastures along with seaweed. By this time, the island became part of the White Estate (Bantry House).

Whiddy Island is comprised of seven townlands. These are Reenaknock (Hilly Promontory), Close (Enclosed Strip of Land), Kilmore (Large Church), Trawnahaha (Strand of the Fort), Curraghy (Garden Enclosure), Croangle (Enclosure of the Cincture) and Reenavanig (Hillock of the Young Women). At the townland of Trawnahaha the hanging tree was located at the place called Gallows Hill. Nobody knows how many who supported Donal Cam after the failed Uprising were hanged here. Many soldiers sailed from Bantry to Spain and France at this time. It is recorded that a Richardo White c. 1652 was instrumental in the transportation of some of these Irish soldiers to northern Spain from Bantry. We do not think that Richard White of Whiddy Island was engaged in this trade. It was probably another man called Captain Richard White who had a smuggling ship and who was also engaged in a bit of piracy at this time.

When a French fleet arrived in Bantry Bay in May, 1689, to land a support force to King James who had landed earlier at Kinsale many of the English settlers fled to the safety of the English fortified town of Bandon. While some of the French were ashore on Whiddy for meat, fresh water, and vegetable supplies, word arrived that an English fleet was approaching the Bay. Immediately all the French longboats were recalled. Some of these had already landed troops and equipment at Gearhies on the south side of Bay. Having the advantage of the south easterly wind the French fleet defeated the English but did not press their advantage. It is said that the sound of so many cannons reverberating through the water drove the pilchards out of Bantry Bay as the pilchard fishery collapsed after this event. This does not seem to be true as the pilchard fishery from Youghal to Valentia faded over the same period of time. Many of the English settlers departed the area including Whiddy Island after the collapse of the pilchard fishing industry and so did the smuggling and pirate activity but a few remained. The possibility of another French fleet arriving also filled English settlers with fear. These included the Whites, Vickerys and Hazels brothers who all had lived on Whiddy Island at one time or another until finally they thought it safer to settle in the town of Bantry from where they could easily make an escape to the English stronghold of Bandon.

Some mention must be made here about the White Family who became the landlords of the Beara and Bantry region. The first we hear of that family is when a parcel of land is leased from Lord Anglesea by a Captain Richard White whose relations had settled in Limerick. Richard move into Whiddy Island where he lived for some time. He married a Miss Hamilton from Scotland and had a son called Richard. Richard Sr. died in 1730 and a few years later Richard Jr. married Martha, daughter of the Rev. Dean Davys, and had a son and daughter. Both Richard Sr. and Jr. took advantage of the lucrative pilchard fisheries and built a Fish Palace near their home on the island as well as getting involved in the export. He bought any land debentures that he could lay his hands on from those officers of Cromwell army who wished to sell. He also bought Blackrock House from the Hutchinson family which had previously been owned by a Colonel Becker. This house was located to the right of the front lawn of the present large house which was built in three sections over the years. This became known as Sea Field House and later Bantry House.

Richard Jnr's son Simon married Francis-Anne Hare, the daughter of Richard Hedges Eyre of Macroom Castle. They had a son, also called Richard who was involved in smeltering, clearance of the forests, fishing and deer farming. He was also that Richard who alerted the English forces in Cork of the arrival of the French Fleet under Tone in Bantry Bay. For this he was awarded the title of Baron and received a peerage. Subsequently, he became a Viscount and then an Earl in 1816. As his finances grew he ruled Bantry and Beara like a serfdom having full power as a judge and jury. During the civil unrest of the Land Wars of the 1820s a large group of Whiteboys numbering about 500 rode up the avenue of Bantry House and after firing some shots departed. This was only a warning not to abuse his tenants. During the Famine in 1846/1848 he donated money towards the cost of the soup kitchens but his income from his tenants fell drastically and by 1882 parts of the White domain was put to auction under the Encumbered Estates Legislation and the vast estates began to shrink in size. As a point of interest part of the main house and the stables were built using the st one and building material of the old Franciscan Abbey. The house and the remaining estate is now run by Egerton Shellswell Leigh White.

Another substantial French fleet under Wolfe Tone arrived in Bantry in December 1796 in very bad weather. Due to the force of the storm all the ships had to leave the Bay and run south with the wind and storm. When the weather abated a number of ships re-entered the bay and the military generals and captains held council. It was decided to abandon the attempted landing and all the vessels sailed back to Brest. Later, however, on the 6th of January, 1797, a number of warships which had been separated from the main fleet entered the Bay and sailed up to the north side of Whiddy. Desperately short of fresh water and food supplies they launched a number of longboats which made their way to Whiddy Island. Here they bartered for cattle, pig meat, fish and vegetables. With the longboats laden down they returned to their respective warships. Seeing no hope of the remainder of the fleet arriving they departed and sailed back to Brest. A more detailed account of these events can be found elsewhere in this volume.

During the Napoleonic wars there was a lot of military building activity on Whiddy, as recounted in the chapter on fortifications, but when the threat receded life on the island began to return to normal. Men returned to fishing in greater numbers. Some engaged in the collection of coral sand which fetched about 40c a load or per ton. Others gathered seaweed off the rocks on the shorelines and deposited it at Bantry where, like the coral sand, it was collected, by farmers with horses and carts to be used as fertilizer on the land especially for the growing of potatoes. At this time it was estimated that over four hundred local men were engaged in the fishing industry. With the arrival of Cornish, English and French steam trawlers in the bay and the destruction of long lines and trammel nets the men of Whiddy felt the blow more than others. Their livelihoods were in danger and four lost their lives trying to save their trammel nets. Commercial fishing steadily improved in the Bay during the last 20 years of the 19th century despite the continuous conflict between the trawler men and those who used trammel nets.

Towards the end of the First World War work commenced on the building of a naval air station which was part of the

Air Wing Division of the American Navy. The site had been taken or leased by the British Admiralty Office in London from the owners who were Mr. O'Driscoll and Mr. Tobin who were compensated. The work commenced about 16th December 1917 by Messrs Moran & Co. who were brought in by the British Admiralty. The construction consisted of a slipway, concrete aprons, and hangars, underground tanks for petrol and water and accommodation for the staff. All of the material was brought to the island by ship or barge from the mainland or by sea from Cork. It is estimated that over 150 local men were employed during the construction. The photos give an idea of the size of the operation.

The base became operational on the 25th of September 1918, when two seaplanes arrived. On the 22nd of October 1918, one plane crash-landed on take-off and one pilot was killed. During

*Bantry House in the days when it had
a conservatory on the south wall*

the month that followed there were five planes based on the island as well as ten submarines. It is reputed that one plane when off the Fastnet encountered a German submarine on the surface and when she attacked the submarine two bombs were dropped, one of which was a direct hit. At the end of the War in November 1918 the planes were withdrawn and the base was finally closed when all the buildings were auctioned off and were dismantled and removed in late January 1919. The concrete radio station next to castle ruins, as well as the water and petrol concrete tanks can still be seen.

After the First World War the men returned to herring fishing during the winter months and fishing for lobsters, crayfish, long lining, and trammelling, during the rest of the year. In all, it is recorded that there were fifteen herring seine boats operating during the winter and over thirty smaller boats involved in summer and autumn fishing. Herrings were landed and barrelled at Gearies and Bantry Pier. Some of the Whiddy boats based themselves at Adrigole Harbour during the winter herring season in the rich herring grounds of Berehaven Sound.

The arrival of Gulf Oil on Whiddy Island is covered in a later chapter, meanwhile, many of the Whiddy men had abandoned fishing and had taking up employment during the construction period. When the Terminal became operational only a handful were employed. Gone were most of their seine boats as a means of fishing the herrings which had returned to the bay. Most of the boats had rotted on the beaches. A few men reverted to fishing for lobsters and mackerel with small half-deckers and punts during the summer months until some fishermen began to experiment with growing mussels on long lines. This became a success and soon most of the local fishermen began to set rafts with long lines. Eventually,

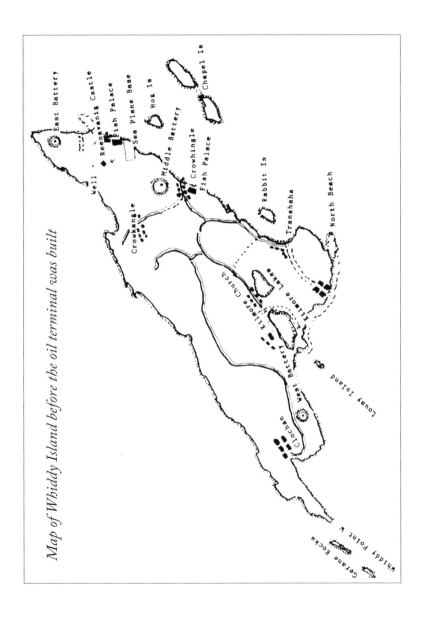

Map of Whiddy Island before the oil terminal was built

Castle ruins and airfield buildings 1918

Hangars on Whiddy Island 1918

this method did not succeed and the use of barrels on a line proved much more satisfactory. Many of the Whiddy fishermen created a co-op and took advantage of working together as the cultivation of mussels is labour intensive. Now, over 6,000 tons of mussels are either processed in Bantry or exported annually.

In recent times the population of the island has dropped to about 15 from 942 in 1831. When most of the islanders moved to the mainland a number of their houses were sold and are now holiday homes. The idea now is to build up a tourist industry on the island provided that our present government takes the necessary steps to make the access to the batteries and make them safe.

XIX

BEREHAVEN AND BERE ISLAND

According to tradition and mythology, Berehaven got its name from a Spanish princess named Beara. It was previously known as Inis Creagraidh and then it was called Insula Magna about 1658. In a map of Bapista Basio in 1599 it was referred to as Beerehaven. In Irish it is known as Cuan mBeara and was part of the dominion of the O'Driscoll Clan who ruled most of West Cork up to the 12th century. From the existence of megalithic monuments it is obvious that Bere Island like the rest of the Bantry Bay area was inhabited from earliest times.

The inhabitants of the area lived by fishing, raising livestock and the cultivation of small plots of land. Their quiet life was suddenly disturbed in the 900s by the arrival of the Norsemen who plundered the religious settlements and the fishing hamlets in the enclosed harbour. Seeing the advantage of Lonehart harbour on Bere Island they built a breakwater to protect their ships from north-easterly gales. This base was an addition to their main fortification on Dursey Island to the west.

With the long association with Northern Spain and France the O'Driscolls engaged in the trade in wine and spirits with these countries and also exported fish, hides, wool and cured meats. This trade was continued later by the O'Sullivans who also engaged in smuggling and trading with pirates. It was not until the 16th century that Berehaven became well known when the O'Sullivan Bere clan moved into the area and their leader, Dermod O'Sullivan, began to build stone castles to protect his newly acquired territory from the advance of the Anglo-Normans who were gradually moving south along the coastline. These castles were Oilean Beag on the small island next to Dursey, Dunboy which was a major fortified tower house, Castledermod which was a square tower house, Carriganass, and Reenavanig on Whiddy Island. When Dermod was killed as he experimented with gun-powder his brother Owen took over the leadership of the clan, despite the opposition of Dermod's sons, especially Donal who was under age. When Donal came of age he disputed the leadership with his uncle Owen and the matter was referred to the English Crown. Eventually, after about five years a judgement was made whereby Donal received all the lands west of Glengarriff and Sir Owen received all the lands around the Bantry region.

An interesting event happened on the 11th of June, 1593, when a damaged vessel called the Desire under Captain John Dean entered Berehaven having sailed around the world. The Captain and crew were almost dead from starvation and only five of the compliment of 16 had enough strength to man the vessel. They had survived on rain water for the last four days before making landfall. Having been fed and looked after by the people ashore the ship was able to continue its voyage to Plymouth after about two weeks.

In this same context it is reputed that the poem 'The Ancient Mariner' by Samuel Taylor Coleridge is based on the voyage from the West Indies to Castletownbere by an English sailor who arrived starving and in a disturbed mental state after such a long voyage.

After the defeat of the Irish forces at the Battle of Kinsale, Donal was nominated leader of the Irish army that still remained in Munster. He departed the battlefield at Kinsale and headed west with what remained of his own force. His objective was his own castle at Dunboy which required to be reinforced. On his way he left the Abbey at Bantry in ruins and attacked his cousin's castle at Carriganass and left some of his force to defend it. When he arrived at Dunboy Castle work was put in hand on the strengthening of the rampart and defences. His spies quickly informed him that the English forces under Carew and Mountjoy were hot on his heels and were already in Bantry camped at Donemark and on Whiddy Island. Donal gathered his army of about 800 men and by night arrived at the north side of Whiddy Island and attacked the English camp just before dawn and routed the force. It is not know how many English soldiers were killed but they were evacuated leaving their arms and baggage on the island.

Donal knew full well that the English would pursue him so he began to fortify his castle at Dunboy. Unable to make progress through the woods and forests between Bantry and Berehaven, the English forces were transported by sea and landed at Loneheart harbour on Bere Island. From here they crossed to the mainland and attacked the castle to the east of the fishing hamlet and quickly overpowered the defenders. They then concentrated on Dunboy castle and brought up their cannon to suitable positions. After a heavy bombardment the castle was reduced to ruins despite the brave efforts of the small defending force who surrendered under a white flag with the guarantee that their lives would be spared. This condition was not adhered to by the English and the survivors as well as some of the local men who had assisted the Irish forces were all hung in the public square of the hamlet.

During this time Donal Cam was at Ardea castle on the Kenmare River awaiting reinforcements from Spain which never arrived. Seeing that further resistance was a lost cause, Donal with about 400 soldiers and 600 followers commenced the long march to Co. Leitrim to his allies. Only about nine survived the epic journey including Donal Cam and his aged uncle (see March into Oblivion by this author). With no further resistance possible, the English departed but not before razing Ardea castle on Kenmare Bay to the ground. As they made their way back to Bantry the encountered a snow blizzard and over 2,500 perished. This event was as if the Lord was taking vengeance for the killing of the innocent in Castletown. Those that survived went to Cork by sea but not before they laid waste the countryside by killing all livestock and burning both crops and huts.

Sir Owen O'Sullivan of Carriganass castle tried to regain that part of the territory that had been administered by Donal Cam who by this time had arrived in Co. Leitrim with the few stragglers including one woman lucky enough to survive the march. Realising that the struggle against the English was lost and that he had no future in Ireland, he took ship with a few of his followers and sailed south to the coast of Kerry where he embarked those who wished to leave and make a new life in Spain.

Meanwhile Sir Owen Jr. was unable to repossess the remainder of the O'Sullivan territory and the arrival of the avaricious Sir William Petty on the scene made it more difficult again. This was an Englishman who wished to acquire as much land as he possibly could and used every means to further this objective. Yet, Sir Owen was not deterred from using what assets he controlled to further his family fortunes. At this time, shoals of pilchard began to show up in the bay and every available boat went fishing. Sir Owen made contact with Cornish fishermen and English settlers to come to Bantry Bay where they could profit from the rich harvest of fish or cultivate the lands.

As in Bantry, 'fish palaces' were built where the pilchard and other types of fish could be processed and barrelled for export. As far as is known there were two 'fish palaces' on Bere Island and some others on the foreshore of the mainland as at Bank Strand. As in Bantry, most of the men were engaged in the fishing industry and when this failed there was widespread hunger. The population decreased over time, mainly due to minor outbreaks of poptato blight. It was not until the English built the Bere Island forts in the early 1800s that the population stabalized. Fishing picked up and Cornish cutters arrived. Many of the crews settled on Bere Island or the adjacent mainland and by 1835 there were about 16 hookers and 90 yawls fishing out of eastern Bere Island. Before the Famine there were over 2,000 living on Bere Island and about the same on the mainland. The Famine had a devastating effect but it was the return of cholera that wiped out most families. Some did manage to walk to the Workhouse in Bantry but few survived the journey. These died on the roadside.

When Lord Bantry almost bankrupted himself collecting antiques on the Continent for his new mansion, he had to seek assistance from the Commission of Encumbered Estates in Dublin like many other major English landowners throughout the country. As a result, the prices for these major estates seriously dropped, much to the detriment of the tenants. The Island of Bere was auctioned as one lot and was purchased by a Charles Clinton along with all its assets and liabilities.

After securing ownership the then Lord Bantry raided the island in 1854 to recuperate the outstanding arrears in rents which were due prior to the sale by sending his agent, Mr. Payne, assisted by bailiffs, cattle drivers and police. The people ran to the hills with whatever they could carry while their cattle were rounded up and secured in pounds. As a result of this action many families were left destitute and many died from starvation during the following years.

Puxley's Mansion

With Clinton introducing higher rents, Tim Healy M.P. objected strongly saying that the rents should be according to the government valuation. Many withheld rent and again found themselves living or surviving on the waste lands of the mountains. In 1906 the Estates Commissioners purchased Clinton's holdings and the rent was fixed at a third of what the people had been charged. Some had earlier taken their case about high rents to the English War Department but they were advised that they were only tenants at will and could be thrown off the land within 24 hours.

When the Troubles or the War of Independence commenced, with the strong presence of English troops on the island, it became a place of internment for those suspected of being members or sympathisers of the Republican Army or Volunteers. The local Volunteers in and around Castletownbere numbered about forty but they lacked arms, ammunition and explosives. These Volunteers devised a plan to raid the explosives stores of the English on the island and carried it out successfully with the removal of explosives, primers, detonators and lengths of wiring. In 1920 the newly constructed internment camp was opened which consisted of four timber huts holding about 60men each. At one stage in May 1921 there were 284 inmates. Before that, those arrested and shipped to the island were imprisoned in the guardhouse of the Lonehart battery. There were a number of successful escapes and also the prisoners went on hunger strike due to ill-treatment.

During the period 1922 to 1938 the island was a British military base and was also subject to Irish civil law. There was a famous incident when the local Gardai raided the pubs on the island. Some of those found included British officers. Many were arrested and charged but the charges were dropped to avoid a major diplomatic incident. During the early 1930s a tariff war commenced between Britain and the Republic but came to an end in 1938. One of the conditions was that the 'Treaty Ports', which included Berehaven, should be returned to the Irish. For various reasons this did not take place until the 26th of September 1938 and the Irish flag was hoisted over the island for the first time since 1797.

After the Second World War, Berehaven slowly began to revive its fishing industry, first with sixty five footers and then gradually by much larger boats. By the late 1960s it had become the second major white fish fishing port in Ireland.

In addition, fish farming commenced to become a major industry. However, now, with the introduction of fish quotas and the decrease of the number of trawlers, the industry is slowly dying and will not survive unless young fish are given the opportunity of growing and spawning.

XX

GLENGARRIFF – THE RUGGED VALLEY

Glengarriff is situated on the north side of Bantry Bay in a secluded harbour with the island of Garinish protecting the inner harbour from southerly winds and seas. Due to its rugged beauty it has become one of the main tourist attractions over the centuries mainly due to Garinish Island with its semi-tropical flora.

Glengarriff was accessible only by sea and by rough paths up to the middle of the 1800s. Before then only animal tracks and rough roads for horse and carts existed through the almost impenetrable forests. From the various types of megalithic monuments in the area it is obvious that the valley was inhabited from earliest times by animal hunters who also availed of the rich supply of fish from the myriad small rivers and streams. They also gathered shellfish from the rocks. One of the oldest shell middens in Ireland was found at Glengarriff. Some say that the standing stones found in the area marked pathways or else tribal boundaries. There are some fine examples of stone circles, standing stones and cist graves as well as circular enclosures. From about the 5th century, many hermit monks made Glengarriff their home. Some lived in isolation on the islands while others came together and built a monastery on a location which is now known as Monk's

Point. They lived here in peace until the Norsemen came up the bay and sacked and plundered the little settlements as well as killing the hermits and monks. Some escaped and sought refuge in the valley where the Magannagan stream flows, where they eventually built up a little stone settlement.

Little of importance has been written about Glengarriff up to the seventeenth century when the English army under the Earl of Desmond attempted to make their way west to Dunboy castle in 1601. Due to the terrain, woods, forests and the guerrilla activities of Tyrell, they were unable to make any progress and suffered high casualties. Since the 13th century the O'Sullivan Bere had ruled over this hamlet which only consisted of a few hundred souls who barely made an existence out of fishing, dredging for coral sand, growing a few crops and keeping one or two cattle. In a way, due to the lack of roads or paths the hamlet was isolated even from the rest of West Cork.

A view of Glengarriff Bay taken from the Eccles Hotel in 1900

In the 1600s some of the English settlers, like Mr. Waters, invited in by Sir Owen O'Sullivan recognised the beauty of the area and settled on the best lands where they built houses and availed of the opportunity of benefiting from the rich pilchard fishing in the bay.

When Lord Anglesea was granted over 94,000 acres in and around Bantry Bay by the Crown, the area was divided into two Baronies – Bantry and Altham. Despite the efforts of Sir William Petty to hold onto his appropriated lands, Glengarriff came under the authority of Lord Anglesea who brought in many more settlers.

By the 1750s a Richard White, who had settled on Whiddy Island, and made a lot of money from the fisheries and from smuggling began to lease large tracts of land from Lord Anglesea. One of these tracts included the greater part of Glengarriff where his descendant built his summer lodge on the north side of the harbour. In 1802 another White, who was called Colonel Simon White, built a stately home in the form of a mock-Tudor castle with a round tower, rectangular section, three battlement towers and archway. The building of the castle was financed by his wife, Sara Newenham of Marleborough House, Cork.

It is said that a tunnel ran from the basement to the seashore and that this was used by smugglers when discharging cargoes of wine and spirits. When I personally inspected the basement in the 1980s, all I could find was an opening which contained a lead coffin.

After the First World War, Glengarriff Castle was owned by a distant relation, called George White, who sold the building and about 48 acres of woodland to the Eccles family who converted the building into a hotel. The building fell into decay shortly after it was sold to a third party in 1978 but over the previous years it had become a thriving business. Plans are now afoot to rebuild the hotel and introduce self-catering apartments on the grounds.

The Earl of Bantry leased the plot of land where the Protestant Church was built. This was completed in 1862 and became a district curacy. Jane, the Countess of Bantry, donated the stain glass windows and the marble pulpit.

From the 1750s onwards there were many famous visitors to Glengarriff including writers and historians such as Charles Smith, Bishop Dive Downes, Bishop Pococke, Rev. H. Townsend, Samuel Lewis, Alfred Lord Tennyson, Froude, Mrs. Hall and Bernard Shaw who was reputed to have written 'St.

Boatmen in Glengarriff Bay with
Garanish Island in the background.

Joan' while resting at the Eccles Hotel. In their writings, they all mentioned the beautiful scenery and the mild climate.

From the middle of the 19th century English and foreign visitors began to arrive in West Cork and especially to Glengarriff where they found a warm climate amidst peaceful and scenic surroundings.

The Prince of Wales visited in 1858. Having travelled by train from Cork to Bandon, he continued his journey by horse and carriage as far as Glengarriff and onwards. His route became known as the Prince of Wales route. This later became the Royal Mail route. With the amount of English visitors it was proposed that a new hotel with a spa should be built near the existing Eccles Hotel but this never came to fruition.

Likewise the plans of C.I.E., in 1946, to build a Great Southern Hotel in the area came to nothing.

Royal Yacht in Glengarriff harbour 1912

Some comments by visitors should be mentioned here – Thackerey said that 'there was a pretty little Inn at Glengarriff'; O'Sullivan in his book on famous and interesting tours said in 1853 'there was one hotel in Glengarriff and that was an indifferent one while the new Roches' hotel was one of luxury'. As in the past, Glengarriff was a place for writers but now it is a place for all of those people interested in the arts.

In 1912, the Prince of Wales came in his yacht to Glengarriff and was joined by his cousin, the German Kaiser in his luxury vessel. They both anchored off Garinish Island and visited the area before journeying on to Bantry, where they disembarked at Bantry pier. This was the last occasion on which they met before war was declared.

Before leaving Glengarriff, a short mention must be made of one of the main attractions for visitors to Glengarriff; Garinish Island, which protects Glengarriff harbour from the

Lord Bantry's cottage in Glengarriff

187

The Eccles Hotel around 1900

winter gales from the south. The island was previously under the domain of Owen and Donal O'Sullivan in turns before it was incorporated in the Barony of Beara which was allocated to the Duke of Anglesea.

It was purchased in 1910 from the Bantry Estate by a Mr. Annan Bryce of Belfast who was very interested in botany and the cultivation of exotic flowers and plants. Bryce hired a Mr. Harold Pinto to develop gardens and over the next three years more than a hundred men were engaged in the work, which also included the construction of pavilions, walled enclosures and a clock tower. The work was completed by Bryce's son, who eventually bequeathed the Island to the Irish Government in 1923. Since the 1930s the island has been open to the public and several ferries make the short sea journey from Glengarriff.

Glengarriff forest was purchased from the Bantry Estate in 1954 by the government. It consisted of about 1,000 acres

Glengarriff in 1918

(404 hectares) of woodland which originally was made up of oak trees but most of these had been cut down by the Whites to fire the ironworks which they had established in the area. Another interesting point is that a glass smelter was established at Reenmeen.

Glengarriff now shows a lot of progress with new hotels, restaurants, shops and the various extensions to the Eccles Hotel and still remains a very popular holiday resort for both Irish and English visitors.

XXI

THE DESPOLIATION OF THE LOCAL FORESTS

Before the English settlers arrived in numbers at the beginning of the 17th century, the woods and forests of West Cork and Kerry were almost impregnable. Only designated pathways controlled by the local chieftains and tribes existed. As a result, at first, the settlers only took up residence near the sea and in the growing villages and towns like Bantry. The native inhabitants of the countryside usually lived in little clusters of houses called 'bothans' in the middle of the land which they had sufficiently cleared to grow potatoes, oats and vegetables and to raise a cow or two.

This all changed with the arrival of the English settlers who immediately saw the great wealth that could be gained by the cutting down of trees and the export of timber which was badly need for the building of warships in England. Having leased or taken possession of some of the lands the settlers began to cut down the trees, hiring the Irish natives to do most of the work which was done by saw and axe. Donkeys and horses as well as manpower were used to haul the tree trunks to a suitable location for cutting into manageable lengths for export by ship. In this way, timber from the Bantry region found its way to England. In this context, it is said that Drake's ship and that of Nelson were built of oak from Bantry and Durrus.

Seeing that a large quantity of waste wood remained, other settlers, especially the Whites, decided to build ore smelters which would use charcoal from the discarded wood in furnaces to breakdown iron ore imported from England. The smelters were located at Adrigole, Glengarriff, Coomhola, Durrus and Bantry.

Iron ore was imported from northern Spain and England and transported to the smelters by large horse drawn carts. It was then smelted into manageable bars and re-exported to Wales and England. This industry continued up to the 1750s when timber began to get scarce. It is said that the Boyles, Petty and the Whites grew rich on the despoliation of the local forest, and such was the rape of the countryside that no wood or forest was offered for sale, in Cork or Kerry.

The major concentration of forest originally stretched from Balingeary to Castletownbere, covering the hills to a height of about 175 metres. Further forests extended from Balingeary to Drimoleague, as well as south-west from Bantry including the Muintir mBaire peninsula. These forests were home to many of the Irish dispossessed who could not prevent the destruction of their temporary hovels. Many new roads and pathways were opened and an act was passed whereby all landowners were obliged to keep all roads clear throughout the kingdom.

Other local industries based on timber sprang up. These included the making of doors, window frames, household furniture, carts, carriages, wheelbarrows and barrels of all sizes. It has been estimated that there were five workshops engaged in making carriages and carts, ten coopers' sheds making barrels, about 12 smiths making iron bands, along with about 30 small carpentry enterprises. In addition, there was a certain amount of small boat building that took place, producing luggers, hookers, seine boats and smaller open boats. At one stage, there were over 600 boats fishing out of Bantry harbour.

Another industry which grew out of the availability of timber bark was hide tanning. Prior to the sixteenth century hides were preserved by salting. It was the custom to strip the bark for tanning from the living tree – especially the oak tree. In 1665 a barrel of oak bark was valued at 6s/8p (about 40c). Late in the 1660s the exportation of live cattle to England was prohibited and the number of tanned hides rose from 100,000 to 220,000 in the space of two years. There were two main tanneries in Bantry. One was situated at the Warner Centre and employed about 400 workers and another was on the site of the present Post Office. The term tanner in those days could encompass a variety of allied trades, such as curriers, skinners, leather merchants, butchers and glue-boilers.

Like the mining industry in the following centuries, most of the iron-works supported considerable colonies of people, most of whom were English or European immigrants brought to Ireland to provide an experienced labour force. An example of this was Sir William Petty, who founded a colony of over 800 English in Kenmare to work his iron foundries. In the Bantry-Castletownbere area, small communities of English ironworkers sprang up near Dunboy, Adrigole, Coomhola and Bantry. The skilled workers were nearly always English while the Irish were employed as hewers and drawers of water, while women carried baskets of charcoal from the tips to the furnaces. As for the wages of those engaged in the various jobs only a few details emerge for that period; £1.12s per 1,000 pit staves; fellers of trees got £1.10p per ton; sawyers received 3s per hundred feet. With the decline of the forests, timber began to be imported on a large scale from Scandinavia and Canada to keep the small local timber businesses in existence.

XXII

THE BATTLE OF BANTRY BAY

In the historical context, the Battle of Bantry in May 1689 was a lost opportunity for the French to seriously damage England's domination of the seas or to cause so much damage to its fleet of warships that it would no longer present an impediment to the growing French sea power. On the day of the battle, all the French needed to do was make a decision on a final 'coup de grace'. However, the French fleet had only one main objective, as ordered by Louis XIV, and that was to land arms, ammunition, supplies and troops to boost the army that had already landed at Kinsale under James II.

Reports are vague as to how many French vessels made up the fleet and how many troops were transported to Bantry Bay, but it seems that there were probably 25 men-at-war, 3 frigates, 6 fire-ships and 8 large troop transporters. As to the number of troops aboard, estimates vary from 1,500 to 6,000. It does seem extravagant that Louis would send such a large fleet to escort transporters carrying such a small number of troops considering that each transport could carry well over 600 men. At dawn on the morning of the 10th of May, the fleet entered the bay and finally anchored a few miles off the south shore, leaving a number of frigates on watch for English warships at the entrance to the bay.

With James in Ireland the Irish Protestants had sent urgent messages to William of Orange for assistance. William was worried. He could not allow two separate French armies to take possession of Ireland. As most of the principal English navy personnel had been nominated by King James, William could only find Arthur Herbert willing to take charge of the English fleet. Due to bad weather, the English fleet did not arrive off the Cork coast until the 12th of April where he was informed that King James was already in Dublin.

While Herbert was trying to make up his mind as to what to do, a severe gale sprang up and drove the English fleet northwards along the coast towards Waterford. Returning to Milford Haven, Herbert sought more ships and new orders from William. On the 26th of April, Lord Nottingham sent a message to Herbert to attack the French wherever he might encounter them as a state of war now existed between England and France. It is interesting to note that King Louis did not in fact declare war until the 17th of May. Herbert sailed on the 27th of May and hearing that there was a French fleet in Bantry Bay he set course southwards to that location.

Meanwhile, the French fleet, under Admiral Chateaurenault, was still at anchor in Bantry Bay. When he was advised of the approaching English ships, by the captains on watch at the entrance of the bay, he ordered that all troops, arms, ammunition and supplies be immediately landed ashore.

The night was spent transferring troops and supplies ashore to the rocks near Gearhies. Some tenders went as far as Bantry to disembark the troops. Meanwhile, as dawn broke, Admiral Chateaurenault arranged his ships in battle formation. With the English fleet encountering difficulty in tacking up the bay against the wind the French admiral, with a strong wind behind him, seized the opportunity and gave the signal to attack.

Over-anxious to engage the enemy, some of the French vessels broke the line of battle. Despite their haste, a number of the English vessels were severely damaged and the order was given to retire to the entrance of the bay where the English would have more room to engage the French. However, Chateaurenault gave the order to cease the engagement and to return to the safety of the upper bay.

Herbert, who had narrowly escaped a crippling disaster, made for Plymouth with his seriously damaged fleet which included the *Ardent, Defiance. Edgar, Cambridge, Portland, Advise, Diamond, Deptford* and the *St. Albans.* Admiral Chateaurenault, meanwhile, completed his task of landing the small invasion force which took two full days.

The majority of the troops slept in the open fields, hay barns and any place where they could put their heads down.

Having secured some horses and carts, the force moved out of Bantry and headed towards Dunmanway passing through the high mountains and deserted countryside. Dunmanway was described as one gentleman's house and a number of cabins. The troops billeted in any straw barn they could locate. On the following day they reached Bandon, described as a considerable walled town inhabited by bands of brigands and lowly classes as all the rich settlers and merchants had fled to Cork.

By the time they arrived in Cork, the main army under James had departed a month earlier so they had no option but to follow and embark on a march of some 300 kilometres through unknown territory.

XXIII

WOLFE TONE AND THE FRENCH INVASION

Over a hundred years later in 1796, another invasion of Ireland by the French took place. This was not ordered by the French Monarchy but by the Revolutionary Council of the Directory and was a part of Napoleon's plans to attack England. However, another venture which Napoleon proposed at the same time, namely, an invasion of Egypt, took preference. However, Wolfe Tone, who was one of the leading figures in the United Irishmen movement and imbued with the tenets of the French Revolution, made several deputations to the Council of the Directory to argue that they send an expedition force to invade Ireland. Tone was successful and preparations were made at the port of Brest for both flotilla and land forces.

The scene was chaotic especially with English spies bribing those in high office to do their utmost in hampering the preparations. Funds from the Ministry of Finance were delayed or not sent at all; expenses for the preparation of the vessels failed to materialise; equipment, food and supplies were not delivered due to non payment. Sailors and troops were left without funds for months on end. Some crews mutinied and took over their ships when they were informed that another invasion of Holland was also being planned. This force was to reinforce the invasion force heading for Ireland bringing the total number of troops to approximately thirty four thousand men under the command of General Hoche while De Galles would be the Admiral of the fleet.

As weeks turned into months, both Hoche and Wolfe Tone spent their time in Rennes away from the noise and dirt of the port. Maybe if they had stayed in Brest, preparations and work would have progressed more rapidly. As the fleet was nearing completion and the troops began to embark, a meeting was held and Morard de Galles was appointed Admiral of the flotilla against the better judgement of Hoche, Tone and Bruix. Morard de Galles was almost blind, suffered from ill-health, was of nervous disposition and completely lacked confidence in himself. In addition to all the funds for the invasion all the principal officers and personnel including General Hoche, Bruix, and Bouvet were assigned to the Fraternité. Aboard the *L'Indomptable*, which was the flag ship of the invasion were Commodore Bedout and Wolfe Tone. It is unbelievable that almost all the principal officers were billeted on the same ship.

The fleet was delayed for a number of weeks due to unsuitable winds and also due to the harbour blockade by a section of the English fleet.

When the vessels finally sailed at night through the various channels they were separated by the thick fog and eventually came together in three groups. The *L'Indomptable* was nowhere to be seen but the *Fraternité*, with Tone aboard, came together with eight other ships of the line.

When enclosed again in thick fog, the sealed orders for the invasion were opened, they explained that all ships were to proceed to the Mizen Head and await five days. If no other ships appeared they were to proceed to the mouth of the Shannon River and remain there for three days. Bouvet was joined by Neilly's section of the fleet so they held a general council and it was decided that if no other ships joined them at the mouth of the Shannon, they were to return to Brest.

With the weather deteriorating rapidly, Admiral Bouvet decided that what remained of the fleet, some thirty four ships in all, should proceed to Bantry Bay which was the ultimate choice to make a landing. If Bantry had to be accepted as the main choice, three locations had been chosen where the ships should anchor. These were at Berehaven Sound, the mouth of Glengarriff or the eastern end of Whiddy Island. In addition, three frigates were to remain at the mouth of Bay in case the English might appear. If a landing was to be made at Snave, all ships' boats were to transfer the troops and supplies and then the army was to proceed to Cork.

Tone was extremely worried at this stage, which is verified in his personal diary – 'Admiral Morard de Galles, General Hoche, General Debelle and Colonel Shee are all aboard the *Fraternité* and only God known what has become of them'. On the 22nd of December, Tone wrote again – 'If this day passes without seeing the *Fraternité* and General Hoche, I fear that the game is up'. He could not fathom why Morard de Galles and Hoche could not follow the instructions that they themselves had drawn up for the invasion. Whatever chances they had of making a landing, with the troops remaining at their disposal, were deteriorating rapidly as the weather began to develop into a full blown gale.

By morning, the gale had turned into a hurricane force storm from the east. Ships dragged their anchors and had to cut their cables and then ran with the weather out of the bay into deeper water. Two days later, on the 24th, the weather moderated and most of the ships returned to the bay and signals were passed that a landing should be made the following morning but by 1800 hours the weather had changed for the worst again.

On the 27th of December, another Council of War was held aboard the *L'Indomptable*. Only fourteen vessels now remained with only 4,000 troops. While Tone suggested that what remained of the fleet should head for the Shannon or Sligo, all the French officers were for returning to Brest. Tone's comment was – 'well, let me think no more about it; it is lost and let it go'. As the *L'Indomptable* ran before a storm later, a rogue wave came over the stern and flooded Tone's cabin. Thinking that he was about to be drowned he went into his bunk and awaited death.

While most of the ships were on their way back to Brest, a number of stragglers arrived in Bantry Bay and within two days there was a sizable fleet in the bay with over 4,000 troops aboard. It was decided that they would wait a further two days and if no other ships arrived they would return to Brest. Being un-seaworthy, the *Surveillante* was scuttled and two foreign ships called the *Beaver* and the *Sisters* were stripped of all materials and supplies and then put to the torch.

There is no satisfactory explanation as to why the Fraternité did not arrive at Bantry Bay or follow the sealed orders as issued by the French Directory. One strong theory has it that the Captain, in the pay of the English, changed course so frequently that Admiral de Galles could not follow the directions.

Before completing this brief summary of the failed Invasion under Wolfe Tone, it should be noted that the French were under the impression that all Ireland would rise up in revolt as soon as they arrived and that there was a rebel force ready to join them. In fact, the only rebel part of the country was Ulster and this was devoid of leadership as the principal United Irishmen who were the instigators of the uprising were mostly in jail. Even those that were at large would not believe that the French had actually landed in Bantry Bay. In Cork city and county there was utter panic as the happy equilibrium between the English and the lowly Irish peasants was in jeopardy. Even the then Bishop of Cork, Dr. Moylan, mindful of what happened to the Church in France during the Revolution exhorted his flock not to assist the French in any way.

Yet, the thought of revolution spread southward to Munster where a state of anarchy was introduced. This did not last long due to the lack of leadership and many atrocities were committed on both sides.

XXIV

THE ENGLISH FORTIFICATION
OF BANTRY BAY

Afraid of further invasions by the French, the Admiralty in London decided that proper fortifications should be built on Bere and Whiddy Island in Bantry Bay to safeguard the south-west coast.

It seems that work first commenced on the fortifications on Bere Island c. 1798. The defensive Martello towers in Corsica served as a blueprint for the construction of four similar towers on the island at Lonehart, Rerin, Clochlann Hill and Ardagh Hill. In addition to these towers, a further square fortification was built at Reendubh. Situated near each tower was a substantial gun battery. For the construction of these towers and fortifications, stone was shipped from the south of England and Cork while any additional material was mined locally on the mainland.

The fortifications built on Whiddy Island were somewhat different from the Martello Towers. They were called 'redoubts' and locally became known as gun batteries. The western redoubt was built at a suitable location to protect the southern entrance to the harbour while the eastern redoubt commanded the north-eastern entrance. The central redoubt was built on the highest point of the island and over looked the harbour and the north side of the island.

Work commenced on the redoubts in December 1803 under the supervision of English Ordinance. The main contractor was called O'Mahony and the engineer in charge was a Mr. Pearson, the father of the engineer who lived at Pearson's Bridge near Kealkil. At the height of the construction period over 500 men were employed. Carts, wagons, horses and donkeys and most of the materials were transferred from the mainland to the island by boat or timber barge.

The western battery was built on rock and shale while the sites for the other two batteries had to be excavated using sledges, bars, chisels and shovels. Where solid rock was encountered, a certain amount of powder was used to clear the obstruction. On the 18th of October, 1804, the western battery was completed and was described at that time as 'a Martello tower of unusual magnitude with an interior diameter of 240 feet'.

The location of the centre battery is quite interesting, as it was previously the site of one of the largest earthen forts in the region.

Early references to the inner bay indicate that this fort had occupied an area greater than the perimeter of the present battery and was surrounded by circular ramps and ditches. It is said that the MacSweeneys, who were gallowglasses to the McCarthys, occupied and defended the inner harbour from this location up to the time when the O'Sullivans built a castle nearby.

The excavation of the sites was carried out by the descending spiral method with most of the material being dumped nearby on the north side. While this work continued, large timber rafts were built on the seashore and with these and luggers, cut stone was transported by sea from the quarries at Ardnagashel and elsewhere on the shoreline. The stones were landed at the slipway at Croangle, transferred to wagons and pulled up the inclines to each site. When the outer and inner walls of the moats were completed the centres were filled in, with the exception of stone-walled wells to store rainwater. Besides the deep well in the centre battery there were also a powder store and a dungeon. On the inner walls, raised platforms were constructed for cannon mountings.

The central battery was the main base, and included officers' quarters, soldiers' barracks, warehouse, cannon and shot armoury. These were built of imported red brick and despite the weathering are still in fair condition. To complete the fortifications, eighteen cannon, powder and balls were shipped from Plymouth to Cork and then to Bantry where they were offloaded onto barges to be taken ashore to the island.

With the completion of the centre battery and the placing of six large guns, a force of seven artillery officers and one hundred and eighty eight soldiers was transferred from Queenstown barracks to Whiddy. An additional timber structure had to be constructed adjacent to the battery on the south side for billeting the large number of soldiers.

These occupied the first floor of the building while the company's horses were confined to the ground floor. On the 29th of December 1804, the whole timber building was burnt to the ground with the loss of 24 horses. No loss of life or injuries was reported amongst the defence personnel. Some months later a decision was made in London to withdraw the defence force from the island and transfer them back to Queenstown. As a result, the batteries were abandoned and were left under the care of a local English merchant called Iremonger, who in turn employed three local Murphy brothers and their families to look after the batteries. With the accommodation so well built within the batteries, the families moved in and were later replaced by the Cotters who took up residence in the centre battery. About a year later only one brother was responsible for the batteries but the families continued to live on the redoubt.

Shortly after Napoleon's escape from the Island of Elba in 1814, the English decided to build a Martello Tower on Garinish Island. This was for show more than defence. It was manned by one officer and ten soldiers who manned a small cannon. This fortification was finally abandoned in 1825.

In addition, a number of signal towers were built around the coast. Included amongst these were watch-towers on Bere Island and on Blackball Head. These were abandoned c.1809 when they became obsolete. Yet, the Martello Towers and the batteries continued to be manned by the English Naval Authorities.

With the arrival of the famous 'dreadnoughts' on the oceans of the world, the English War Department examined the defences of Berehaven and came to the conclusion that improvements were absolutely necessary. Compulsory Purchase Orders were issued on the 17th of March, 1898 and the tenants

Dreadnought in Bantry Bay

who occupied the lands required were moved off and the building of massive gun batteries commenced. When work was completed huge guns were landed at Laurence Cove. During the period 1898 to 1911, six gun batteries were built. Some 500 men were employed during the construction.

With the major part of the English fleet guarding the south-west approaches Berehaven and Bantry Bay was usually full of warships of all shapes and sizes. An anti-submarine underwater net was located just north of the Piper Sound to protect the western entrance.

As all the warships were steam powered it required about 48 hours for them to get up a head of steam before the anchors could be hauled aboard and the ship could move. Admiral Jellicoe was stationed at Castletownbere for some time and was accustomed to be seen walking the hills and byways for exercise. It was from Berehaven that he sailed to Jutland with his fleet to engage the German warships.

During the 1930s Britain was engaged in an economic war with the Irish Free State. This ended in 1938 with the Anglo-Irish Agreement.

One of the conditions was that the 'treaty ports' of Queenstown and Berehaven be handed back to the Irish State. Much to the disgust and anger of Churchill, the fortifications of Bere Island were included as part of the agreement of April 1938 but the hand-over did not take place until September 1938. With war looming, the Irish government did not want armed forces of any nation on its soil.

An Irish force arrived at Bere Island on the 22nd of September to take over the installations, having travelled down the bay on the *Princess Beara*. As the English were loading their equipment onto the Marquis of Harrington, orders arrived (from London) that the island fortifications were not to be handed over. After about two hours of negotiation between Dublin and London, the English force finally departed. It is obvious that the Naval War Office did not want to lose such a vital cog in the defence of Britain.

Michael J. Carroll

XXV

THE FAMINE IN THE BANTRY REGION

Before we recount the history of the famine in this area, we first have to examine the overall background in Ireland leading up to this disastrous period. In 1829 'high farming' was introduced into Ireland by the English. This was a system which changed the Irish landscape from small holdings of a few acres, which sustained the majority of those who lived in the countryside, to large farms of wide open spaces for the cultivation of grain and the raising of substantial herds of cattle.

Nearly all landowners, both large and small, endeavoured to take advantage of the change in land use. Amongst the means of getting rid of the small land-holders was to pay their expenses for the voyage outwards to the Americas. In 1832 the potato crop failed which caused much hardship amongst the small tenants and cottiers. This was a forewarning of what was to come during the next decade. By 1844 the Poor Laws were in operation, whereby all those, rich and poor, who had a roof over their heads, had to pay a tax for the relief of those less well-off. Of course, this burden, as usual, fell on the poor Irish who were trying to exist on their small holdings.

Around the same time, the Devon Commission decided that the only way of getting rid of the Irish peasantry was by forced emigration, 'peculiarly applicable as a remedial measure'. To accomplish this, the Commission decided on the consolidation of all farms less than eight acres. This proposal aimed to 'rid' the country of over a million Irish peasants.

Even though the Irish harvest of 1845 was one of the best on record, it was nearly all exported to Britain, and no notice was taken by the authorities of the re-appearance of the potato blight late that year.

A few 'experts' came over from Britain to examine the situation and reported back that 'there was nothing to worry about'. When questions were asked in Parliament around two months later about the seriousness of the situation in Ireland, and the plight of the starving masses, the government of the day pretended to be surprised at the arrival of a serious famine. It is interesting to note that, even at this time, the official numbers recorded of those who had died of starvation and famine had been 'doctored', and only represented less than a tenth of the actual figures.

High Street Bantry

In June 1846, Peel, the British prime minister, introduced the Coercion Bill for Ireland. This involved the imposition of a curfew, from sunset to sunrise, on the population, and anybody found outdoors during this period was considered to have broken the law, and was therefore liable to transportation for 15 years or else serve three years in prison. It should be remembered that up to 40 per cent of those living in the countryside at this time were now destitute and living at the side of the road.

Things were further exacerbated by the repeal of the Corn Laws, which allowed corn to be imported into Britain from other countries. This automatically lowered prices in Ireland with the Irish farmers feeling the brunt. As the bottom fell out of the market, the English buyers and shippers made a 'killing' on the market by shipping out cheap grain to an English port, transferring it to another vessel and transporting it back to Ireland where it was subsidised by the British government. It is estimated that over £8 million worth of Irish grain was imported in this manner during the Famine years.

To relieve the poor in Ireland, Parliament granted the sum of £50,000, an amount equal to the grant given to the British Museum in London that same year. The grant was to be used for 'public works' which were to be unproductive and which would provide the poor with cash to purchase the basic overpriced foods for their existence. With the withdrawal of the Coercion Bill various Acts were passed to give the impression that the starving masses in Ireland were being assisted. In the countryside additional public works were commissioned but the substantial numbers of civil servants appointed to oversee these works were the main beneficiaries.

The plight of the peasants became unbearable. Before the harvest was brought in, the bailiff and his henchmen were at the door of his little cabin to collect the rent. In addition, there were the collections for Public Works, Labour Rate Acts, the 'country cess' collections and payment to the Preserver of Decrees. If the peasant sold his lands he would be considered homeless and liable to transportation. Many decided to slave on and eventually perished in their bothans.

The situation worsened during 1847. Those who had been able to obtain employment on public works and still had land were immediately dismissed. Many, therefore, had to sell their holdings to get work and to be able to purchase food for their families. At about this time, the charity food began to trickle into the Irish ports where it was stored or distributed by the agents of the English government who were the local important merchants. Very little of the grain reached the starving people as it was sold on the open market at the going rate.

Having explained the general situation in Ireland up to and during the Famine we should return to the Bantry region during this period. From the early 40s Bantry was a very prosperous town enjoying a lucrative sea trade, fishing industry, grain production, tanneries, breweries and an abundance of livestock. The population of the town, despite the dire housing shortage, was increasing drastically, with people sleeping in the streets, hovels, yards sheds and barns. From 1835 the number of ships clearing outwards with corn and general cargo was about 30 vessels annually as well as about the same number entering. Amongst these were the '*Kingston*' and the '*Deeley Bridge*' which brought timber from New Brunswick, and transported emigrants back to Newfoundland and Quebec.

Bantry Porter brewery, owned jointly by Mr. M. Murphy, Mr Plomer and S. Young as well as the cider brewery were in full production. New Street and part of the new Square had been filled in while work had commenced on the stone pier. In addition, the work on Bantry Workhouse which was to serve Bantry and Castletownbere had been completed. It had been built to hold 976 inmates with the sexes divided. It was funded by the Poor Law rates which were levied on all buildings and lands within the Bantry Union area which embraced the entire region between Dursey Island to the north and Schull in the south.

The next nearest workhouse was in Skibbereen. All those admitted to the Workhouse were required to discard their own clothes and wear the workhouse uniform which was a type of prison garb.

The Workhouse was run by a Board of Guardians elected from the local merchants and traders. Amongst these were J.W. Payne (agent of Lord Bantry), Arthur Hutchinson (Ardnagashel Manor), William Pierson (civil engineer), George Bird (lawyer and agent for Bantry Estates), Richard White (Coomhola Lodge), Richard O'Donovan (fish exporter), Timothy Murphy (mill and brewery owner), Arthur Hutchins (landlord), William Vickery (inn-keeper), Robert Warner (merchant), Michael Murphy (mill owner), Samuel Hutchins (landowner), Patrick O'Sullivan (landowner at Ballylickey) and James Downey (merchant). The clerk was Henry Spencer and the medical officer was Thomas Tisdall of Donemark. The official in charge of the Workhouse was a Mr. Roberts, whose wife acted as matron.

The summer of 1845 showed signs of a promising potato crop but the blights struck almost overnight, casting the poor into further misery. In 1846 the crop failed again and the people became destitute. Soup kitchens were set up – John O'Shea-Lawlor of Gurteenroe and Samuel Hutchinson of Ardnagashel were the main instigators. These soup kitchens were located at Ardnagashel, Newtown, and the Rope Walk and at the Black Bridge. Other minor soup kitchens were set up by the Board of Works near Dunmanus Castle, Caheragh, Durrus, Drimoleague and Ballydehob These soup kitchens must have had some effect as in August 1846 there were 400 vacancies in the Workhouse. The soup kitchens were doing their job. They halted the steady stream of starving families from the countryside from entering Bantry but those who could not afford to pay 8d per month for two pints of soup per day were left to starve. But this situation was about to change and by January 1847 there were 746 inmates in the Workhouse.

As for employment in the town, only the Bantry Mill was working part time. The Rev. Alex Hallowell and the Catholic curate, Thomas Barry, worked together and helped as best they could to alleviate the suffering of those dying on the streets. The situation deteriorated to such an extent that bodies were left on the streets. Those fit enough to move the bodies refused to do so, fearing that they also might catch cholera and fever which had became rampant at this time.

With funds for the soup kitchens running low, Lord Berehaven, heir to the Earl of Bantry, donated the 'magnificent' sum of £20 towards the soup kitchens in his domain while those who could afford it, financed their own soup kitchens.

At about this time, the Labour Relief Act, at sessions in Bantry, granted the sum of £3,540 to the Barony of Bantry in November 1846. This money was used on the drainage on the Bantry Estate, work on the Square, road works on the approaches to town and a section of road from the present West Lodge Hotel to Gearhies.

Toward the end of November 1846, the Poor Law Rates were not sufficient to purchase food for the Bantry Workhouse with its over nine hundred inmates. The Bantry traders refused to give further credit.

In addition the Munster and Leinster Bank in Skibbereen refused to honour any cheques drawn on the Poor Law Rates' account. It was only the generosity of some of the guardians and other charitable people that enabled the Workhouse to remain open.

Diseases became rampant around this time and even reached inside the wall of the Workhouse. There were outbreaks of fever, typhus, dysentery, diarrhoea and cholera. The outbreak of cholera was the worst. It is said that more people died from cholera in the Bantry region than from starvation. Deaths averaged about 20 per week in the Workhouse. With the situation deteriorating, the local merchants began to store corn and grain at the mill at Donemark, the warehouses on the quayside and the English Market at Main Street.

It was decided that when all corn and wheat in the area was either given out or sold, these emergency supplies would be sold 'at cost'. By September 1846, the situation became so critical that crowds of starving and sick people began to arrive at Bantry. The destitute begged for admittance to the Workhouse which by now was filled to capacity. To alleviate the problem a number of annexes were opened by voluntary groups at the mills on Main Street and Donemark, at two warehouses on the quayside and the warehouse at the site that is now occupied by the Bank of Ireland. The Rev. Alex Hollowell could be seen trying to help the infirm on the streets and alleyways. At that time, the Protestant population of Bantry was given as 396.

Those people who had some money and were in reasonable health decided to seek refuge in the West Indies or the Americas on the 'coffin ships'. The going rate was £3 per person or £10 per family and people had to bring their own food and water for the voyage. Those who had no money negotiated for passage with local agents acting for planters in the West Indies or with the ship's skipper. Contracts were signed for free passage outwards in exchange for a period of work on the plantation which could last up to 15 years. Little did they known it but they were signing their lives away.

What followed late in 1846 became known as 'the Black Winter'. The Workhouse was overflowing and the staff were unable to cope. Inmates were required to assist with the sick thus further spreading disease. In January 1847 a fever hospital adjoining the Workhouse was opened. It was designed to hold 26 patients, but within a week there were 160 people within its cramped confines. It is interesting to note that this fever hospital stayed operational until 1949 due to the continuous outbreaks of contagious diseases in the region.

There is no exact record of the number of people who died in the Bantry region during the Famine (1845-1847), probably about 2,000, except that it is reputed that the majority died from fever and cholera and not starvation and were not natives of the town. Many came to Bantry from the outlying areas such as Skibbereen, where the workhouse was overflowing. The demand for coffins became so great that the 'hinged coffin' (a coffin with iron hinges on the bottom which opened when a bar was pulled) began to be used at the two famine pits which were dug at the Abbey graveyard. Only one of these is marked by a Famine Cross.

While the majority of the Irish population was suffering due the Famine, it is recorded that during 1846 exports of corn, beef, butter, pork, hides etc. totalled a value of £8 million. In addition, there were 127,000 acres under oats, 114,000 under wheat and 44,000 under barley and the majority of these crops were exported to Britain. So while Ireland starved, 95 per cent of its products were exported by English landowners, settlers and farmers.

With the effects of the Famine continuing into 1847, the relief work for the starving poor could not be sustained by the rates collected. Even the donations of the volunteer committees were not sufficient to meet the expense of buying food. There was utter chaos and deaths increased and it took until 1849 before life returned to some sort of normality with the potato blight slowly disappearing from the countryside.

Sea traffic increased and ships arrived with further cargoes of grain while the fishing increased, with the assistance of the merchants who financed the purchase of nets, despite the lack of markets where the fish could be sold. About twenty boats were also engaged in the dredging of coral sand and the collection of seaweed to fertilize the lands for the new harvest. In addition, some nine seine boats recommenced fishing but this number fell to four due to poor fishing. Only £600 worth of butter was sent to the market in Cork in 1850.

In the summer of that same year, the number of inmates in the Workhouse fell to about 100.

During the following decade the imports of corn increased, mainly from Odessa and the Americas. Two of the ships engaged in this trade were the *Margaret Anne* and the *Ellen*, while the *Haimkringla* was engaged in the timber trade from Canada (Quebec).

XXVI

THE BANTRY FAIRS

It is interesting to note that the Irish word for fair – aonac – also means anger or rage. This, quite possibly, derives from the ancient fairs or 'gatherings', which were not only the occasion of commerce, but also of family and tribal rivalry. These fairs were usually held on hill tops or high ground such as the southern area under Curran, Coomhola, where there is a gentle slope and some flat land. The ancient year was divided into two seasons which commenced on the first day of May and the first day of November. These were the main dates on which the 'gatherings' were held for the division of land (commonage) and the imposition of tithes. These dates, on which land tenure is based right up to the present day, were referred to as 'Gale Days'.

The first area in Bantry used as a location for the fairs was known as 'Pig's rock' and is an area adjoining the present Bridge Street, to the right as you go up the hill. Here, pigs, sheep, goats and cattle were bought and sold. With the growth of Bantry, this area became too confined and seizing the opportunity the then Lord Bantry built and operated the 'English Market' at the end of Main Street in addition to a 'cattle pound' nearby. He had the authority to do this as a result of an Act passed in 1431 whereby control of all fairs was passed to the local English landlord. Unable to cope with the vast number of livestock, the cattle fair extended from New Chapel Street to Market Street and the area in front of the Catholic church.

When Bridge Street and New Street were reclaimed from the river the fairs extended downhill until the area down as far as the Courthouse was covered in and surfaced. Eventually, half of the Square, as we know it today, was reclaimed from the sea and when this work was completed Bantry fairs grew in importance. From the latter half of the nineteenth century up to the 1950, Bantry became known for having one of the major fairs in Ireland.

Some fairs were of more importance than others during the course of the year. The months October and November were an important period for the farmers and country people, with the approach of the long winter period. It was time to sell the good cattle in order to raise enough money or items of barter to maintain a family and the remaining livestock through the winter. The fairs of February, March, July, August and September were mainly dedicated to horses, pigs, sheep and farm products.

With Lord Bantry having jurisdiction over the Bantry fairs, his toll and tariff collectors were stationed at the various roads leading into town. These locations were at the West Lodge, Custom's Gap, Brewery Cross and the Chicken Loft on Glengarriff Road (opposite Quick Pick). In addition to the activity of trading livestock the fair was also the occasion for the monthly excursion into town for the country folk. It was a time to meet relations, renew old acquaintances, encounter distant relatives and pass on news of important events. Paper money and coinage were extremely scarce in those days, so most negotiations were carried out either by barter or by the weight of butter which was the main item of trade.

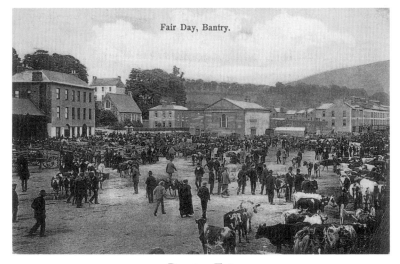

Fair Day, Bantry.

Bantry Fair

Fair goers living over 40 or 50 kilometres from town would commence their journey the morning prior to the Fair Day. Some of the cattle drives arrived in town late that night but the sound of cattle mooing early in the morning signalled the arrival of the majority of the drives which could be of up to 20 cattle.

The sight of a herd of cattle driven by a farmer accompanied by his children in bare feet, while his wife handled the horse or donkey pulling the cart carrying the younger children covered in rough blankets, was familiar on every approach road. In the cart would be a small churn of country butter, baskets of eggs, chickens in wicker creels and rabbit skins. Others arrived with just a young calf, a few sheep, or a large sow or boar in a creel.

The noise on the approach roads would gradually intensify, until the early dawn air was filled the lowing of cattle, the bleating of sheep and the grind and rattle of carts on the rough ground. The shouting of farmers to their older children, or the whistling to their dogs, could be heard echoing through the narrow streets as they scrambled to the most advantageous location to sell their cattle or goods.

When a good spot had been found the animals were gathered together in a confined space while the cart was unloaded and the products or young animals for sale were unloaded and put on display. Small fires were lit with some dry kindling, and cans of water were boiled to make porridge or tea which was accompanied by junks of dry bread. Any butter brought to the market was weighed before being used for barter.

By 5.30am the hotels and eating houses were already opened and serving food to those who could afford it especially the buyers and jobbers who had come from afar. Those who had slept in the doss houses ate their porridge and drank some tea before emerging into the morning air. The pubs or shebeens did not usually open until about 7.00am but the back doors were always open for those with an early morning thirst.

The local blacksmiths, wheelwrights and saddlers would have been working through the night to take advantage of the trade which only came once a month. In those early post-Famine times there were seven hotels and about 20 eating houses, 20 to 30 pubs or shebeens, 18 blacksmiths and three large tanneries in the town.

By dawn, the Square, as well as the adjoining streets and lanes would be crowded with people. Buyers and farmers haggled over prices until a deal was struck by a slap of the hands. No deal was completed without 'luck-money' – a coin if available – and a slap on the back or a tap on a child's head.

Meanwhile, the townspeople descended on the farm market in droves to purchase butter, fowl, fresh eggs, vegetables, a junk of bacon or a skinned rabbit or hare. A long line of meat stalls extended down Main Street, while the fish-mongers, including

Ety Hurley, Donovans and the Downeys, sold their wares on New Street.

Bantry Fairs always seemed to be damned by inclement weather, either heavy rain or gales. This was sometimes ascribed to the time when these gatherings or the accompanying patterns (dancing) were banned by the local Catholic clergy as they were occasions of 'profanities, fights and lewd pagan customs'. Some of those who came to town for the Fair only used the excuse to drink spirits or stout. Drinking on an empty stomach all morning they would emerged on the streets arguing and fighting. This behaviour was based on the old 'faction fighting' when families fought with stones and blackthorn sticks over some inter-family dispute like land division, the non-payment of a dowry or an engaged bride left at the altar.

With the introduction of the railway at the end of the 1890s most of the livestock was shipped out of town in cattle wagons, with train loads departing nearly every hour from 10.30am onwards. It has been estimated that up to 1,000 cattle were dispatched by train on the main Fair Days in July, August and September. Those herding cattle to the railway station were usually met outside the Terminus Hotel by an agent of Bantry Estate who collected a tariff of one shilling per beast on each animal. By early afternoon, most of cattle had been sold and dispatched either by train or by road transport and it was time to make some small purchases at the stalls and local shops.

Amusements began on the streets with minor circus acts and by 4pm the country people began to gather up their possessions and head for home. By 7.00pm the town was once more deserted except for a few stray animals, lost dogs and a few drunks lying in a stupor on the dung-covered ground. There was no school on Fair Days in case any children might be hurt coming through the cattle on the streets. This gave young boys the opportunity of minding cattle and animals for the farmers if they were short-handed. A three-penny bit or a six=penny piece was the usual compensation for a few hours.

Those days are now gone and only the horse and sheep fairs in September are still held. Instead the famous fairs have been replaced by a vibrant weekly market of foodstuff and the spectacle of hawkers of all nationalities selling their wares on the first Friday of each month.

XXVII

RECENT FESTIVALS AND CUSTOMS

Leaving the fairs, which had their origins in the ancient 'gatherings', we should look at the old customs and festivals which are now fast disappearing. Unless they are recorded they will be lost to future generations. Having described the ancient druidic customs and traditions in an earlier chapter, I shall now deal with the customs, beliefs and festivals which still existed locally up to the 1950s. These contain a mixture of old druidic and early Christian practices.

There were two methods of dividing the year into four seasons, one which consisted of the 'true quarters of the year', and a second which was called the 'crooked quarters of the year'.

The True Quarters

    A quarter from Lunasa to Samhain
    A quarter from Samhain to St. Bridget's Day
    A quarter from St. Bridget's Day to Bealtaine
    A quarter from Bealtaine to Lunasa

The Crooked Quarters

    A quarter from St. John's Day to St. Michael's Day
    A quarter from St. Michael's Day to Christmas
    A quarter from Christmas to St. Patrick's Day
    A quarter from St. Patrick's Day to St. John's Day

The true quarters are derived from the ancient druidic calendar year, while the crooked quarters represent the early Christian calendar of the feasts of the important saints. There were various customs observed with the celebration of the main quarter days.

'La Coille' – First Day of January
Children would be up early in the morning so that they could ask the first person they met, for a New Year's gift. Most commonly the gift was a brass coin – a halfpenny or maybe even a penny.

'La Brideog' – 1st of February – St. Bridget's Day
On St. Bridget's Eve, children were accustomed to go from house to house with their faces blackened with soot. One of the young girls would hold a straw doll in her arms. In olden times this straw doll had a dress of oat-straw with a binding string around the waist, a similarly made jacket and a peaked cap of straw on its head. When the children came to the door, the woman of the house would approach the doll and stick a pin in the chest. Then the children would start dancing and singing, and if the woman was satisfied she would give them a present of some kind. St. Bridget's Day is a renaming of an ancient pre-Christian festival and it is possible that the custom of sticking a pin in a doll came originally from the Ivory Coast where Voodoo was practiced. The local custom became known as 'a Penny for the Biddy' and was practiced in Bantry up to the early 1950s.

St. Bridget's Cross
On the days and nights leading up to St. Bridget's Day, many hours were spent in each household making St. Bridget's Crosses. They were given from one family to the other for good luck and

were usually tied up to the rafters or over the fire. They were supposed to protect the family from fire, accident and sickness. This type of cross had its origins in ancient pre-druidic culture and is also found in Hindustan.

St. Patrick's Day (17th of March)

Before the practise of wearing a sprig of shamrock on a dress or lapel was introduced, the custom in the not too distance past was somewhat different. Little girls wore a multi-colour band of cloth around their arms. The boys, men and older women wore fire-blackened sally (willow) twigs in the shape of a cross on their right arm to indicate that Lent was still in force.

Good Friday

The practice of visiting local graveyards to pray for departed family members and others is still followed countrywide, including visits to old cillineach where un-baptised children were interred. This custom was handed down from old times when the inhabitants worshipped their dead ancestors. As for the custom of eating fish, there were many variants. A lot of the population would not have freshly caught fish but would be cooking salted ling, cod or haddock which had been left hanging for some time. If salt fish was not available, then families would go to the beaches and rocks to collect periwinkles, clams, limpets and any other type of shell fish to make a soup. It seems that the custom of eating fish during Lent was introduced by the Christian church as a method of penance. Now, however, fish is regarded as a delicacy so the opposite would be true.

May Day

On the eve of May Day, children went out to collect green leaves. When the sun had set, these sprigs of green were tied to the doors or onto the eaves of each house to signal the arrival of summer. The type of green twigs collected did not matter – it was often bog-myrtle, hazel, ash or holly. However, ash and hazel were considered luckier that other types. These sprigs were left in place until the following year. Originally, this was an ancient custom introduced by the druid priests as a means of cleansing the abodes of our ancestors.

St John's Eve
St. John's Day was a reminder of one of the old pagan customs. On the eve, bonfires were lit in every clochan, village and settlement. It was a night of celebration, with music, dancing and merriment. In olden days the old women recited the rosary around the fires and took a lighted ember home for luck before the festivities commenced.

St. Stephen's Day
During this celebration on the 26th of December various groups of boys or men called to all houses in their locality with a dead wren hanging from a stick with green twigs tied to the top. The bird usually had a coloured ribbon tied around its neck. As these groups made their way around the countryside, they played various instruments and sang songs including the 'Wren's Song'. The original source of this custom is not known but is sometimes said to relate to the legend of a wren pecking on a drum to alert the English forces of an Irish attack. It seems to me that this solution is too modern to account for a practise that appears to have a longer history. It seems that the wren was a bird of ill omen and brought death to a household.

Shrove Tuesday – Skelligs Night
Marriage was prohibited during Lent so some young couples took the opportunity of getting married on the Skellig Rock as the monks there still followed the old calendar by which Lent

would start later by 15 days. As Shrove Tuesday approached, one of the two methods of conveying the message from the community to a couple that it was time to make a decision was by a 'listing'. The 'listing' was a type of comical matchmaking put together by some of the local wits. This would contain a list of the most incompatible bachelors and spinsters in the area, and be posted on the doors of the local shops and pubs. The other method was when groups of young boys and some girls would pull a collection of old pots, pans and baths around the streets of the town with fires burning, on Shrove Tuesday night, to alert any young couple that it was time to go to the Skelligs if they wanted to get married.

MICHAEL J. CARROLL

XXVIII

EMIGRATIONS AND TRANSPORTATION

L ittle is known about emigration by the Irish up to the seventeenth century but as ships departing from Liverpool, Bristol, London and Portsmouth, called into Youghal, Cork, Kinsale, Baltimore, Crookhaven, Bantry and Dingle for water and fresh vegetables, it is more than likely that some Irish did join up as crew or else sought passage with a view to starting a new life in the West Indies or the Americas.

Searching the available English records we find that during the 1570s, two English ships called into Crookhaven for supplies on their outward voyage to the West. On both of these vessels Irish families embarked, seeking a new life in the far away Colonies. One of these exploration vessels which had a Jesuit aboard ended up at the mouth of the Amazon River where the Irish disembarked and began to set up a settlement on a large island called Sapanopko which became known as 'New Ireland'. The other vessel ended up at the mouth of the Maracaibo where they built a settlement on the north bank.

A number of years later we encounter a Sir Walter Harcourt obtaining a charter from King James I to sail to Guinea in 1609. In 1612 Sir Thomas Roe commenced his expedition to the 'Indian Gates' (West Indies) having taken on board a number of Irish families who wished to settle somewhere in the West

Indies. In the same year, the brothers, Philip and James Purcell arrived at the Amazon and built a settlement on the banks of the Toureque river, which in time exported tobacco, dyes and hardwoods to Europe on Dutch ships. These were followed in 1620 by a group of Irish emigrants led by a Bernard O'Brien of Clare who built a wood and earthen fort to protect them from the natives and also, a Peter Sweetman, who lead a group of some 400 immigrants and settled at Para, south of the Amazon.

With the increase of shipping from England to the West Indies and the Colonies during the early part of the seventeenth century, it is almost certain that many Irish did voluntarily leave to find a new life in the Colonies. Most made the voyage on English ships, but a number availed of the opportunity of embarking aboard pirate ships on their way to the Caribbean to plunder.

After the defeat of the Irish at Kinsale many men departed to both France and Spain to fight on against the English in those countries. Amongst these were Donal Cam O'Sullivan and his followers, who sailed to La Corunna in Spain and eventually settled in Madrid. Many others went to France where they enlisted in the French army. Many never returned to Ireland or were killed, leaving wives and children to fend for themselves back in Ireland. We can only imagine the tears and anguish as the men departed.

As far as the western Colonies were concerned, most of the English vessels sailed to Barbados, which was regarded as the gateway to the other islands. Making the voyage were people who wished to make a new life and included adventurers, sons of wealthy gentlemen, farmers, general craftsmen, potential settlers and servants.

Between 1612 and 1642 the early English emigrants who had sailed westward established the most perfect colonial aristocracy in the Americas in the colony of Barbados. They had brought with them the English common law, and institutions, the system of English parishes and the English Church.

In 1653, a Captain John Vernon, acting on behalf of merchants Sellick and Leader, offered his services to the Crown to transport Irish children (mainly orphans) to New England. We don't know if this undertaking was ever completed. Meanwhile, in June of that year, a Colonel Phair advertised in Irish ports, especially Kinsale and Cork, for men to work in the English Colonies. A sum of fifteen shillings was offered to those who wished to avail of the opportunity. The small print in the advertisement added that each man would be 'free' after four years, having worked off the cost of his passage, clothes and food. Also, during that month a Colonel Stubbers, who was governor of Galway, tried to organise the transportation of over one thousand Irish from Connaught. There is no evidence as to whether he was successful or not. All of the above could not be defined as emigration but forced transportation.

It was in 1627 that a Sir William Courteen organised the first real settlement in Barbados. He sent two shiploads of emigrants to Barbados under the command of John and Henry Powell. Up to this time, various wealthy individuals had organised privately funded expeditions to the West Indies but these had run into financial difficulties. No semblance of law and order was established until Courteen's associate, the Duke of Carlisle, installed Henry Hawley as governor of the island in 1639. He organised the distribution of land, which was covered in rainforests and was extremely difficult to clear and so only fetched the low price of £1 per acre. The clearing of the land was mainly undertaken by the young indentured servants or those who had bound themselves to work for a period of time before they could purchase land themselves. During the 1630s there was an annual average of sixteen vessels sailing from London to Barbados. Most of these called into the ports of the south coast of Ireland on their outward voyage.

From the records available in Barbados, we can see that Ireland was a prime source for the supply of servants during this period. In 1636 a ship was listed as having transported fifty six Irish men and women from Kinsale to Barbados. A Thomas Anthony also organised two further ships from Kinsale that same year. Unable to recruit enough young Irishmen, he signed up more women than required, assuring the ship-owners that all these women were 'between seventeen and 35 years of age with lusty and strong bodies'. Those that survived the voyage were sold as slaves for 500 pounds of tobacco each. In 1638, a Thomas Rous lost 80 of his 350 'passengers' during a voyage to Barbados. There were seven more ships listed around this time carrying 'emigrants' to Barbados.

At this time the main export from Barbados was tobacco but it was of poor quality and prices dropped in England when better quality tobacco from Virginia became more popular. The planters of Barbados, with the loss of their tobacco market, changed to the cultivation of sugar cane which during the following ten years became a lucrative export. However, the indentured white servants were unable to cope with all the work so the planters negotiated with the privateers to supply them with African slaves. Soon the white indentured servants found themselves toiling in the fields with black slaves. Those who could, bought their freedom and went north to the other colonies of Virginia, New England, while the Irish moved to the Leeward Islands, Montserrat and St. Kitts where they eventually made up over two-thirds of the population. These were mainly farmer's sons, carpenters, smiths and masons who had left Ireland for a new life.

To Hell or Barbados

The history of the transportation of the Irish to the West Indies and the American colonies after the Cromwellian conquest of Ireland is poorly documented. Initially, it was mostly a clandestine practice operated by the London and Bristol slave traders in collusion with a number of English families who had established themselves in the south-west of Ireland. Oral tradition in the south-west is very strong on the subject, and the phrase 'to Hell or Barbados' supercedes that of 'to Hell or Connaught'.

While subduing the south in the spring of 1650, Cromwell sacked the majority of the Irish strongholds and castles. One section of his army marched into West Cork and plundered the whole area. Those captured alive were taken to the ports and imprisoned. The overflow was shipped to Barbados on the first available ship. The going rate for male prisoners was 1,500 lbs of sugar or the equivalent. The rate for young women was somewhat less.

This ethnic cleansing of Ireland really began in August 1652 when a Proclamation was issued giving the Commissioners of Ireland power to transfer the Irish to the overseas colonies. The Commissioners could seize and transport anybody of whatever standing judged to be a danger to the Commonwealth. This included the Royalist landlords and settlers, Irish soldiers who had refused to emigrate to foreign armies, and the dependants of those who had already gone abroad. This action left a vast number of women and children in a desperate situation.

A further Act was passed in which it was stated that 'Irish women, as being too numerous now, and exposed to prostitution, are to be sold to merchants, and to be transported to Virginia, New England, or other countries where they may support themselves by their labour'.

With nowhere to go, the women and children crowded into the towns. Only the orphans, whose fathers had left for foreign fields and whose mothers had died from starvation remained wandering the countryside. The work of rounding up people for transportation was carried out efficiently by the so-called 'man-catchers' who herded the unfortunate people, bound together by ropes around their necks, into holding pens outside the towns where they were branded with the initials of the ship that would take them to Barbados or Virginia. Young women of marriageable age and 'not past breeding' were sold to the ship's captains for £4 or £4 10s. They were sold on for double this amount to the planters. The captains and crews of the transportation ships treated the Irish the same as the black slaves who were packed into the ship's holds like sardines in a can.

As to how many children were transported the records are not very reliable. A Sir John Clotworthy was given a licence to transfer 1,000 children to Virginia. Thomas Emmet stated that 'over a hundred thousand children were sent to the colonies of West Indies, Virginia and New England'. This practice of rounding up Irish women and children for transportation ceased after about four years when the English landowners and settlers objected when the 'man-catchers' began to pick up their own wives, daughters and children for transportation.

Some of the vessels engaged in this human trade from the south-west coast of Cork were the *Jane, Susan and Mary, Elizabeth* and the *Two Brothers*. Amongst the families mentioned on the island of Monserrat, in 1632, were the O'Sullivans, O'Donovans, O'Lynch, Gibbons, O'Shea, Croghan, Leahy, O'Callaghan, Murphy, Scully, Shannahan, and Sugrue. There were 22 O'Sullivan families, 16 McCarthys and 12 O'Donovans on the island. Irish was the unofficial language of the island.

With the great influx of black slaves into Barbados the island became known only as a slave colony. Many of those English who had decided to sail to that island now changed their minds and sought passage to the other islands and to Virginia and New England. Instead of making the round trip to Barbados and then up the east coast of the States, captains sailed their ships direct to these locations.

The Irish Immigrant or Coffin Ships

This phrase was first coined in 1787, which was eleven years after the Declaration of Independence in the United States. It is not known how many people emigrated to the States between 1600 and 1795. The so-called Puritan Migration between 1628 and 1640 totalled only about 20,000, with the averages for the following years put at 10,000. Total emigration from Ireland during the eighteenth century could be estimated at 450,000. Even with this many people leaving, prior to the Great Famine Ireland had the highest population density in Western Europe.

The emigrants to North America fell into two categories: those pioneers who settled in the wilderness and helped to establish a new society, and those who arrived later when the country's laws and customs had been established. The first mass movement to America commenced after the Napoleonic Wars, reaching its peak in the 1850s. The second was in the 1880s and the last was in the decade prior to the outbreak of the First World War. It is estimated that some 35 million people emigrated to America during these three periods.

In the hundred years from 1820 to 1920, it is estimated that over 4.5 million Irish emigrated to the United States. The main destinations of the Irish were Baltimore, Boston, Detroit, Chicago, Cincinnati, St. Louis, New Orleans and

San Francisco. Between 30 and 40 million Americans now claim Irish descent.

'For their Country's Good'

Before leaving the history of transportation we must mention the transfer of convicts to Australia. These convicts were the overflow of the English and Irish prisons which had become overcrowded. The situation became so bad that old hulks moored in the principal ports were used as temporary prisons before the convicts were escorted aboard ships destined for Australia and Tasmania.

The first penal settlement was established by Captain Arthur Philip, R.N. at Port Jackson in 1788. A total of some 160,663 male and female prisoners were landed in Australia from England and Ireland. During the long and dangerous passage many died from scurvy, dysentery, typhoid, fever, smallpox and other diseases but the numbers did not compare with those who successfully made the voyage to the West Indies or the Americas. Also, those involved in the transportation of convicts across the Atlantic were mindful of their charges because each one landed had a value. The contractors employed to transport convicts to Australia had no such incentive. The majority of those transported were landed in New South Wales.

Transportation of convicts was abolished on the 22nd of May, 1840, and Tasmania, which became known as Van Diemen's Land, was chosen as the new destination, but within some ten years the local colonists objected to the landing of convicts on their shore and in 1853 the transportation of convicts to Tasmania was halted. This decision left only Norfolk Island and Western Australia as destinations for convict ships. Records indicate that 84,000 were sent New South Wales, Tasmania received 67,000, Western Australia got 9,720 and several hundred landed at Norfolk Island.

In Ireland ships or hulks were moored in Dublin and Cork harbours to take the surplus of convicts before they were placed aboard ships destined for New South Wales. Amongst them were many youths and young girls. Between 1812 and 1817 some 1,116 young people were transported and for the other years there was an average of 45 aboard each ship sailing to New South Wales. Some of these had been found guilty of stealing food or lady's apparel or some other minor offence. In this context mention must be made of a number of ships, including the Lady Kennaway, which departed from Cork with women transported to Port Elizabeth in South Africa, where they were supposed to 'entertain' the English and Prussian soldiers.

Finally, a William Cotter, who was fighting for Brazil against Argentina in 1826 recruited about 2,400 men with their wives and children to sail from West Cork to Brazil but the conditions were so bad that most of the people moved on to Argentina or sought passage to Canada. Another group that emigrated to Brazil were some 400 people from Wexford under the guidance of a Father T. Donovan. These also moved on to Argentina and Uruguay.

As far as emigration to the States during the period 1846 to 1925 is concerned we find that over four and a half million left these shore for a new life in the Colonies.

XXIX

MINING IN THE BANTRY REGION

The copper mines at Mount Gabriel, near Schull, were worked during the Bronze Age (c.1,500 to 1,300 BCE). This coincided with the exhaustion of the copper mines in the Mediterranean countries. It is estimated that over 4,500 tons of rock were extracted from 32 mines during this period. Primitive means were used to extract the copper. The basic method was to light fires against the rock face and wait for cracks to appear before prizing the pieces out. The main use of copper at that time was to make bronze implements and arms such as swords, daggers, axe-heads and arrow tips. This was achieved by mixing copper and tin in extreme heat. The largest worked tin deposits around this time were to be found in Cornwall so this must have created a certain amount of sea-traffic between Cornwall and the south-west of Cork. More than likely it was the early Phoenicians who exploited both types of mines.

It is not known who worked these early mines – whether it was a native population trained or obliged to work as slaves by 'foreigners' or the 'foreigners' themselves. There is no evidence of smelting taking place at Mount Gabriel but indications of these sites are to be found on the Muintir mBaire Peninsula. This would indicate that copper was also extracted on this peninsula during that early period.

It took until the 1830s before mining recommenced on the Muintir mBaire peninsula by English adventurers or entrepreneurs who descended on the region, imbued with a get-rich-mentality but with little financial backing. Their decision to explore for minerals was probably based on the success of the mines at Allihies across the bay, which reached the peak of production in the 1830s. A number of companies were incorporated by an Act of Parliament to work mines throughout Ireland, and their main objective was to carry out trials with a view of opening up old mines. Many companies were formed, some of them fraudulent and merely designed to profit the promoters and directors who had purchased old leases cheaply and then sold them to a company in which they were shareholders.

As to these 'shady operators' it is not known how many of these operated on the Muintir mBaire peninsula. However, the amount of local subscriptions to the various undertakings indicates that those involved were considered trustworthy.

In 1845, a Captain William Thomas is said to have 'discovered' the Gortavallig copper seams on the Sheep's Head peninsula. It is not known if he was a geologist, had mining experience or was just an adventurer. Also, it is not known if these seams were worked in the distant past. Captain Thomas was joined by a Colonel Beamish, who became the chairman of the mining company. Work initially commenced with a small capital investment, but as the location was inaccessible by sea, a road ten miles long was built in eleven weeks from the mine location east to the sheltered inlet to the south of White Horse Point where a strong stone pier was built. It is reputed that over 90 tons of copper ore was mined during the first year of operation and shipped to Swansea in Wales. If this is true, then the Gortavallig seams were more productive than the mines at Allihies. Despite this apparent success, the mine was closed and abandoned in 1847. This might have been due to a shortage of workmen during the famine years or because of sea water entering the main shaft works.

Despite this setback, various other mines were opened on the peninsula – Killeen North (on the water's edge), Glanruin (Cuas), Lissaremig and Rooska as well a number near Kilcrohane. A Mr. Walter Woods and a Colonel Swart were involved in the opening of the Lissaremig, Cuas and Rooska seams. It is interesting to note that the assayer's report on these seams revealed that:

a) Lissaremig and Cuas yielded 32 per cent copper and two grams of silver per ton.

b) Rooska yielded 12 per cent copper and 73 ounces of silver per ton.

Bearing in mind that the mines at Allihies were producing ten per cent copper per ton, the above were exceptional figures which had been verified by Messrs. Bath & Sons Ltd, a well known and respected copper smelter at Swansea, who had received the first shipment of ore. Despite the great potential of these mines – now operated by the Bantry Silvermining Company – no government funding or financial assistance was forthcoming, so the mines closed when funds ran out.

With no further work available, the Cornish miners who had moved to the area and set up their own little villages, departed for the States, leaving their newly constructed houses abandoned. When a Mr. Rathbone, Director of South Berehaven Mines, wrote to the Geological Survey Office, in Dublin, requesting up-to-date geological survey maps for the Muintir mBara Peninsula, they were not released. This would lead one to believe that there were people in high places preventing any further development of the mines on the Muintir mBaire Peninsula.

Additional information on the mines can be found in an article by F. O'Mahony, in the *Bantry Journal* and also in the *History of the Berehaven Copper Mines* by R.A.Williams.

Slate and Barytes Mining

During the 1880s other types of mining commenced in the Bantry area including quarrying for very good slate. The earliest slate quarries were operated by a Captain O'Flaherty of the Bantry Slate and Slab Quarries at Gouladoo, about a mile and a half west of White Horse Head. These were subject to a lease of 92 years at a rent of £11 per annum. Employing about 50 men and producing over 40,000 slates per week, it appeared to have been a prosperous business. Slates were exported by sea to Cork and were used locally. There were also a number of other slate quarries in the area especially that located at Dromkeal, near Snave Bridge. This was operated by a Mr. Lissabe and had direct access to the sea for shipment.

After a short time, the quarry was taken over by the Belfast Slate Company, with a Mr. W. B. Ritchie as the local director. The lessee of the property was the Earl of Bantry (White). When he realised the success of the quarry he drew up a new agreement whereby a down payment of £300 had to be made to him and also one twentieth royalties. After two years in production the quarry ceased to operate in 1866 and the 50 men were left unemployed. No doubt, this was due to the exorbitant demands made by the Earl of Bantry. All the plant, machinery and stock piles of slates were auctioned off. In addition to the above, there were also slate quarries on the south side of Vaughan's Pass where slates were extracted mainly for use in the Bantry locality.

The barytes mine at Derriganoch was located outside of Bantry, off the road to Lough Bofinne. It is said that this was the first to open in Ireland and was operated by the Liverpool Barytes Company Ltd., and later became known as Storer's Mines and Mills from the name of the company representative, a Mr. Storer. We do not have an exact date as to when the mine was opened but it seems that it was about 1890. A special railway siding was constructed to facilitate the mill, the rail line having been extended around the town in 1882. From the siding the barytes was loaded onto wagons and was transported to Cork where it was loaded onto vessels destined for England. The barytes was used in the production of pottery and paint.

During the height of production at the mines there was a 24 hour shift system in operation – 30 men in each eight-hour period. The rate of pay for those on shift work, working six days per week, was £1. 10s, while men working on the separation of the barytes from impure rock were paid 12 shillings per week. The work was labour intensive as the men had to remove the barytes from the rock face by crowbar and sledge. The holes for the dynamite were made by a miner and driller. After the holes were cleaned out by a 'buchee', dynamite was put in place, the siren was sounded, and the mine was cleared. Situated over the main mine shaft was a boiler house and steam winch which was used to transport the workers up and down and also to hoist up the barytes in large iron buckets. On the surface, the barytes was loaded into large carts which were pulled by teams of horses to the crushing mills near the town. A J. J. Crowley, grandfather of Jimmy Crowley, the Square, was the main haulage contractor. When the main shaft began to run out of suitable barytes, a number of extra cuttings were made nearby. Some of these were up to eighty feet deep but they were not very productive.

When the Troubles commenced, Mr. Storer, fearing for his life, left Ireland and was replaced by a Captain Daly. Together with a Mr. Henry Downey, they continued to operate the mines until 1922. A point worth noting about this period is that the late Ned Cotter. T.D. and Ted (Reagh) O'Sullivan, T.D. worked in the mines during their early years.

During the early 1950s an attempt was made to reopen the mines. New machinery, winches and pumps were installed and, as soon as the mine shaft was emptied of water, barytes was once again brought to the surface. When a sufficient amount of barytes had been stockpiled it was then transported by trucks to Bantry Pier where it was loaded onto cargo ships of about 600 tons. The mining continued for a few years but then closed down completely either due to lack of financial support or else because the water level in the main shaft could not be controlled.

As to the other mining operations in the Bantry region, there are various ambiguous references principally to the mining of

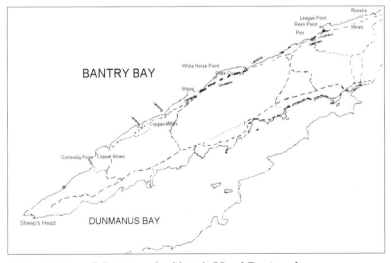

Mines on the Sheep's Head Peninsula

iron ore by one of the Whites for their smelters in the area – at Castletownbere, Adrigole, Glengarriff, Coomhola and Bantry. It seems that the main source of iron ore were located near the smelter at Coomhola, at Glengarriff and at another location on the shore of Roaring Water Bay. These were soon exhausted and ore had to be shipped in from England.

Lastly, there was once a glass-smelting furnace at Reenmeen East, Glengarriff. Little is known about this operation except that it was worked by one of the Whites who found suitable raw material in that area.

Many geological surveys have been carried out in the Bantry region over the past few years and even though the results were promising, no new mining operation has taken place to date.

XXX

ROAD, RAIL AND SEA ROUTES TO BANTRY

Before dealing with road, rail and sea transport in the Bantry region we should first glance back at the developments, events and general improvements that took place between 1855 and the end of that century. According to the records, the number of inmates in the Workhouse decreased to about 100 people, while the fever hospital still remained opened due to fever which was still present in the locality. It is interesting to note that the fever hospital did not close its doors until the early 1950s.

As for fishing, funds were made available to those who were still engaged in the industry, to purchase nets and ropes, yet, due to the lack of proper markets, prices were extremely poor for catches landed. The number of seine boats further decreased to four as a result. Total income for 1859 was a meagre £600 in total. Some fishermen had to be content in dredging coral sand and gathering seaweed to make some sort of a living. Some fishermen continued using trammel nets for cod, hake, pollock and ling.

In September 1865 the potato crop failed once again and there was a short famine which lasted until the following harvest when the fears of the local people abated. One of the direct results of this famine was that the growing of flax, which had begun the previous year, ceased.

However, after a delay of some six years, the building of a stone pier commenced. The main contractor was William Martin Murphy. Meanwhile, slate was being exported from White Horse Point and Snave on small schooners. With the lack of fresh drinking water in the town, an underground reservoir with a capacity of some 350 cubic metres was built across the stream from the Priests' houses. Pipes were laid to the English market and to a number of pumps in the town plus a fountain on the Square.

In 1871 Bantry enjoyed a mini trade boom. £2,000 worth of butter was exported or dispatched to Cork from Warner's Buttery at William Street. John Capithorne re-opened the Bantry Mills for the dyeing of imported wool from Australia. G.W. Biggs imported grain for its mills on the quayside, William Murphy imported timber from St. Johns, Newfoundland and a Mr. Harris commenced the manufacture of paint at the mills of Donemark. He was also involved in the export of barytes to England. As for the lighting of the town, the area around the Bantry Mill had a supply of electricity from a dynamo on the water wheel while oil lamps were placed at strategic locations on the street corners.

Yet the population of the town had not increased to pre-Famine numbers. In a census of c.1871 the population was 2,830, which was about a third of the 1842 figure. This was a slight increase from the previous census and was mainly due to the improvement in fishing and the employment of extra men.

In the 1880s the country suffered from a serious depression and employment suffered severely mainly due to the return of the potato blight. Of all the areas around Bantry Bay, Bere Island suffered most.

The Bantry Fairs became the mainstay of the town and the building of a rail-link from Dunmanway to Bantry increased trade. The rail-link cost £109,000. The original station or terminus was located in front of the present hospital where carriages from Vickery's and Water's Hotels collected visitors in horse and carriages and goods were brought down to the town in merchants' carts.

It was also during this period that the Bantry Bay Steamship Co. was established by a Mr. Payne, with the purchase of the *Countess of Bantry*. Further details of this company are included in the following pages.

From the late 1850s until about 1905, a steamship service operated between Cork and Dingle, calling in at various ports, including Castletownbere, on the round trip. The *South Western* was the first vessels to be used on this service. In 1876, this vessel was replaced by the *Ria Formosa*, which was owned by the Clyde Shipping Co. This ship was later joined by the *Rockabill*, *Skelligs* and the *Valentia*. There was no fixed schedule for these ships until the 1890s when a weekly round trip from Cork to Dingle was introduced. When there was sufficient cargo the ports visited included Schull, Castletownbere, Bantry, Kenmare, Sneem and Cahirciveen. When the SS *Fastnet* was introduced on the run, she departed Cork on Tuesday morning and returned on the following Sunday. Some passengers were embarked and the cost of the round trip was 22s 6d, excluding food. In order to maintain this valuable sea link, the Congested Districts Board paid an annual grant of £500 to Clyde Shipping Co., but when this grant was terminated in 1940, the service was terminated.

According to the records, the Cork and Bandon Railway Company was formed in 1844. Amongst the members of the Board were the Earl of Bandon, Lord Carbery and the Earl of Bantry. On his journey to Bantry and Glengarriff in 1858, the

Prince of Wales availed of the train journey as far as Bandon before changing over to horse and carriage.

The West Cork Railway Company was incorporated in 1860 and during the next 20 years the towns of Balineen, Dunmanway, Drimoleague, Skibbereen, Clonakilty and Kinsale were all connected by rail to Cork. In November 1879, work began on the railway line between Drimoleague and Bantry, and this link was officially opened on the 4th of July, 1881. The terminus at Bantry was situated in front of the present hospital buildings. The cost of this extension was £105,000. The further extension from the hospital site to the north side of the Square was built during the period 1891–1892 by William Martin Murphy, contractor.

With the completion of this link between Bantry and Cork trade increased. With a further small extension to the north pier, a thrice-weekly cargo service from Bantry to Castletown and other small ports in the bay was introduced by the Bantry

The Inner Harbour and Station, last quarter of nineteenth century

Steamship Company with the *Countess of Beara* which had been chartered by Mr. Payne. As a result of the building of timber pier facilities at Glengarriff and Adrigole with the assistance of Congested Districts Board in 1906, the service increased to these small ports. Many of those forced to emigrate from Beara made the sea journey to Bantry and then either waited for a ship destined for Nova Scotia or else travelled on to Cork to join a vessel sailing to the Americas. To cope with the additional services required in the bay, the *Lady Elsie* was purchased.

During the famous Cork Exhibition of 1902, many visitors enjoyed the daily round trips by rail to Bantry and then to Glengarriff by boat which had been introduced in 1899. This Sunday Excursion Special from Cork to Bantry became extremely popular between 1902 and 1913.

Loaded with day-trippers, the train arrived at the pier head at 12.30 pm to catch the sailing of the boat to Glengarriff which cost 1s 6d per adult for the round trip. There was the added pleasure of a brass band aboard. In addition many people availed of the boat trip to catch the coach journey from Glengarriff to Kenmare and Killarney.

Normally, the sailings on weekdays connected with the train's arrival and departure at Bantry. During the First World War, there was a period of interruption of the sailing to and from Castletown and Bere Island but it continued later with the *Lady Elsie* until 1936 when the *Princess Beara* was introduced on the route and continued on the route until 1946 when the service was withdrawn mainly due to the improvements of the road from Glengarriff to Castletown. In 1931 the road over the Healy Pass and the Tunnel Road were completed. Workmen came from as far as Eyeries and Allihies for work. The going rate for a day's work was 1s 6d.

*Bantry Piers in the early 1900s with
Countess of Beara and Lady Elsie*

The *Princess Beara* was laid up in Bantry harbour until 1949 when she was purchased by a Spanish concern and towed to Vigo. She was eventually cut up on the beach at Bouzas, near Vigo. It is not known if she served as a cargo boat from the time of her arrival or not.

In 1946 CIE proposed a new hotel for Glengarriff, but this never materialised. Due to lack of usage and the poor condition, the railway pier at Bantry was dismantled. Despite the introduction of diesel-engine trains in 1954 the West Cork railway was closed in March 1961, thus depriving the region of one of the vital means of transport to Cork.

XXXI

A TIME OF CIVIL UNREST

Before discussing the 'Troubles' which commenced during the second decade of the nineteenth century we must first mention the efforts of Daniel O'Connell to abolish the Penal Laws in Ireland. Due to continuous efforts in the British House of Commons he became known as the 'Liberator'. He visited Castletown and especially Bantry many times as his sister was married and lived at Reendonegan House.

In the fight for Home Rule for Ireland at the turn of the century there was a group of Bantry men who became M.P.s and members of the Irish Parliamentary Party. These were known as the 'Bantry Band'.

This group was made up of relations of both A. M. Sullivan and Tim Healy, namely Tim Harrington, Edward Harrington, T. D. Sullivan, Donal Sullivan. Thomas J. Healy, Maurice Healy, William M. Murphy, and James Gilhooly. A.M. Sullivan became the owner of the Nation newspaper while William M. Murphy became the owner of the *Irish Independent*. They were like a clan of politicians who did their utmost to disrupt normal business in the House of Commons requesting that the Irish Question must be solved. A. M. Sullivan aided the rise of Parnell, but Tim Healy manufactured his downfall and later became the first Governor General of the Irish Free

State. Tim Healy was born in the premises now occupied by the Bank of Ireland.

The Irish Volunteer Movement was formed in December 1913. Most of those who joined were already members of the Ancient Order of Hibernians which was founded in 1909. In Bantry, the Volunteers, who numbered over 40, carried out training exercises in the local Town Hall and, as numbers increased, training took place on the adjoining road, now known as Parade Field. However, as a result of a controversial speech by Redmond, on the 29th of September 1914, there was a major split in the Volunteer Movement. As a result, the membership in Bantry fell to about 20 men. The Volunteers broke into two groups – one called the 'O'Brienites' and the other the 'Redmondites'. The 'O'Brienites' made the 'Molly Hall', next to the old Terminus Hotel their base while the 'Redmonities' remained in the A.O.H. or Town hall. Both locations were used for dances, playing cards, meetings and Irish dancing lessons for young girls. Later, the 'O'Brienites were joined by Tim Healy.

On the Saturday before Easter 1916 people from all over West Cork made the journey to Drimoleague to hear Terence McSwiney speak.

A group of some 15 Volunteers travelled from Bantry in a horse-drawn cart which carried a rowing boat with a flag flying from its mast.

The following Saturday, the Volunteers received orders that they were to march to Kealkil by noon on the following day which was Easter Sunday. After parading at first Mass, they made their way unimpeded to Kealkil where they were to receive orders to join up with Balingeary contingent. However, a Sean O'Hegarty arrived with instructions to disband and return home much to the chagrin of all those present.

With no other option and disappointed at not seeing any action they made their way to Bantry without being stopped or arrested by the R.I.C(Royal Irish Constabulary). After this event, the group became disheartened and the majority of the Volunteers ceased to be members especially when they heard that the Uprising had been a failure in Dublin.

After the failed Easter Rising, the Irish people saw things in a different light. The Irish Parliamentary Party, which ruled the country, was finally identified in its true role as a puppet of the English Government. During the following years those elected to represent the people were those who had the welfare of Ireland at heart. These included Count Plunkett, Joseph McGuiness, Eamon de Valera, William Cosgrave, Arthur Griffith and others.

During the early months of 1917 the Irish Volunteers in Bantry and elsewhere were reorganised. In Bantry, under a Battalion Commander, the following were elected: Captain – Ralph Keyes; First Lieutenant – Robert Lynch; Second Lieutenant – Michael Crowley; Adjutant – Michael Harrington;

Naval personnel in Bantry Square

Quartermaster – Jack O'Mahony. The company became known as the 'A' Company of the 14th Battalion, Cork Brigade. Other companies were formed in Glengarriff, Coomhola, Kealkil and in other towns and villages.

The British Government maintained order in the country, in addition to the armed forces, with a large force of R.I.C. who were nicknamed 'Peelers'. These provided a network of outposts in every town and village which were nothing more than a network of spy bases to keep watch on the population. The main objective of the Irish Volunteers was to break the power of the R.I.C who were nothing but a well-armed military force whose purpose was to keep the country under British rule. The R.I.C. was made up of Irishmen who had sworn allegiance to Britain and who spied on their neighbours. In fact, messages were dispatched to Dublin everyday from each R.I.C. barracks outlining the activities of those who might cause trouble or civil unrest.

Michael Collins, Countess Markievicz and Geroid O'Sullivan arrived in Bantry on the 7th of October 1917, and a large meeting was held in a field at Newtown. They all spoke on the necessity of getting the country free from the domination of the English Government. Countess Markievicz, who was from a Protestant gentry family, asked for women volunteers for a branch of Fianna Eireann which became known as Cuman na mBan. After a meeting of the Volunteer Movement near Dunmanway it was adopted that the Movement should be known as the West Cork Brigade and a system of communication was established whereby men on bikes would travel between towns and villages.

On the 16th of April 1918, Britain introduced a Conscription Bill which included Ireland. This was due to the severe troop losses on the Continent. To free British soldiers for war duties many leaders of the Volunteers were arrested and marshal law was introduced. Conscription was never enforced but many joined the English forces. These were mainly from the settled English and the gentry classes.

Two months after the end of the war, in January, 1919, a directive was sent to all Volunteers by the newly constituted Dail Eireann that all members of the R.I.C. should be ostracised from society. This had an immediate effect as some of the members retired or resigned and returned to their native homes. A new recruitment drive failed and only a few joined the R.I.C. To get over this problem, the English government sent thousands of troops to Ireland and two Companies of the King's Liverpool Regiment, some 200 soldiers, were sent to Bantry. These were billeted in the Bantry Workhouse after those inmates still on the premises were thrown out. On hearing of their plight, Mrs. Shellswell White of Bantry House took them in and they were accommodated in the Stables.

At that time there were about 32 R.I.C. barracks in West Cork, including Bantry, Glengarriff and Durrus, Castletownbere and Bere Island. The Volunteers decided to mount a major offensive against these early in 1920, but the lack of arms and explosives was a major obstacle. In the Bantry area, various raids and attacks were carried out including on a Naval Sloop moored at the old railway pier and on Durrus and Ballydehob barracks. In addition, any small groups of R.I.C. who were on their way to or from other outposts were attacked and their weapons taken.

Also, Derryganoch Mines were raided for dynamite. Ted O'Sullivan, who had worked in the mines, had a good knowledge on the use of gelignite explosives.

With the increase of Volunteer activity, a number of the officers were arrested and sent to Cork gaol. These included

Sean Cotter and Ralph Keyes. A short time later they were sent to Belfast and finally ended up at Wormwood Scrubs in London where they commenced a hunger strike. They were released after 23 days and eventually returned to Bantry where attacks on the R.I.C. continued. Armaments, labeled as machinery parts, were dispatched from England addressed to the loyalists G.W.Biggs and then collected from the train by Volunteers without the knowledge of the R.I.C. or Biggs.

To bolster the numbers of the R.I.C., recruits were dispatched from England. It turned out that those recruited were criminals and dregs of society who wore Khaki uniforms and black R.I.C. belts and became known as the 'Black and Tans'. The King's Regiment of some 200 soldiers under the command of Colonel Jones, who would not accept any excesses by his men, only patrolled the roads, the towns and villages.

Plans were drawn up by the local volunteers, who were now part of the West Cork Brigade, to attack various R.I.C. barracks in the region. Two R.I.C. returning from Glengarriff on their bicycles were ambushed at Donemark by a group of Volunteers led by Dan O'Mahony, who removed a rifle and two hand-guns. A similar attack took place at Snave Bridge where a lone R.I.C. man was attacked, killed and his rifle and revolver were taken.

The R.I.C. and the Tans took revenge by raiding all houses of suspected members of the Volunteers and those belonging to sympathisers. When they didn't find Michael Crowley at home they went upstairs and shot his invalid brother who was confined to his bed. Then they threw incendiary bombs in through the windows of many houses including that of David O'Mahony which went up in flames just after his family escaped. Soon after these atrocities the Volunteers came out of hiding and began to patrol the town to prevent any loss of innocent lives or damage. To avoid any direct confrontation the R.I.C., Black and Tans and the British army remained in their barracks.

At that time there were a number of barracks in Bantry, including at the top of Barrack Street, on the Square with a jail (part of Bantry Bay Hotel), Glengarriff Road (next to Murphy's workshop) and the officers' quarters on the north side of Square (O'Sullivans). In addition to these, there were barracks at Glengarriff, Castletownbere and Durrus. In all, there were over 60 members of the R.I.C. in the locality who were well-armed with rifles and handguns. In contrast, there were 154 Volunteers in Bantry alone but these were badly armed, possessing only a few rifles and handguns.

Keeping up the pressure on the R.I.C. four who were patrolling the town and on their way up the 'steps' to the Hospital barracks were met by a burst of gunfire and one of them fell dead while the others ran back towards their barracks on the Square. Despite a search by the Auxiliaries and the 'Black and Tans' no suspicious characters were found. Systematic searches of the houses of all know possible Volunteers commenced. All the Volunteers having received word of what was about to happen, vanished into the countryside to safe houses.

When things returned to near normal, the R.I.C. rounded up a number of the Volunteers including Sean Cotter who they paraded around town in a cart. This was an open invitation to the Volunteers to attack but they did not take the bait and things gradually returned to normal. The outcome of this was that the R.I.C. had to move up to the Hospital barracks of the British army and 'Black and Tans'.

In April 1920 orders were given that all income tax offices all over the country were to be raided and all documents, as well as premises, to be burned. On the same night 315 vacated R.I.C.

barracks were torched. A few nights later those that remained standing were also burnt to the ground. In addition, the houses and mansions of the gentry and all those sympathisers of the English cause were also put to the torch. In Bantry these included the R.I.C barracks and prison on the Square, the officers' office and rooms at the north side, Vickery's Hotel where the British officers were accustomed to drink and many other houses.

Martial law was introduced in the town but despite this move the Deal Yard was burnt to the ground in revenge by the R.I.C. or the Black and Tans depriving over 100 men of their jobs.

XXXII

THE STRUGGLE CONTINUES

The 1916 Proclamation was a declaration which stated that the Irish Republic was a sovereign Independent State and was also a call to arms. During the following years, the combined forces of the British Army and the police force in West Cork was about three thousand men who were well-armed and who could seek refuge in their barracks at any time. Against these were mostly unarmed young men. The people rallied behind these young men but knew that open armed conflict against the British was out of the question.

These young men were the kernel of the newly formed Irish Republican Army which was untrained and unarmed for the most part. This army was called the Third Brigade in West Cork and was divided into seven Battalions covering every major town in the area. These had only 35 rifles, 20 revolvers and some ammunition between them.

In the General Election, held in 1918, over 70 per cent of population voted only for those candidates who pledged to abstain from the British Parliament. Those elected came together in Dublin and formed the Dail Eireann as the Parliament of the Irish people, but two opposing governments could not exist side by side. The Irish Volunteer Army became the army of the newly formed Irish Republic.

To prevent this new body from becoming stronger, the English Government proclaimed the Dail Eireann and all its departments were illegal. To support any further action against this newly formed body the English government sent large numbers of 'Black and Tans' and Auxiliaries to assist the existing forces.

Subject to continuous harassment, searches, and the odd arrest, the Volunteers did not retaliate in West Cork until the 12th of February 1920, when simultaneous attacks were mounted against a number of R.I.C. barracks and various patrols. Many arrests were made and those captured were sentenced to hard labour. These were released some time during their internment but were subject to be picked up and jailed again at any time.

The Brigade Vice-O.C. for Bantry and Castletown was Ted O'Sullivan and various meetings were held in secret locations where progress, locations of the British forces, arms and future activities were discussed. In preparation for any possible outbreak of hostilities the British Government sent 2,000 extra troops to West Cork. These landed in Bantry before leaving for various locations in West Cork.

To counteract this movement of troops, orders came from Dublin that a Flying Column be formed in every Brigade in West Cork to engage the enemy when they harassed or intimidated the local people. The number of men in each Flying Column rose to about 150 men.

After a successful attack on the British Forces at Toureen, rifles and ammunition were sent to Bantry for those training and for any possible attack on British personnel. Some of the rifles were then sent to Dunmanway for training purposes. By this stage, everything was pointing to a possible major encounter between a Flying Column and the English forces.

This came at a place on the road about a mile and half south of Kilmichael when three lorry loads of Auxiliary soldiers were ambushed resulting in the death of about 16 Auxiliaries and four Volunteers. The lorries were set on fire and all arms which consisted of 18 rifles, 2,000 rounds of ammunition, 30 revolvers and a quantity of Mills bombs were captured. After the encounter troops were moved in from all over Munster to apprehend or shoot those who had carried out the attack but the culprits were never located due to the network of safe houses in the countryside.

Around this time, Skibbereen was well-garrisoned with a number of companies of the King's Liverpool Regiment and about 80 R.I.C.

The Commander was Colonel Hudson, who was an honest and fair man with an utter dislike of the R.I.C. When Maurice Donegan, Ralph Keyes, Sean Cotter and Cornelius O'Sullivan from Bantry were arrested on November 30, 1920, and brought to Skibbereen, the R.I.C. wanted to execute them there and then but Colonel Hudson protected the men and sent them off to internment camp.

Despite the deaths of a number of the Volunteers, the efforts to dusrupt the English forces continued. Only the direct rail link with Bantry was serviceable. All branch lines had been blown up. All bridges and roads were either blown up or had trenches dug, so that the army vehicles could not drive through the countryside. Yet, some 11 Volunteers were killed or executed by the members of the Essex Regiment, who were based at Bandon, during the following months. A subsequent attack on Bandon, in revenge, caused the deaths of four members of the Essex Regiment and four others seriously wounded.

With vital information on the movements of the Volunteers being passed on to the British Authorities and the subsequent arrests of members, widespread raids were made. Many informers were killed or executed whether they were Loyalist sympathisers or Catholics eager for money. With the lack of information arriving to the British forces it was decided that the houses of possible Volunteers or their sympathisers in West Cork should be burned to the ground. When notice of these burnings reached Dublin Headquarters the reply was that for every house put to the flame that two houses of those loyal to the British cause would be burned in reprisal. Soon castles, mansions, and residences of the British supporters went up in flames. This 'tit-for-tat' continued for a few months until the English forces were restrained by their commanders.

One of the major actions of the Volunteers was the attack on the R.I.C. barracks at Rosscarbery which was taken after a few hours using Mill bombs and dynamite which had been removed from the internment camp and British Base on Bere Island, transferred to Bantry by sea and loaded on horse and cart destined for divisional headquarters. What remained of the dynamite and fuses were used during the following year during the attacks on other R.I.C. barracks in West Cork.

While the British army and the Auxiliaries were tolerated in the towns of West Cork, the R.I.C. and the Black and Tans were detested and ostracised. They were cursed by the woman, spat upon by the men and called names by the children. Even though they burned down or wrecked shops that refused to serve them, the people still treated them like the scum of the earth. The British forces were almost confined to barracks in Bantry. Trenches had been dug on all the access routes into town and when these were filled in they were soon opened again. On one occasion dynamite was placed in the culvert near the Kilgobbin Inn but it was deemed too dangerous for the local population to detonate this when a British lorry or armoured vehicles passed over it. The same went for telephone wires, these were regularly cut and poles pulled down and removed. Communication was very limited to the outside world and to headquarters at Bandon except by a convoy of armoured trucks or by train.

It is difficult to imagine that the West Cork Brigade which only consisted of a small force of 300 riflemen and another 400 with just a few rifles and handguns could instil such fear and panic into a combined British force of some 2,000 men. No soldier or member of the R.I.C. could walk alone outside his barracks but was usually accompanied by two or three others fully armed in fear of snipers. In Bantry, these were usually located in Blackrock Road, Reenrour and Church Road. During this period the local Volunteers used the attics of Hazel's fish shop, O'Donovan's pub on the quay and the pigeon house on Glengarriff Road as places of refuge and bases of operations. As mentioned earlier, the Pigeon or Chicken House was used by the English over the centuries as a base to collect rents and dues from those entering town.

When the British forces began to round up and imprison all those suspected of being members of the Volunteers, they were sent a message that for the execution of every one of those held two British sympathisers would die. The same applied to the burning of houses. Matters deteriorated to such an extent that every British outpost in West Cork could be attacked at any given time. To counteract this situation, some 20,000 additional British troops were brought in from surrounding counties and a three branch offensive was launched which would gradually enclose and capture the West Cork Brigade.

Travelling by night over mountains and rough terrain the Flying Column found themselves in the dead of night at Ballylickey Bridge and headed up a by-road to Coomhola where they could rest up for awhile.

Having located the house of Marcella Hurley, a safe haven, they ate and rested. Knowing that the British forces were all around them including the last escape route over the Priest's Leap they were in a dire situation. Then one of the local men said that he would take them east across the mountains and bogs to Gougane Barra by an old route which was used by Donal Cam O'Sullivan when he avoided the English during his March to Leitrim in 1602. At nightfall, they departed carrying some food supplies, water and a long rope. At the bogs they all had to following in each other's footsteps while holding onto the rope in case they took a stray step. Eventually, they all arrived safely at Gougane Barra and set up a small camp in the rocky terrain.

After the visit of Michael Collins and Countess Markievicz, there were only three women volunteers to Cumann na mBan, which increased to nine members in Bantry. However, as hostilities increased this number grew to between 20 and 30 in the Bantry region. Their job was to help the injured, wounded and the hungry. They also carried messages on their bikes between different Brigades often covering ten or twenty miles. They also ran 'safe houses'.

In June, when the British gave up in their quest to apprehend the members of the West Cork Flying Column and returned to their barracks in Cork, Macroom and Bandon, a concentrated offensive by the Volunteers commenced. Most of the Loyalist's houses and mansions that remained standing were burnt to the ground including Puxley's Mansion at Castletownbere and Castle Bernard at Bandon as well as all buildings which could be used for new contingent of British forces which were soon to arrive. About this time, to cope with the numbers of suspected Volunteers and sympathizers apprehended, an internment camp was opened on Bere Island

and manned by the Yorkshire Light Infantry. These were also based at Furies Pier and Castletownbere. The guardhouse in the Lonehart battery was used in the beginning before a proper camp was built which had four timber huts holding about 60 men each. Despite permanent guards and barb wire there were at least five successful escapes from the camp before it finally closed on the 10th of December 1921. To support the R.I.C. in Glengarriff a number of Auxiliaries were assigned to that village. Knowing that the village was a hotbed of discontent, a raid was organised by the British forces and twelve armoured tenders full of Auxiliaries who searched every house and bothan for arms and suspected Sinn Fein members. Meanwhile, even though the West Cork Brigade was continuously on the run they still managed to attack the British forces at Crossbarry and Kilmichael where the British suffered substantial losses of both men and arms.

About this time the Brigade headquarters was moved from house to house including Hurleys of Coomhola, Crowleys of Trenamaderee and Sweeneys of Maughnaclea.

Soon news filtered through from Dublin that a number of Dail Eireann members were having tentative talks with representatives of the British Government concerning a possible Truce and a cessation of hostilities but everyone knew that this could only be a temporary lull in hostilities.

XXXIII

CIVIL WAR

The Civil War lasted from June 1922 until May 1923. It was caused by the negotiated Anglo-Irish Treaty which was accepted by Michael Collins, Arthur Griffith and the Sinn Fein delegation in London. De Valera did not travel as he thought that the probable outcome would not be favourable to the Irish people. The Treaty as negotiated declared that 'Ireland would become a free state under Britain and that the six counties of the North would remain part of Britain'. The Free State would become like other members of the Commonwealth such as Canada and Australia with the English monarch ruling as sovereign to whom all representatives of the people had to swear allegiance. These conditions caused a split in the Nationalist Movement resulting in one side been supported by De Valera and the other by Michael Collins who became the commander-in-chief of the Irish Free State Army.

One of the major effects of the establishment of the Irish Free State was the disbanding of the R.I.C. and the returning to Britain of the Auxiliaries, 'Black and Tans' and the British Army who did not want to get mixed up in the confrontation of the two antagonists in the Civil War who both called themselves Sinn Fein. To sort out this problem, Michael Collins established a National Army to replace Sinn Fein.

The conflict between the two sides commenced when De Valera's Sinn Fein forces occupied the Four Courts in Dublin. After borrowing some field guns from the remaining British Army, Michael Collins gave orders to his troops to dislodge the opposition forces from the building. This resulted in the deaths of many of the opposition and the burning down of the Four Courts.

Having gained control in Dublin, Collins ordered, in August 1922, that all the major towns in the country be taken over by his forces. This involved sending troops by boats to the various important ports around the country to avoid conflict on the roads, towns or villages. Not long afterwards, De Valera set up his own Republican Government with most of his support in Munster where the Sinn Fein or Irregulars as they were now called, were against the English Treaty especially those in West Cork who had fought so hard to defeat the English forces.

Now that their comrades were either killed or wounded by the National Army under Collins the Cork Brigades began to mobilise their forces once again. Now, the atrocities began with revenge killings and executions by the Irregulars which were met by similar actions by the National Army. Soon father turned against sons and sons against each other, depending on which side they took. Neighbours fell out and fought against each other and in Bantry where the two sides were fairly well represented a vendetta began with sniper fire from one side of the town to the other resulting in the dispatch by sea of the 30th Battalion of Nationalist soldiers numbering about 200 men. These made their headquarters at the vacated workhouse. General Eoin O'Duffy was appointed by Michael Collins as the commander of the South West Command.

On the 30th of August 1922, the Irregulars mounted an attack on the workhouse but after about four hours had to

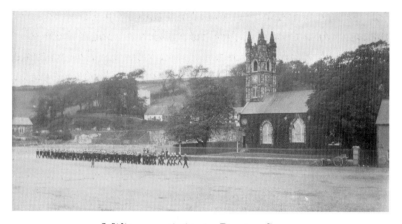

Military activity in Bantry Square

retreat leaving four officers and a number of fighting men dead. Only one Nationalist soldier was killed and a small number wounded in the encounter.

After this, the streets of Bantry were patrolled by the army in groups of eight or ten soldiers under the command of an officer on the orders of Ted Sullivan who had now become a Brigadier of the National Army. He was now in direct opposition against Liam Deasy and Dan Breen, his former comrades. Bantry was no longer a 'hot bed' of revolt against the forces of the Free State. Yet, the Irregulars remained in the area in safe houses including O'Driscoll's house at Reenvanig on Whiddy island from where they used to come ashore at Cove during night hours. Then the whole situation was exasperated by the arrest of De Valera in Dublin by the National Army. Unable to create a solid opposition to the National Army, the Irregulars changed their objective and began to take their vengeance on what remained of the old landlord classes by burning them out of their houses.

Things took a dramatic turn when Michael Collins who had been touring West Cork trying make contact with the

Irregular commanders, Liam Deasy and Dan Breen, and at the same time to consolidate his position amongst those who supported him, was ambushed and shot dead at Beal na Blath which is located between Dunmanway and Macroom, by members of the Irregulars who were following his movements and knew that the only road open to Macroom was the one from Dunmanway.

In fact, there were only five Irregulars who were waiting in ambush as the remainder of the group, thinking that he had taken some other road, had departed. Collins seems to have been killed by a 'dumb-dumb' stray bullet which hit him on the back of his skull killing him instantly. The only one of the Irregulars who had this type of bullet was an Irregular from Dunmanway whose identity was known all over West Cork. In fear of further reprisals, the body of Michael Collins was transported to Cork in an armoured vehicle and then placed on the 'M.V. Classic' which took the remains to Dublin by sea where he received a State funeral.

Some say that De Valera, who had been released from prison, ordered the West Cork Irregulars to kill Michael Collins.

XXXIV

THE SPANISH FISHING FLEET IN BANTRY

From time immemorial Spaniards were fishing off the south coast of Ireland. In the Book of Innisfallen we find a reference to three Spanish sailors being washed ashore on the coast c. 1200 BCE and Spaniards fishing and curing fish in some of the ports of the South West including Baltimore, Crookhaven, Bantry, Castletownbere, Valentia and Dingle. Then there is the reference to Princess Beara, daughter of the king of Breogan, which related how the Prince of Munster went to Spain and married her c. 200 BCE. Returning to Bantry Bay, he named the north peninsula Beara in honour of his wife who had passed away at a young age sometime after their arrival.

The next reference is more 'modern' and relates that many ships departed from Bantry with cured pilchards for the ports of the north of Spain from c. 1558. This renewal of contact generated trade in wine and spirits. Further contact was made in 1601 when the King of Spain sent a fleet of ships with troops and ordnance to assist the Irish in their conflict with England under Queen Elizabeth.

The next sighting of ships from Spain was just after the Second World War when the Spanish fishing fleet ventured across Biscay to our coast. The first pair arrived on a calm May morning when the sea was like a sheet of glass. In the distance at the northern entrance they appeared like phantom ships with their long funnels belching black smoke and their white hulls reflecting against the background of the wooded area of Ardnagashel. When they were eventually guided to and moored to the stone pier, it took some time for the local fishermen to realise that they were Spanish trawlers from Galicia.

Soon the local townspeople congregated on the pier to observe these strange men who had arrived from a far away country. After a doctor visiting aboard a sailor with a broken leg was transferred to the Mercy Hospital in Cork. The sailor was collected some ten days later and both ships sailed off to their home port in Galicia, Spain, loaded with fish.

We thought that this was just a visit of necessity and that we would never see the trawlers again. How mistaken we were in our false predictions.

About two weeks later the silence of the dawn was broken by a cacophony of ships' steam horns blowing in the distance. Soon eight or nine trawlers were being guided into the harbour. In time, they were all moored at the pier each abreast of one another. As soon as their particular needs were understood they were taken care of by the Harbour Master whether there were injured or sick crewmen aboard or if there were some mechanical problems. This was the beginning of some 25 years where the Spanish fishing fleet would use Bantry as their base or home from home.

During the rest of that summer, more and more trawlers came into port. Word had spread around the fleet that Bantry was a place of refuge where most of their problems would be solved. Nearly all of the vessels were of timber and painted in white with steam propulsion.

They carried coal and fresh water tanks for their boilers and had little or no navigation aids. A dry paper sounder was used for fishing and communication was by radio transmitter which only had a range of a few hundred miles. The accommodation aboard was forward and consisted of a space with about ten bunks where the crew slept, if they had a chance, and where they ate during bad weather. Most of the crew worked on deck, gutted fish and slept in the same clothes regardless of the weather. Using ropes and wires in poor conditions and steam winches which could not cope with the strain of hauling in the trawl there were many accidents including deaths. The sick and the injured were brought to Bantry for medical attention and if they were in a serious condition they would be transferred to a hospital in Cork. The dead were either buried in the Abbey graveyard or else transported back to Spain in the ice hold of the trawler.

Many of the trawlers remained on the fishing grounds for the winter of 1948. Towards the end of December the weather seriously deteriorated and the fishing fleet began to seek shelter in Bantry.

By the 23rd of December trawlers were entering harbour at every hour of the day and night until there were 127 vessels in the harbour. With the extreme hurricane force winds no one ventured outside of the harbour. Everyone realised that they would have to spend Christmas on foreign shores far from their families at home. With the scarcity of food many of the crews had to put up with the barest essentials of bread, fish and vegetables. On Christmas Eve most of the crews came ashore and spent the time walking the street singing Christmas Carols in Spanish to pass the time away. With over 1,500 sailors in town the local population was outnumbered by strangers.

A few of the trawlers ventured out during a lull in the weather about the 29th but the majority remained in port for the New

Year. The majority departed either for their home ports or to the fishing grounds during the first week of the New Year and the town had a short period of peace and quietness. But this lasted only a few weeks until a number of trawlers came into port having suffered wheelhouse and bulwark damage during a sudden storm. They were the lucky ones as we were informed that two trawlers had vanished without sending out a distress call or signal. These tragedies were not going to be the last ones as some twelve trawlers went to the bottom during the following few years. Some of the crews were rescued but the majority went to a watery grave.

From the early 1950s some 50 trawlers entered Bantry each week for one reason or another. As they commenced to trawl individually from the side many ended up with a wire, rope or trawl on the propeller. This necessitated that they be towed to the nearest port, like Bantry, where the obstruction could be removed by a diver. In those days the divers used a hard helmet, dry suit and weights with air supplied by an air

Four pairs of Trawlers on Bantry Pier

pump either on the deck or else on the quayside. When scuba diving gear was introduced sometime later these were used by experienced divers.

With the increase of crewmen dying from injuries or sickness, in addition to the bodies picked up at sea, the Spanish burial plot at the Abbey became over-full and another section of the graveyard was dedicated to foreign seamen. In time, many of those interred were removed and sent back to their families in Spain. Those who had survived serious accidents and had lost limbs were flown home to Spain, lucky to be alive, and spent the rest of their lives doing menial and easy jobs like mending nets on the quayside.

In time Spanish became the second language of the town where everyone knew some Spanish words and sentences. It was quite normal to be greeted in the morning with 'buenas dias' or for the evening with 'buenas tardes'. Even the swear words came into common usage. Many of townspeople made friends with some crewmen and captains and invited them to their houses for an Irish meal which consisted of a pigs head and cabbage or a rabbit stew as it was extremely difficult to get proper food in those days after the war.

When some trawlers were confined to port during fine weather due to some serious mechanical problem it was not unusual to see the local boys and the crews, always playing with bare feet, playing a game of soccer on the sandy Square. It was always Ireland against Spain but the crews always won.

In the 1960s the timber trawlers were withdrawn from the fishing grounds and a new type of trawler emerged. Instead of steam or oil fired boiler power they were propelled by diesel engines and had all the modern fishing and navigational aids which were most foreign to Spain. All of these caused major problems as the captains and engineers didn't know how to

Steel Trawler on Bantry Pier in Winter

use them so they came into Bantry for guidance on their first fishing trips. In the majority of cases their problems were solved by calling in the manufactures representatives from various countries.

The numbers of trawlers entering Bantry gradually decreased in the mid 1960s due to the complete modernisation of the fleet. They only entered when it was a case of utmost necessity. The loss of fishing time was serious and they tried to avoid this at all costs. With the congestion of service boats involved in the building of the Gulf Oil Terminal, space at the pier to moor was non existent. This automatically convinced the captains to locate another port where they could berth and get attention. This port was Castletownbere which was on the north side of the entrance to Bantry and was one of the main fishing ports of the country. Except for the occasional visit the Spanish fishing fleet had abandoned Bantry.

273

XXXV

GULF OIL AND THE SUPER TANKERS

When the representatives of Gulf Oil first visited Bantry Bay in December of 1965 with a view of building a crude oil terminal with adjoining deep water, they first looked at the suitability of the eastern part of Bere Island. They found that the location was unsuitable due to the dangerous entrance between Roancarrig Lighthouse and the Dog Rock and the large swell running on the south side of Bere Island.

Returning up the bay, they then looked at the western end of Whiddy Island and seeing that the heavy swell had subsided and that there was more than adequate depth of water on the north side, concluded that this was a more suitable location. Within about 12 months the equipment and heavy machinery moved in and work commenced. Few realized at that time that Bantry would be changed dramatically from a dead seaside location into a 'boom town' and once again figure on the world map.

With the influx of Irish, English, Belgian, Swedish and those of other nationalities, local accommodation was at a premium, from Bantry to Glengarriff and beyond. Hotels and guesthouses were taken over, houses and garages were quickly converted and restaurants sprung up overnight. When accommodation was no longer available, caravans and mobile homes were used. These were parked on the Square and suitable fields in the locality.

With over 750 additional workers in the town, business picked up, especially the outlets for food and drink. Working 24 hours per day, seven days a week, severe pressure was brought to bear so that the terminal would be completed in time to coincide with the arrival of the first mammoth tanker, the *Universe Ireland*, which did arrive amidst much celebration and fanfare.

From 1968 onwards, there were an average of 17–20 tankers each month, some loaded with crude from the Persian Gulf and small tankers engaged in the distribution to the European refineries. The tanker traffic brought a certain amount of revenue to the town as crews came ashore and made some purchases to eventually take home to their families. In addition, the Terminal employed about 150 men employed directly and some 50 part-time workers.

At the beginning of 1975, the price of crude oil dropped due to the use of the Suez Canal by tankers up to 125,000 tons and the viability of the Terminal came into question. The number of tankers using the Terminal dropped dramatically and there was a general cut back on services. Many people came to the conclusion that the Terminal would close. However, due to damage to the jetty at the crude oil terminal at Leixeos, in Portugal, a number of tankers were diverted to Bantry Bay. Two of these were the *Casiope* and the *Betelgeuse*, both of approximately 220,000 tonnes. After a delay of a few days, the *Betelgeuse* was berthed at the jetty, at 23.30 hours on Saturday, the 7th of January 1979, and began pumping crude oil ashore.

Sunday, the 8th of January, was a normal day with the usual service boats running to and from the tanker and the terminal. Many of the tanker crew came ashore and spent time purchasing some goods in the shops that were opened. What happened later that night will remain in the minds of every Bantry person as long as they live.

At midnight, the discharge of the *Betelgeuse* was proceeding normally. The service boat to the tanker was completing its last trip with crew while the service boat to the Terminal and the boat on standby were mooring to the service pier at the island. Nothing seemed out of the ordinary.

Sometime around 00.40 hours a rumbling sound was heard by a number of people on the mainland, which seemed to come from the location of the Terminal with the wind from the south-west. This was followed by flames from the vicinity of the jetty/tanker. This was immediately followed by an immense explosion and the whole sky was lit up with black smoke billowing over the island and town. Other minor explosions followed as the town's fire siren was sounded. There was major bedlam in the town as people emerged from their homes and hearing that there was a fire at the Terminal ran towards the local pier, especially those with men-folk on duty that night

Whiddy Terminal with the wreck of the Betelgeuse

either on the jetty or on the island.

Very few people knew what exactly had happened. Most of them thought that tanks on the Terminal itself had caught fire and exploded, but those who had VHF radio contact with the island knew that the tanker *Betelgeuse* had exploded and caught fire. Within minutes Bantry pier was in a state of mayhem, with cars and people arriving from every direction, who immediately commandeered the service boats moored for the night at the pier. Soon, most of the boats departed with fire-personnel, fire officers, terminal workers, managerial staff and volunteers. Quickly, the word was passed around that the fire was on the tanker and the mooring jetty and everyone wondered about the fate of the tanker crew and jetty personnel, who were all local. As soon as the emergency personnel were dropped off at the service pier, some of the boats headed out to the north side of the island. What greeted them was a sight not easily forgotten.

Both the tanker and the jetty were engulfed in a raging inferno of burning crude oil. The sea was on fire to the north and east for a distance of about a mile with flames leaping upwards 20 to 50 feet. A dense black pall of smoke moved slowly north-east with the light wind while the fumes and the lack of oxygen made it difficult to breathe. Skirting the flaming sea, a service boat approached Dolphin I and then searched for any survivors who might have escaped the inferno. This boat was joined by a tug and they both searched together, but neither survivors nor bodies were found or floating in the water. It seemed that those on the tanker and the jetty had made their way to Dolphin 22 to wait to be picked up by a service boat which never arrived. Acting as skipper on a air-sea rescue launch I was the first to arrive on the scene.

With the early light of dawn the magnitude of the disaster became evident with the pall of smoke now extending inland

The remains of the Betelgeuse

and the flames could still be seen overlapping the storage tanks. As soon as crews had been changed on both the tugs and the service boats, the search for bodies began. Relations of those who were on duty on the Terminal huddled anxiously on Bantry pier, hoping against hope that their loved ones had somehow survived. Shrunken and oil-covered bodies began to be recovered about mid-day and were removed to Bantry Hospital.

Gulf management ordered a complete blackout to the Press and only prepared statements were released mainly due to the exact time that the fire started. In fact, there was between ten and fifteen minutes of a difference between reports from the mainland and when the alarm was raised. Not long afterwards, the Government decided to hold an Enquiry into the disaster.

With no further tanker traffic entering the bay, crews and personnel were laid up except the few who were engaged in the salvage work undertaken by Smit-Tak, from Holland. The Betelgeuse had broken up into three sections due to the force of the explosion and these were removed one by one until work was completed that September. The Terminal was put in moth balls with only a number of security men employed. As for those others that were employed, they found themselves redundant and seeking new jobs. As for the findings of the Enquiry, the question of the lost time in sounding the general alarm was never solved or fully explained.

The Terminal was handed over to the Irish Government and then the oil company Texaco-Chevron took over. The storage tanks were repaired and the whole installation received a complete overhaul. Instead of rebuilding the Jetty, a single buoy mooring installation was placed about a mile north of the ruins of the jetty and a pipeline to the tanks on the island was placed on the seabed. Since then, the Terminal has been used by a number of tankers each month which nowhere approaches the volume of tanker traffic of the early days.

XXXVI

BANTRY SINCE 1980

As a parting settlement Gulf Oil Inc. 'donated' ten million Punt to the Irish State for the damage that had been caused to the economy of Bantry and West Cork by the tanker disaster. Expecting new industries that would give jobs to the unemployed, the people of Bantry waited in vain. Hopes had been high for the rebuilding of Bantry pier and the dredging of the inner harbour so that the port of Bantry could attract maritime industries and sea traffic. However, no funds were forthcoming for Bantry and the money was spent on developments in other West Cork towns and infrastructure. Bantry was left to its own devises as usual. This was nothing strange as each government, over the years, treated the town in the same way and left it to survive on its own.

Knowing that Bantry harbour had a thriving oyster industry in the past, a number of individuals including Sean O Luasa and Brendan Minihane built a timber raft and began to experiment in the cultivation of mussels. This enterprise became a success and many more rafts were used until eventually the inner harbour area became one large cultivation area using rope lines and 45 gallon drums as floats. After a year or so, a small factory was set up to handle the mussels and then later two large factories were built at Gearhies near Bantry where about a hundred people were employed. In addition, as the industry is labour-intensive, many part time jobs were created in the cleaning and grading of the mussels. This industry continues with an annual export of between 5,000 and 10,000 tons per annum.

In addition to the mussel industry, a small industrial park was set up where small business enterprises could commence production. Murnane & O'Shea Ltd. became one of the largest building contractors in Munster employing over 200 workers. They were joined by many other small building firms, as well as ancillary firms who operated in both Cork and Kerry. Now, however, with the recession in the building trade, many of these small firms will find it difficult to exist.

With the remodelling of the Square and the building of the new hotel at the Docks, Bantry has come to be regarded as a place of prosperity. With the long awaited improvements to the local beach, Bantry will once again take on the appearance of a holiday resort. All that is required now is the development of the inner dock area as a marina and the dredging of the area adjoining the pier. Lets hope that these projects proceed in the near future.

APPENDIX 1

Down Survey 1855

For those interested the following is a list of inhabitants for the lower part of the town after the famine.

Donovan's Lane (next to Bantry Bay) .... 8 tenants

Tom's Lane (Cinema) .... 11 tenants

Stormy Lane (Evans' Corner) .... 7 tenants

Aghalane Road (Scart Rd.) .... 30 tenants

Piper's Lane (off Scart Rd.) .... 5 tenants

Orchid Lane (off Blackrock Rd.) .... 15 tenants

Water's Lane (behind J.J.Crowley's) .... 12 tenants

New Chapel Road (as existing) .... 28 tenants

Fair Green (original village – off Bridge St.) .... 5 tenants

The Quay (B. of I. to J. J. Crowley's) .... 5 tenants

New Road (Evans to Tom's Lane) .... 3 tenants

Blackrock Lane (J. J. Crowley's Lane) .... 3 tenants

Young's Point (House at Nr. Side of Slob) .... 3 tenants

Marino Lane to Bantry Beach (Old Reenrour Rd)) .... 21 tenants

Marino Tce .... 3 tenants

Marino House .... 3 tenants

APPENDIX 2

LIST OF WRECKS IN BANTRY BAY AND NEARBY
(Including Dunmanus and Kenmare Bays)

YEAR	SHIP'S NAME	CARGO	LOCATION
1613	*'Pearl'*	General, with silver	South side of Dursey Island or Deenish West?
1665	*'Bonaventure'*	General	Indigo Rock
1683	*'Infanta'* (Spanish Galleon)		Bantry Bay S. of Bere Island
1692	*'French Privateer'* (32 Guns)		Outer Bantry Bay in 47 fathoms
1732	*'James West'* (English Sloop)	Indiaman	White Horse R.
1770	Unknown	Mixed cargo	Bantry Bay
1778	*'John and James'*	Light	Ballycrovane
1781	*'William and Anne'* (English Sloop)	Tobacco & general	Ballycrovane
1781	*'Nuestra Senora de Palerma'*	Wine/Port	Ballycrovane
1782	*'Peter'* (Brig.)	General cargo to West Indies	Piper Sound
1796	*'Sisters of Liverpool'*	Unknown	Outer Bay
1797	*'Surveillante'*	Transporter	Whiddy Island

1797	'Beaver'	Timber	Whiddy Island
1797	'Sisters'	Timber	Ardna Point
1797	'Fille Unique'	Transporter	South Bere Is.
1800	'Betsy'	Unknown	Garinish West
1811	'Canada' (Brig)	Mahogany	Off D. Castle
1814	'Baring'	Guns/Ammun.	Piper's Sound
1822	'Unity'	General	Piper's Sound
1822	'Argo'	General	Piper's Sound/ Bere Island
1827	'Martin'	Unknown	Berehaven
1830	'Joseph Shaw'	Timber	Bere Is. SW tip
1830	'Sally'	Unknown	Blackball Head
1830.c.	'Valliant' (Brig)	Unknown	Crow Head
1830	'Josias'	Unknown	Blackball Head
1831	'Effort'	Unknown	SW Dursey Is.
1831	'Vittoria'	Unknown	Bere Island
1835	'Fitzroy'	Unknown	Dunmanus Bay Dunkelly
1837	'Oralia'	Unknown	S. Bere Island
1838	'Triphena'	Oats	Piper's Sound
1839	'Henry?'	Unknown	Bantry Bay
1839	'Elisa' ?	Unknown	Bantry Bay
1840	'Emmeline'	Timber	Off Garnish E.

1842	'Leon' (Sloop)	Spirits	Outside Piper Sound
1835	'Earl of Leicester'	Unknown	Dog Rock
1849	'Ocean' (Brig.)	Timber	Dursey Island
1849	Derelict Brig.	Cotton	SW Bere Is.
1850	'John Bull'	Light	E. of Bally Donegan
1850	'Ranger'	Wheat	Dunmanus Bay
1850	'Caroline'	Salvage	E. Dunmanus Bay
1850	'Mountaineer'	Timber	Carbery Is.
1851	'Jolly Tar'	Coal	Piper Sound
1852	'Eliza'	Coal	Dog Rock
1853	'Luisa Christina'	Unknown	Cleinderry
1859	'Wizard' (Brig.)	Guns	Roancarrig Beg
1860	'Miner'	Copper Ore	Ballydonegan
1861	'Emily' (Brig.)	Light	Dog Rock
1867	'Pencalenick'	Timber	Ballydonegan
1867	'Naiad' (Brig.)	Timber	Dog Rock
1874	'Kate Dawson' (Smack)	General	Dog Rock
1874	'Shamrock' (Schooner)	Coal	Palmer;s Rock.
1874	'Cardross' (Schooner)	Mahogany	Bantry Bay
1876	'Joseph Howe' (Brig.)	Mahogany	S.W. Bere Is.

1876	*'Florence'*	Coal	Ballydonegan
1876	*'Felix'* (Barque)	Cotton	Adrigole
1878	*'Bessie Young'*	Coal	Dog Rock
1878	*'Rio Farmosa'*	General	Bantry Bay
1880	*'Sophia Margaret'* (Schooner)	Coal	Ballydonegan
1882	*'David Jenkins'* (Schooner)	Coal	Ballydonegan
1882	*'Commodore'* (Brig)	Guano	Piper Sound
1884	*'Three Brothers'*	Light	SW Bere Is.
1886	*'Augusta'*	Unknown	Dunmanus Bay
1888	*'Karen Elsie'*	Light	Ballydonegan
1889	*'Fancy'*	Light	Garniah West
1893	*'Esperance'*	Fish	Piper Sound
1893	*'John Stonard'*	Slate	Lea Rock/Dursey
1896	*'Iberian'*	Cattle	S. of Bird Island
1904	*'Areil'* (Ketch)	Copper ore	Piper Sound
1907	*'Evyln'* (Trawler)	Fish	SW Piper Sound
1908	*'Reggio'* (Cargo vessel)	Coal	Dog Rock
1908	*'N.D. de Bologne'* (French trawler)	Fish	Dog Rock
1908	*'Bonnie Lass'* (Trawler)	Fish	Dog Rock
1914	*'Irish Girl'* (Schooner)	Fertiliser	SW Bere Island

1917	'Ina Williams' (Fishing boat)	Fish	Bull Rock
1918	'Petrel' (Schooner)	Coal	Piper Sound
1921	'John Casewell' (E. Trawler)	Fish	Dog Rock
1930	'Caliph' (Trawler)	Fish	Dursey Island
1930	'Aranvale' (Trawler)	Fish	S. of Roancarrig
1952	'Mass 19' (S. Trawler)	Fish	Donavan's Point
1962	'Josepha Lopez' (S. Trawler)	Fish	Roancarrig Rock
1974	'Monte Izazkun' (S. Trawler)	Fish	SW Piper Sound
1986	'Contessa Viv' (S. Trawler)	Fish	N. Piper Sound
1988	'Talay Mendi' (S. Trawler)	Fish	N. Piper Sound
1990	'Garadosa' (S. Trawler)	Fish	Roancarrig Beg

Other possible wrecks with incomplete details:

Two English trawlers off Gearans

One trawler west of Sheelane Island

Unknown wreck off Sheep's Head, possibly Spanish + plane

Small brig on Portuguese Rock

'Arantes' off Leal Point

Two unknown wrecks in bay south of Bere Island

APPENDIX 3

Rail and sea links

Vessels of the Bantry Bay Steamship Company

SS Countess of Bantry
This vessel was built in Belfast in 1884. She was an iron vessel with a Compound Steam Engine and was 92 feet long with a beam of 17 feet. Withdrawn from service in 1935.

SS Lady Elsie
This vessel was built in Greenock, Scotland, in 1906. She was a steel-plated vessel with a Compound Steam Engine. Dimensions were 87 feet long by 19 feet beam. She was withdrawn from service in 1936.

SS Princess Beara
This vessel was also built in Greenock in 1901 and was also a steel plated vessel. Dimension were 115 feet long by 21 feet beam. Withdrawn from service in 1948.

SS Lady Betty Balfour
She was built at Paisley in 1884 and was also a steel-plated vessel with a Compound Steam Engine. She was 70 feet long and had a beam of 14 feet. She was withdrawn from service in 1922.

The following are some extracts from the Press regarding the Bantry Railway Terminus.

FIRST TRAIN TO BANTRY
(*Skibbereen Eagle* – 4th of July 1881)

A Special train ran from Cork(Albert Quay Depot) on Sunday, 3rd of July, for the Directors' party. The line was opened to the public on the following Monday, the 4th.

The Bantry terminus is an exceedingly neat and handsome structure. The contractor, Mr. Dowling, exceeding what he had to do in erecting such an edifice, and on coming under its friendly shelter (it was a two-storey building, with a roof over the platform and tracks) one was sheltered from the wind and rain. Mr. McBirney, Dublin (CBSC Chairman), was the first person to step out onto the platform, followed by the Directors, Lawyers and commercial men. A wagonette from Vickery's Hotel collected the passengers and transported them down to the town.

SERIOUS ACCIDENT,
BANTRY TRAIN WRECKED, FOUR INJURED
(*Cork Constitution* – 8th of July 1887)

The Mail train, which left Cork at 3 AM yesterday morning, on approaching Bantry terminus, moved rather faster than usual, running over the turntable at the end of the line and in doing so knocked away the buffer stop. This portion of the line was built on an embankment, some six feet high, over which the engine fell, pulling with it the carriages, van and wagon. So great was the speed that the engine and carriages were partly embedded in the ground. The driver, Mr. Kiely, was thrown off and seriously injured, as was the fireman Mr. Twomey. The guard of the train, who was at his brakes, was thrown against the brake levers and suffered only from shock.

There was only one passenger, a Captain Shea, who was to join the *Augusta.* He was thrown down and received some back injuries.

News of the accident was telegraphed to Cork, and the services of Dr. Cotter, the Company's consulting physician, and a Dr. Guiseni, resident physician of the South Infirmary Hospital, being secured, a special train was sent immediately to Bantry.

ROYAL TRAVELLER

On Monday the 16th of July, 1888, Prince Edward of Axe-Weimar travelled the Prince of Wales route, joining the 8.55 am train Bantry to Cork.

OPENING OF NEW STATION AT BANTRY
(CBSC Advertisement in *Skibbereen Eagle*)

On and from Saturday, the 22nd of October, 1892, the new station at Bantry, near the pier, will be opened for public travel, and the present station will be closed. All trains leaving from Bantry will depart ten minutes earlier than at present, and all down trains will arrive at Bantry ten minutes later than present.

For particulars see timetables.

All that remains to be said about the railway is that if it did not cease to operate in 1961, it would have benefited from the construction of the Gulf Oil Terminal when over 1000 workmen were employed and over 250,000 tons of materials were transported to Bantry.

APPENDIX 4

Fifth Battalion of the Cork Volunteers – Bantry

1917   Battalion Commandant, Michael Murray

1918   Battalion Commandant, Dan O'Mahony

1919 (16th of August)
Battalion Commandant, Ted O'Sullivan
Battalion Vice-Commandant, Maurice Donegan
Battalion Adjutant, Sean Cotter
Battalion Quartermaster, Michael O'Callaghan

1920 (January)
Sean Lehane succeeds Maurice Donegan as Vice-Commandant

1920 (March)
Maurice Donegan, succeeds Sean Lehane
Michael Harrington, succeeds Sean Cotter

1920 (June)
Sean Cotter, succeeds Michael Harrington

1920 (August)
Battalion Commandant, Maurice Donegan – captured 21/11/'20
Battalion Vice-Commandant, Tom Ward, Durrus
Battalion Adjutant, Sean Cotter – captured 21/11/'20
Battalion Quartermaster, Michael O'Callaghan

1920 (Nov)
Battalion Commandant, Tom Ward
Battalion Vice- Commandant, Denis Keohane, Caheragh
Battalion Adjutant, Michael Harrington
Battalion Quartermaster, Michael O'Callaghan
Battalion Intelligence Officer, Tom Reidy
Battalion Transport, Miah Houlihan
Battalion Engineer, Dan Sweeney

APPENDIX 5

Company Captains of the West Cork Brigade

Fifth Battalion – Bantry	*Glengarriff*	*Coomhola*
R.P.Keyes	Jack Downey	Denny Jer O'Sullivan
Jim Sullivan	Tim McCarthy	Denis Cronin
Jerh. Sullivan	Michael O'Brien	Michael Driscoll
Jerh. McCarthy		
Cecil Keyes		

Kealkil	*Pearson\s Bridge*	*Drumsullivan*
Patsy Sweeney	Jerh. Mullins	Denis Cadogan
John Wrynne	Tim O'Connor	Denis Hurey
William Dillon	Pat Crowley	Con Manning
Paul Sullivan		

* * *

Cumann Na mBan – Women Auxiliaries of the Volunteers

Bantry

Bridie MacSweeney	Kate Ann Coughlan	Molly O'Donoghue

* * *

Details of the Strength of the English Forces based locally

Bantry:	15 R.I.C. and 200 Military
Kilcrohane:	8 R.I.C.
Glengarriff:	6 R.I.C.
Whiddy Island:	4 R.I.C. and 12 Military
Bere Island:	150 Military
Castletown:	13 R. I. C. and 80 Military.

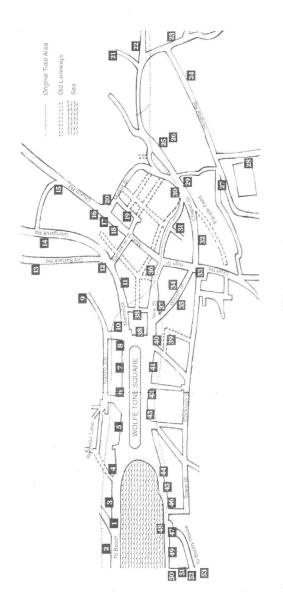

Plan of Bantry Town

APPENDIX 6

Key To Bantry Town Plan

1 *The Road to Beach*
This road leads to what remains of the Railway Pier. Built of timber in 1893–4, it was used by The Bantry Bay Steamship Company, who operated a service to the other ports of Bantry Bay with *The Countess of Bantry*, the *Lady Elsie* and the *Princess Beara* from the 1890s and for the first 20years of the 20th century. All that remains is a section that has been turned into a promenade.

2 *Site of the Bantry railway station*
The original station of the Cork, Bandon & South Coast Railway was up near the hospital (28) and opened in 1880. The extension down around the town was completed in 1892 by the Bantry Extension Railway Company. This station operated until 1961 on a site originally reclaimed from the sea.

3 *Terminus Hotel*
This hotel operated during the years of the railway station and was owned by the O'Sullivan family. The duty levied on livestock leaving the area by rail was collected here on fair days by the agents of the Earl of Bantry.

4 *Protestant School*
This was built c. 1853 by the 'Board of First Fruits' and was opened in 1855.

5 *'Áras Beanntrai'*
This building was once the Bantry Technical School. The site was reclaimed from the foreshore of the inner harbour and was called Beach Strand during the 19th century. It was the location of Mr Meade's Fish Palace during the 17th century.

6 *Protestant Church*
Work started on the building of the church in 1818 and it was extended in 1858. The church clock chimed for the first time at midnight to welcome in the 20th century.

7 *Church Grounds*
The area from the church grounds to the end of the block is the site of the 'Palais de Peche' (Bantry Fish Palace) where from the early 1700s until 1842 over 1000 people worked in processing and barrelling pilchards, herrings etc. Boats loaded with fish landed on the beach in front of the present buildings. The present grey house was the location of a later Customs House and then an R.I.C. office.

8 *Bantry Arms Hotel*
The western part of this large building was the residence of the Bantry House land agent and the last two buildings comprised the Bantry Arms Hotel or Godson's Hotel. The hotel had a short existence between 1852 and 1862 as the owner went bankrupt.

9 *Old Convent*
This site was previously occupied by a large house of the Hutchinson family but was almost in ruins by 1865. It was taken over by the Sisters of Mercy from Cork who used it until moving to their new convent building in 1859. The building is now the Revenue Commissioners office.

10 *Methodist Church*
This was built by the local congregation and opened on the 13th of September 1866. It is now a doctor's surgery.

11 *Tannery Yard*
The location of one of the largest tannery yards in Bantry with an area of around 900 square metres.

12 *Barracks*
The early English army barracks gave its name to Barrack Street.

13 *Old Barrack Road*
This was the original north road out of the early town and in the 18th century was densely populated with cabins and huts.

14 *Glengarriff Road*
Originally called New Barrack Road and afterwards Glengarriff Coach
Road and the Royal Mail Road.

15 *Boy's Club (Bantry Community Centre)*
The main part of this building was constructed in 1950 by volunteers from
the town on a site known as the 'Corn Field'.

16 *Garryvurcha Church & Graveyard*
The church was built around 1720. A number of the Earls of Bantry are
buried here as are members of prominent protestant families.

17 *Cattle Pound*
Below the graveyard was the Cattle Pound where livestock seized from
defaulting tenants of the Bantry Estate were held for sale in lieu of rent. It
gave its name to the lower part of the street opposite (Pound Lane) which
is now called Market Street.

18 *Kingston's Hotel*
This hotel was one of the first in Bantry and existed prior to the 1830s.

19 *New Lane*
Running south from Market Street to Bridge Street, this was one of the
earliest commercial streets in town and the location of Murphy's Flour Mill.

20 *The English Market*
The stone frontage of the Market built by the Earl of Bantry can still be seen.
The upper section of the street consisted of Ash Lane and Chapel Road.

21 *Convent of Mercy*
The land was donated to the sisters by Mr J Cotter. The foundation stone
was laid in 1859 and the chapel built in 1878.

22 *Original Catholic Church*
The original thatched church was where the priest's houses now stand.

23 *Young's Brewery*
One of the cider breweries of the locality was on the site now occupied
by the old people's homes (Cuan Mhuire).

24 Boys' National School
There is a housing estate where the Ard Mhuire school was built in 1899. It was extended in 1929 and closed in 1980.

25 Original School
This was where the middle church gates now stand and was built in 1824. Around that time there were over 20 private schools in the town.

26 Catholic Church
The central long structure was built in 1826 and the wings added in 1846.

27 Original Railway Station
This was the station before the line was extended round the town to the beach area.

28 Hospital
This was the location of the Bantry Workhouse completed in 1845 which during the famine years was the refuge of up to 950 people. Nearby was the Fever Hospital and to the south the paupers' graveyard where many were buried in the famine years.

29 Bantry Town Hall
This is now part of the Centra Stores near the church. It was built by voluntary labour of the farming community c.1880 as a meeting hall. It was later used as a concert and dance hall.

30 Bantry Mills
The Bantry Woollen mills occupied the site of the present library and part of the car park below. With its reservoir above the church grounds and its large wheel overlooking Bridge Street it was an important landmark in the town.

31 The 'Fair Field'
Up the laneway to the side of Bridge Street was the original site of the hamlet of Bantry where some twenty huts were located around the Fair Field where the early markets were held.

32 Godson's Folly
This is the rock-cut on Chapel Street which facilitated coach access to the newly filled in Square and to Godson's Hotel (Bantry Arms Hotel). The only other access to the lower town from the east was via a bridge opposite the

lower church gates. This was privately owned by Mr Kingston who owned a hotel and who denied access to Mr. Godson's clientele. This private undertaking bankrupted Mr. Godson.

33 *Customs Gap*
This is where dues and tariffs were levied on livestock entering town from the south. Scart Road or Aghalane Road was the main access route from the south.

34 *Tanneries*
There were two tanneries in this vicinity – one to the left going up Scart Road and the other occupied the site of the present Post Office.

35 *Butter Exchange*
Warner's Butter Exchange was located where the present car park operates on William Street. Opened around 1880, it became the biggest butter market outside of Cork.

36 *Vickery's Hotel*
This was one of the first hotels in Bantry and occupied the section of building nearest the laneway. The hotel was burnt down in 1921 and later rebuilt and extended. At the rear is a network of small lanes which date from the 18th century. Retaining the façade the whole building is due to be demolished and changed into apartments.

37 *Anchor Bar and Hotel*
This was originally called the Railway Hotel c. 1893 and then became known as Canty's Hotel.

38 *Bridewell Jail and Courthouse*
The jail was located between the present courthouse building and the Bridewell Lane. It was a high walled compound with two buildings in the centre. The courthouse was built at the same time as the jail in 1842 and was burnt down in 1921. The existing building now changed to a Tourism Office was built in 1924.

39 *Tannery Yard and Warehouse*
These were located on some old quays on the site of the present Bank of Ireland and the area to the rear of J. J. Crowley's pub. A laneway at the rear was called Water's Lane.

40 *Lannin's Hotel*
This occupied part of the premises of J. J. Crowleys and was constructed on the original quayside.

41 *Flour and Grain Warehouses*
These occupied the area where the Allied Irish Bank is situated. It was later changed into a garage premises by a Mr. Kelly. Also in this area, Coen's pharmacy was once the Garda station with the customs office upstairs.

42 *R.I.C. Barracks and Jail*
This was situated at the section of the Bantry Bay Hotel which adjoins the lane. It was burnt down in 1921.

43 *McCarthy's Hotel*
The hotel occupied the centre section of the present Bantry Bay Hotel.

44 *The Central Hotel*
This occupied the building which is now the Brick Oven and restaurant.

45 *The 'Rink'*
Occupying the area of the present Garda Barracks this consisted of Lyon's chicken and egg packing enterprise. On the second floor was a dance hall/cinema.

46 *Flour and Salt Warehouses*
These were located on the site of the new apartments and retail units and were owned by the MacCarthys of Scart.

47 *East Gate to Bantry House*
Prior to the building the gate house, access to Bantry House was down Blackrock Road and through Tower Lane.

48 *Bantry Docks*
These were planned in 1829 but due to lack of finance they were not built until c. 1847 as a famine relief project.

49 *The New Road*
This road from the town to the graveyard was built in two stages – the first part as far as the 'Black Rock' and then the continuation to the graveyard. It became known as the Royal Mail New Road.

50 *The Stone Pier*
This pier was built after the Famine by W.M.Murphy. Before the adjoining area silted up large sailing ships berthed on the east side.

51 *The Black Rock*
Situated off the road to the graveyard under the cannons of Bantry House was the original pier where sailing ships moored to a timber extension. It was the location from where the emigrants sailed to the New World.

52 *Bantry House*
Originally known as Blackrock House and then Seafield House, Bantry House was built in three stages and is now one of the major attractions for visitors from all over the world.

53 *The Abbey Graveyard*
This was originally the site of a Franciscan Monastery which was built c. 1460. It was occupied by the O'Sullivan forces on their retreat to Dunboy after the Battle of Kinsale in 1601. It was destroyed by the O'Sullivans to prevent it being used as a fortification for the English forces.

APPENDIX 7

The Barony of Bantry

Parish of Kilmacamogue

The parish derives it name from one the Camoge brothers who lived for a time in the area and was regarded as a saint. A religious settlement was built at the location of the present graveyard and ruins. This was later replaced by stone monastic buildings later to be taken over by the Church of Ireland at the time of Henry VIII. Earlier in pre-history this was a Druidic site with a Stone Circle, souterain, and a holy well.

TOWNLANDS

This list is not alphabetical order but roughly follows the various regions of this extensive parish. A townland was originally an area of land which was rented out for a period of a month or more by a tenant.

Cloonee – *Cluain an Fhiaidh* – Plain of the Deer
Like Parkana, which follows, it was a deer park used for the breeding of deer by Lord Bantry or a place where wild deer could be found. The townland has roughly 294 acres.

Maulinvard – *Meall an Bhaird* – Hillock of the bard
This townland includes the ruins of the ancient church of Durrus which has a standing stone with a Christian motif. It is reputed that this church is one of the oldest in Ireland. About 200 metres further west is an ancient boulder burial.

Parkana – *Pairceanna* – park or fieldsAs mentioned, this was another area which was dedicated to deer raising.

Aghagoonheen – *Ath a'Ghoithin* – the ford or timber bridge across the fast running stream.

Dunbittern West – *Dun Beanain* – Benan's western fort
Benan must have been a local tribe leader.

Cappanaloha West – *Ceapach no Luaithe* – place of the ashes
No human ashes are mentioned in this context but the burning of wood, probably for charcoal.

Cappanaloha East – as above

Shanvally Beg – *Sean Baile Beag* – small old settlement

Dromclogh – *Drom Cloch* – the stony hillock

Beach – *Traigh* – beach or strand
This townland has a fine beach which is known as the black strand from deposits of slate as well as about a kilometre of rough beach including Blue Hill. Near the southern end of the townland is a holy well known as Our Lady's Well which is a place of local pilgrimage.

Abbey – *Ard na mBrathar* – friar's height
The Franciscan abbey was founded in 1460 on the invitation of the chieftain of the O'Sullivan Bere. To prevent its occupation by the English forces it was destroyed by Donal Cam O'Sullivan in 1601. The stones of the abbey were used to build a section of Bantry House. The location later became the town's graveyard.

Seafield – *Garrydubh* – *Garrdha Dubh* – black garden or enclosure
Bantry House and gardens are built on this townland. The townland also contained a deer park.

Clashduff – *Clais Dubh* – black hollow

Kilnaruane – *Cill na Romhanach* – church of the Romans
Here are the remains of a carved pillar stone which was probably an Ankh. There are also signs of an early settlement and a burial ground.

Dromleigh North – *Drom Liath* – the grey ridge

Dromleigh South – as above

Dromacoosane – *Drom a'Chausain* – ridge of the caves or caverns

Ardyhoolihane – *Ard Ui Uallachain* – Holland's height

Gortacloona – *Gort Tighe Cluana* – field of house between ridges

Keilnascarta – *Coill na Scairte* – wood of the whitethorns
There are a number of standing stones and builder burials in this townland.

Hollyhill – *Cnoc a'Chuilinn* – hill of the holly
This townland contains the remains of a ring fort and a possible crannog.

Scairtbawn – *Scairt Bhan* – rough ground with white hawthorn

Ardragh – *Ardrath* – the high fort
Here are the remains of a three ringed fort with a souterain. Also, in this townland are the remains of a castle that belonged to the Mac Carthy Scairteen. There were also some barytes mines which were worked in the 1880s.

Letterlicky East – *Leitir Lice* – slatey hillside

Letterlicky Middle – as above

Letterlickey West – as above

Glanlough – *Gleann a'Locha* – glen of the lake
The lake is situated on the west side of this townland.

Derryvahalla – *Doire Ui Mhothlaidh* – Mohilly's wood
Mohilly was an ancient surname in the Bantry region.

Caherogullane – *Cathair o gCoilean* – stone fort of the Collin's
The stone fort is situated on the south side of the townland.

Derreengrenagh – *Doireen Greanach* – little oakwood with gravelly surface
Substantial barytes mines were worked here until about 1920. The loose barytes on the surface of the ground might have led to the name.

Baurgorm – *Barr Gorm* – blue hilltop
The name derives from the blue slate quarries. It was also the location of another castle of the Mac Carthy Scairteens. There is a stone circle and two ancient graveyards also in the townland.

Sheskin – *Seisceann* – marshy boglands

Carrignagat – *Carraig na gCat* – rock of the wild cats

Kilathafineen – *Kil Atha Fhinghin* – church of the bridge of St. Fineen
There were remains of an early Christian settlement in this townland.

Knocknamuck – *Cnoc na Muc* – hill of the pigs

Ardnageehy More – *Ard na Gaoithe* – fhe windy height

Ardnageehy Beg – *Ard na Gaoithe Beag* – small windy height

Derryginagh East – *Dearg Eanach* – the red marsh
Location of Loch Bo Finne (Lake of the White Cow) which supplies Bantry with water. On the north side of the lake is an ancient graveyard.

Deeryginagh Middle – *Deargh Eanach* – the red marsh
This is the location where the major barytes mines of Bantry were located and which were closed c. 1921 at the time of the Troubles.

Derryginagh West
A section of this townland of some 87 acres was called *Gort na Sagart* – field of the priests. This location was probably used to celebrate Mass during the Penal Times.

Glanbannoo Upper – *Gleann Ban Uath* – glen of the witch/spectre

Glanbannoo Lower – as above

Tooreen South – *Tuairin* – sheep walk/path

Coomanore North – *Cum an Phobhair* – hollow of the well

Coomanore South – as above

Glancreagh – *Gleann Craobhach* – woody glen

Dromclogh East – *Drom Clumbach* – height of the wild grass

Dromcloch West – as above
This townland of some 108 acres has two ring forts and a Famine graveyard for children.

Clonygorman – *Cluain na Garman* – plain of the gallows

Derrenkealig – *Doire an Chaolaigh* – wood of the saplings

Cahernacrin – *Cahair an Ao'Chrainn* – stone fort with the single tree

Raheen – *Raithin* – small fort

Slip – *Fanan* – incline

Reenrour East – *Rinn Reamhar* – fat, thick headland

Reenrour West – as above

Newtown – *Baile Nuadh* – new town
This name was given to the growing settlement which grew near Cromwell's son's fort or fortification, which became known as Ireton's Fort.

Lahadane – *Leath Eadan* – small breasts of land

Dunnamark – *Dun na mBarc* – fort of the ships
This was the location, according to legend, where Cesair, sister of Noah, and her followers landed after the Deluge. Here also is the Viking fort with souterain and water dyke for protection. Nearby were flour mills, dye factory and brewery in the 1800s.

Caher – *Cathair* – stone fort
This is sometimes referred to as *Cathair Ruadh* or the Stone Fort on the red coloured land. The stones of the fort have been used over time to build bothans and outbuildings.

Gurteenroe – *Goirtin Ruadh* – little red piece of land
In this townland there were two ring forts.

Reenydonagan – *Rinn Ui Dhonnagain* – Donegan's promontory
This townland contains Reenydonagan Lake.

Laharn East – *Leath Fhaerann* – small holding

Laharn West – as above

Dromdaniel – *Drom Domhnaill* – Domhnaill's ridge

Gortagarry – *Gort a'Ghoraidhe* – field of the smelting
As the name implies there was a smelting operation in this townland in the 18th century.

Gouree More – *Guairi* – rough land

Gouree Beg – as above

Dromacappul – *Drom a'Chapaill* – ridge of the horse

Carrigboy – *Carraig Bhuidhe* – yellow rock

Dromnafinchin – *Drom na Fuinnsin* – ridge of the ash tree

Dromadooneen – *Drom a'Duinin* – little fort on the ridge

Dromadooneen East – as above

Dromadooneen West – as above

Cappanavar – *Ceapach na bhFear* – the men's tillage plot

Loughdeeveen – *Leaca Dhiomhaoin* – untilled land

Shanaknock – *Seana-Chnoc* – the old hill

Inchiclogh – *Inse Cloch* – stony river run

Drombrow – *Drom Brugh* – ridge of the crossing
Drombrow lake fed from adjoining townlands.

Skahanagh – *Sceachanach* – area of white thorns

Skahanagh More – as above

Skahanagh Beg – as above
Near the centre of this townland is an old fort.

Gortroe – *Gort Ruadh* – the red field/soil
In this townland there a number of standing stones as well as St. Bartholomew's Well.

Shandrum More – *Sean Drom* – the old ridge
Here we have another ring fort.

Shandrum Beg – *Sean Drom Beg* – the small old ridge

Dromsullivan North – *Drom Ui Shuilleabhain* – O'Sullivan's ridge

Dromsullivan South – as above
At the eastern side of the townland is a large pool where horses were washed.

Ards More East – *Arda Mor* – the great height

Ards More West – as above

Ards Beg – *Arda Beag* – the small height
This townland contains the ruins of a ring fort.

Gortnacowly – *Gort na Cabhlaighe* – field of the old wrecked house

Coomleagh East – *Cum Liath* – the grey hollow
There are many standing stones in this townland.

Coomleagh West – as above

Glanycarney – *Gleann Ui Cheithearnaigh* – Kearney's glen
In this townland there is a stone circle and also two ring forts.

Cousane – *Cousan* – little hollow
A stone circle in located on the north side of this townland

Laharnshermeen – *Leath-Fhearann Searmin* – half-farm of Searmin

Ardragh – *Ard Rath* – the fort on the hilltop
A large earthen fort is situated in this townland.

Maughanaclea – *Macha na Claimhe* – field of the sheep enclosure
There are two stone circles in the townland. Also, an ancient burial ground and a small lake.

Kealkil – *Caol-Choill* – narrow woodlands
The famous stone circle can be found on the south side of the townland. There is also a small lake.

Maulikeeve – *Meall Ui Chaoimh* – O'Keeffe's knoll

Derryyarkane – *Doire Orcain* – oakwood of the pigs.

Breeny More – *Bruidhne* – fairy castles
Here we encounter two ring forts and a large stone circle

Breeny Beg – *Bruidhne Beg* – small fairy castle

Dromlickacrue – *Drom Lice Cruaidhe* – ridge of hard slate

Dromanassa – *Drom an Easa* – ridge of the waterfall

Cappanaboul – *Ceapach no bPoll* – cleared hollow
There is a stone circle on the south side of this townland.

Kealcoum – *Caol Cam* – the crooked stream

Dromloughlin – *Drom Maoilsheachlainn* – Malachy's ridge

Dromaclarig – *Drom a'Chlaraigh* – hillock with flat top

Crossoge – *Crosog* – narrow cross-roads
On the north side of this townland is *Leaba no Caillighe* or the Hag's Bed.

Ballylickey – *Beal ath Lice* – the ford of the flagstone

Dromkeal – *Drom Caol* – narrow ridge
On the north side of the ridge is a stone alignment which indicates the equinox or the top of spring tides.

Reenadisert – *Rinn a'Disert* – headland of the hermitage (St Canera)
Also in this townland are the ruins of a fortified house of the O'Sullivans.

Barnageragh – *Barr na GCaorach* – hill of the sheep

Snave – *Snamh* – swimming
Cattle swam across river before the bridge was built.

Ardnagashel – *Ard na gCaiseal* – height of the stone fort or castle
This townland was inherited by Philip O'Sullivan, brother of Donal Cam. It is reputed that he built a small castle here.

Ardnamanagh – *Ard na Manach* – height of the monks
According to tradition a group of early monks had a monastery here. To the north is a cillin burial ground.

Ardnaturrish More – *Ard na a'Turais* – height of the pilgrimage
This townland contains a holy well where 'rounds' were performed. There is also a small lake and an old burial ground.

Ardnaturrish Beg – *Ard na a'Turais Beg* – the small hill of the pilgrimage
This townland contains a sizable lake.

Iskanafeenla – *Eisc na Faoilinne* – marsh of the seagulls
Off the shore is the island called *Oilean Craoibhin* or the island of the small trees.

Dromgarriff – *Drom Garbh* – rough hill side
This townland contains the ruins of the Gothic style Glengarriff Castle.

Derrycreigh – *Doire Creiche* – wood of the rustled cattle

Kealanine – *Caol an Oighinn* – stream through the marsh into hollow
This townland contains a number of ancient sites..

Coorycommane – *Cuairi Coimead* –round peaks of the outposts

Maularaha – *Meall a'Reithe* – mound of the ram

Mill Beg – *Poll a'Mhuilinn* – hollow of the mill
This was the location of the iron smelting mills of Lord Bantry. Also location of a stone circle.

Mill Little – as above

Cooryleary – *Cuar Ui Laoghaire* – round hillock of the O'Learys
This townland contains a stone circle.

Dromduff West – *Drom Dubh* – the black ridge

Dromduff East – as above

Ardnacloghy – *Ard na Cloiche* – height of the stone
Pearson's Bridge over the Ouvane River is in this parish. The original timber bridge was known as the Bridge of the Fairies.

Lisheens – *Lisini* – place of the little forts
In this townland are the ruins of the old church of Kilmacomoge which was previously part of a monastery which was suppressed by Henry VIII. Nearby is a holy well. There are three ring forts in the townland as well as a souterain running west from the church in ruins.

Lackareagh – *Leacha Riabhach* – furrowed hillside

Maulavanig – *Meall a'Mhanaigh* – monk's knoll
Unfortunately, there is no information on this settlement of monks.

Cahermuckee – *Cathair a'Mhuicodhe* – fort of the pig herder
There is a large fort in this townland.

Ballynamought – *Baile na mBocht* – living area of the poor

Coomclogh – *Cum Cloch* – stony hollow

Cahermoanteen – *Cathair a'Mhainntin* – stone fort of the narrow gap

Gortloughra – *Gort Luachra* – field of rushes

Kilnaknopoge – *Coill na gCnapog* – wood of the mounds

Cappaboy More – *Ceapach Bhuidhe* – yellow wood clearance
In this townland there are a number of standing stones and a stone circle.

Cappaboy Beg – as above
Here, there are two stone circles and a number of standing stones.

Maugha – *Macha* – night enclosure for cattle

Derryfadda – *Doire Fada* – long oakwood

Carriganass – *Carraig an Easa* – rock of the waterfall
Here, on the river side is the O'Sullivan Castle of Carriganass.

Ahil More – *Aichil* – high ground
On the north side of the townland is the Bull's Pocket where a bull was trapped for a winter and survived his ordeal.

Ahil Beg – *Aichil* – high ground

Ahildotia – *Aichil Doighte* – burnt strip of high ground

Tooreen – *Tuairin* – green sheep path
Lake Atooreen is situated on the east side of the townland.

Rangaroe – Reanga Ruadh – red ridge

Kippaghingergill – *Ceapach Ui Iongardail* – Harrington's wood

Coorloum East – *Cuar Lom* – round bare hillock

Coorloum West – as above

Coorloum North – as above
Here we have a stone fort and an open space of ground where the 'gatherings' were held.

Derryduff More – *Doire Dubh* – dark oakwood
Also in this townland we have Meall an Lobhair or the Leaper's Knoll.

Derryduff Beg – as above

Gearagh – *Gaorthadh* – wooded glen

Cappanabrick – *Ceapan a'Bhruic* – land of the badger

Knockanecosduff – *Cnocan Cos Dubh* – black-footed (turf) hillock

Illane – *Aillean* – little cliff face
There are two stone circles in this townland.

Maughanasilly – *Macha na Sailighe* – field of the willows
In this townland there are two standing stones.

Shronagreehy – *Sron na Gaothe* – nose of the wind

Inchinarihen – *Inse an Airchinn* – river boundary

Coomacroobig – *Cum a'Chrubaigh* – rough hollow

Lackavane – *Leaca Bhan* – white hillside

Curraglass – *Corra Ghlas* – round green hill

Cullenagh – *Cuileannach* – holly patch

Inchiroe – *Inse Ruadh* – rough river

Currakeal – *Currach Caol* – narrow bog

Derreencollig – *Doire a Choiligh* – oakwood of the woodcock

Deerynafinchin – *Doire na Fuinseann* – ash thicket

Deeryclogher – *Doire Cluthmhar* – sheltered oakwood

Curramore – *Coradh Mhor* – big waterfall

Trawnamaddree – *Trian no Madrai* – land of the wild dogs

Carran (Curran) – *Carn* – stone mound (cairn)
Very little of the cairn remains. Stones mostly used for building. To the south of the cairn was an area of the 'gathering'.

Derrynakilla – *Doire na Cille* – church in the oakwood
There are remains of a church and an ancient graveyard.

Inchinagoum – *Inse na gCeann* – river of the heads (battle)
In this townland there is a dolmen, stone circle, souterains, caves and ancient mines.

Farranfadda – *Fearann Fada* – long townland

Cooleenlemane – *Cuilin na Loman* – little recess in rock

Coumaclavlig – *Cum a'Chlamhlaigh* – crevasse of the bones
Here the peasants used to throw the discarded bones from rustled cattle.

Derrograne – *Doire O gCorran* – Curran's oakwood

Derreenathirigy – *Doirin a'tSiorraidh* – cold wind little oakwood

Caherdaniel East – *Cathair Domhnaill* – Daniel's homestead

Caherdaniel West – as above

Milleencoola – little knoll of the stake

Whiddy Island

Reenaknock – *Rinn a'Cnoic* – hilly headland

Close – *Clos* – yard or narrow strip of land

Kilmore – *Cill Mhor* – big church
This townland has ruins of an old church and graveyard.

Trawnahaha – *Traigh no hAtha* – beach of the ford

Gurraghy – *Garrdhtha* – garden, apple garden

Croangle – *Cro Ceangaill* – enclosure of the cincture

Reenavanig – *Rinn a Ban Oige* – headland of the young women
In this townland was located a priory and a castle of the O'Sullivans.

Chapel Island

Chapel Island – I*nis Cuinge* – island of Cong
The monks from Cong occupied this island for some 70 years and had a
small church, living quarters and a graveyard.

.

BIBLIOGRAPHY

Analecta Hibernica. No.4.
Anwly. E. *Celtic Religions*.
Archives de la Marine. *Journal de Morard de Galles*.
Archives de las Guerre, *Carton de L'Expedition de L'Irlande*.

Bennett, G. *History of Bandon*.
Berleth, R. *The Twilight Lords*.
Bonnechose. E. *Lazare Hoche*.
Bradley, P. Brendan. *Bantry Bay, Ireland in the days of Napoleon*.
Brady. W. Maziere. *Clerical and Parochial Records of Cork, Cloyne and Ross*.
Burke, Rev. U.J. *The Aryan Orgins of the Gaelic Race and Language*.
Burke's Landed Gentry of Great Britain and Ireland.
Butler, W. *Confiscation in Irish History*.

Caesar. *De Bello Gallico*.
Chadwick, N.K. *The Druids*.
Chausee, Le Comte de la. *Memoire Sur Bantry*.
Childe, V.G. *Pre-Historic Communities of the British Isles*.
Clarke & Piggot. *Pre-Historic Societies*.
Clarke. G. *World Pre-History*.
Connellan, *Annals of the Four Masters*.
Croker. T.C. *Fairy Legends of Ireland*.
Curry, E. *The Battle of Magh Leane*.

D'Alton, Rev. E. *History of Ireland*.
D'Arbois de Joubainville. *Les Druids*.
De la Gravoere. *La Marines des Anciens*.
Deasy, L. *Towards Ireland Free*.

Eliade. M. *Shamanism.*
Ellis, P.B. *Hell or Connaught.*
Everett Hale, E. *Letter on Irish Emigration.*

Fallon, N. *The Armada in Ireland.*
Ferguson, Lady. *The Story of Irish before the Conquest.*
Fernandez-Armesto F. *The Spanish Armada.*

Gibson, Revd. *History of the County & City of Cork.*
Gordon, C. H. *Riddles in History.*
Gwynne Revd. Aubrey. *Cromwell's Policy of Transportation.*
Gwynne Revd. Aubrey. *Early Irish Emigration to the West Indies.*

Hawkes, Dr R. *The Last Invasion of Ireland.*
Holland, Revd. E. *History of West Cork & Diocese of Ross.*
Homet, M. F. *On the Trail of the Sun Gods.*

Joyce, Dr. I*rish Names and Places.*

Keating. G. *History of Ireland.*

Lanigan, Revd. *Ecclesiastical History of Ireland.*
Le Roy. *Les Navires des Anciens*
Lewis, S. *Topographical Dictionary of Ireland.*
London Records Office. C.O.I. to 1688.

MacDermot, Frank. *Theobald Wolfe Tone.*
Martin, C. P. *Pre-Historic Man in Ireland.*
MacAllister, R.A.S. *Ireland in Pre-Celtic Times.*
MacAllister, R.A.S. *Ancient Ireland.*
Murphy, Revd. D. *Deportation of the Irish to the West Indies in the Seventeenth Century.*

Nilsson, N. P. *Primitive Time Reckoning.*

O'Brennan. *Ancient Ireland.*
O'Brien, H. *The Round Towers of Ireland.*
O'Brien, H. *Phoenician Ireland.*
O'Callaghan, S. *To Hell or Barbados.*
O'Curry. *Manuscript Material of Irish History.*
O'Donoghue, B. *Parish Histories and Place Names of West Cork.*

O'Donovan, J. *The Four Masters*.
O'Donovan, J. *Miscellany of the Celtic Society*.
O'Flaherty, Ogygia.
O'Halloran. W. *Early Irish History and Antiquities of West Cork*.
O'Hanlon. Revd J. *Irish American History*.
O'Mahony, J. *West Cork and its Story*.
O'Riordain, S.P. *Antiquities of the Irish Countryside*.
O'Sullivan. Don P. *Ireland Under Elizabeth*.

Phene, Dr. *Serpent Worship*.
Piggott, S. *The Druids*.
Prendergast. J.P. *The Cromwellian Settlement of Ireland*.
Prichard, J.C. *The Eastern Origins of the Celtic Nations*.

Rawley, J. A. *The Trans-Atlantic Slave Trade*.
Rawlingson. G. *Religions of the Ancient World*.
Rushe. Revd. J. *A Second Thebaid*.
Rutledge *Anglo-Irish Trade in the Sixteenth Century*.

Savory, H. N. *The Pre-History of the Iberian Peninsula*.
Shaw. A.G. *Convicts and the Colonies*
Shearman. J. *Loca Patriciana*
Smith, Rev. *The Ancient and Present State of the County and City of Cork.*.
Stuart Jones, E.H. *An Invasion that Failed*.
Summerville-Large. P. *The Coast of West Cork*.

Taylor and Skinner. *Maps of the Roads of Ireland*.
Toor. *Ancient Ships*.
Tucker, F. *Cork Remembrancer*.

Wakeman. W.E. *Archaeologia Hibernica*.
Wilde. Lady. *Ancient Legends of Ireland*.
Wilkes. Mrs E. *Ireland – Ur of the Chaldees*.
Williams. R.A. *The Berehaven Copper Mines*.
Wood, J.E. *Sun, Moon and Standing Stones*.

INDEX

Abbey 70-72, 110, 132, 161, 164, 167, 176, 214, 270, 272, 300, 302

Adrigole 21, 37, 47, 58, 65, 111, 116, 137, 170, 191, 192, 242, 247, 286

Ardnagashel 70, 103, 117, 124-125, 159, 202, 211-212, 269, 307

Ashtoreth 29

Astronomy, 27, 31-32

Atlantis 22-23, 48

Baal 29, 73-75, 79-80, 82

Ballylickey 68, 98, 102, 104, 122, 132, 211, 261, 308

Bandon 110, 119, 122, 141, 161, 165-166. 186, 195, 245-246, 259, 261-262, 294, 312

Banshee 81-82

Bantry Bay Steamship Company 152, 288, 294

Barbados 5, 124, 228-232, 313

Barytes 98, 152, 239-241, 244, 303, 304

Bealtaine 29, 73, 222

Beara 24, 51, 56-57, 59, 61, 116-117, 149, 158, 166-167, 174, 188, 205, 247-248, 268, 294

Bere Island 5, 111, 174-176, 178, 201, 204-205, 244, 247, 253, 260, 262, 274, 283-284, 287, 292

Betelgeuse 13, 275-277, 279

Blackrock House 122, 124-125, 141, 166, 300

Borlin 21, 66

Brehon Laws 79, 85-87, 116

Bronze Age 19, 40, 46, 63, 65-66, 236

Butter 122, 152, 154, 214-215, 217-219, 244, 298

Caha 21

Calendar 31-32, 42, 44-45, 75, 77, 122, 223, 225

Cappanaboul 64, 307

Carnac 24, 32

Carriganass Castle 69, 117, 122, 131, 162, 177

Castledonovan 69, 118

Castletownbere 5, 110, 116, 128, 135, 157, 175, 180, 191-192, 205, 211, 242, 245, 253, 262-263, 268, 273

Celtic 32, 45, 51, 53-54, 88. 94-95, 312, 313, 314

Celts 18, 51-52, 54, 88, 92-95
Cessair 10, 14, 35-38, 48
Cholera 145, 178, 212-214
Christianity 9, 35, 49, 59, 79, 87, 96-102
Civil War 264-267
Colomane 46, 58-59, 63, 77-78, 98
Coomhola 21, 33, 46, 60-61, 63, 65-66, 89, 105-106, 191-192, 211, 216, 242, 252, 261, 263, 292
Cures 78, 83-84
Cycladic 17, 30-31, 66, 88-89

Danae 49
Donamark (Donemark) 10, 21, 66, 69, 107, 111, 122, 136, 147, 152, 162, 176, 211, 213
Dorians 54-55
Druids 17, 24, 28, 54, 85, 90, 312, 314
Dunboy 61, 68, 71, 111, 116-117, 158, 161-162, 175-176, 183, 192
Dunmanway 152, 195, 244, 246, 252, 258, 267
Durrus 108, 119, 143, 159-160, 190-191, 212, 253, 255, 291, 301
Dursey 11, 51, 56, 68, 110-111, 119, 148, 157, 174-175, 211, 283-287

Egyptian 15, 26, 29, 34, 41, 54-55, 91, 100, 102
Emigration 227, 229, 233, 235, 313

Fairs 117, 122, 139-149, 216-221, 222, 244
Famine 105, 134-135, 145, 149, 151, 154, 164, 167, 178, 207-210, 214-215, 219, 233, 238, 243-244, 282, 297, 299, 300, 304

Festivals 28-29, 73-82, 222
Fir Bolg 41, 49
Fishing 12, 119, 125, 129, 130-138, 140-141, 144, 147, 149, 152, 158-160, 163-164, 166-168, 170, 174, 176, 178, 180, 183-184, 192, 210, 215, 243-244, 268, 271-272, 287
Formorians 48-49, 56
French 11-12, 14, 133-134, 140-141, 143-144, 165-168, 193-195, 196-200, 201, 228, 283, 286
Fulachta Fiadh 66

Gael 16, 109
Gearhies 136, 165, 194, 212, 280
Glengarriff 21, 68, 70, 111, 175, 182-189, 191, 198, 217, 242, 245, 247-248, 252-255, 261, 263, 274, 292, 296, 308
Goddess 33, 59, 81
Greek 15-17, 22, 30, 49-50, 54-57, 59-60, 66, 81, 86, 90-91, 93, 95, 100, 107, 113, 156
Gulf Oil 170, 273, 274, 280, 290

Hebrew 15-16, 44-45, 53, 55

Irish Republican Army 257
Irish Volunteers 251-252

Kealkil 43, 63, 66, 98-99, 105, 202, 250, 252, 292, 307
Kenmare 15, 116-117, 177, 192, 245, 247, 283
Kilmocomogue 104, 106
Kilnaruane Stone 7, 99-101, 302
Kinsale 51, 109, 117, 121, 161, 165, 176, 193, 227-230, 246, 300

Manannan 57, 59-60, 76-77, 80, 100

Martello Towers 201-202, 204

Michael Collins 252, 262, 264-267

Milesians 11, 41, 48, 50-53, 58, 82

Millbeg 43, 58

Mining 151, 192, 236-242

Minoan 15, 55, 78

Mount Gabriel 159, 236

Mussels 171, 173, 280-281

Nemedians 49

Neolithic 19, 21, 40, 42-44, 66

Newgrange 21, 24, 31-32, 41-43, 45

Newtown 60, 70, 123, 132, 140, 212, 252, 304

Nile 22, 30, 36, 42

Normans 8, 11, 115, 119, 175

Ogham 59, 88-90

Osiris 30, 34, 100

Palladius 96-97

Patrick 7, 9, 55-56, 87-90, 96-97, 222, 224

Phoenicians 15, 17, 25-27, 29, 73, 75, 86, 88, 90-91, 236

Pirates 126-129, 140, 163, 175

R.I.C. 252-256, 258-261, 263, 264, 292, 295, 299

Roman 15-17, 64, 85, 87, 95, 97

Scart 39, 43, 46, 63, 69, 135, 282, 298-299

Souterains 33, 58, 68, 310

Spain 8, 18, 25-26, 30, 41-42, 54-55, 64, 71, 92, 117, 119, 127-129, 130, 133, 157-158, 163-165, 174, 177, 191, 228, 268-270, 272

St Brendan 102, 107, 112-113

Transportation 13, 165, 209, 210, 227-229, 231-235, 313

Tuatha 11, 15, 41, 48-50, 54, 58, 67, 82

Vikings 23, 108, 109-114, 115, 157

West Cork Brigade 252, 254, 261, 263, 292

Whiddy 15, 69, 71, 102-103, 104, 111, 120, 121-122, 124-125, 129, 131-132, 136-138, 141, 147, 149, 152, 156-173, 175-176, 184, 198. 201, 203, 266, 274, 283-284, 292

Whitsuntide 76, 80

Wolfe Tone 11, 154, 167, 196-200, 313

Workhouse 104, 148-149, 151, 178, 211-215, 243, 253, 265, 297

ALSO AVAILABLE BY THE SAME AUTHOR

Irish Pirates and Privateers

ISBN 9780955203923

The lives and exploits of Irish pirates and the ports they sailed from.

The Knights Templar and Ireland

ISBN 9780955203909

A survey of the Templars' holdings in Ireland including a history of the order as a whole as well as in Ireland and a look at what happened to Templar property after the dissolution of the order. Lavishly illustrated throughout and also available in hardback.

The Castles Of County Limerick

ISBN 9780951941591

A studiously researched reference to the medieval history of Limerick and the castles built between 1200 and 1700 CE. Over 140 individual entries detailing the position, remains and history of each castle. Contains colour photographs, pen and wash drawings, plans and map.

The Castles and Fortified Houses Of West Cork

ISBN 9780951941584

An Indispensable, illustrated reference to the history of West Cork from 1150 to 1700 with details of the history and legends surrounding the castles of the region.